Praise for *In Wolf's Clothing*

"Everything you thought you knew about this 'Russian Spy' caper is wrong. Read *In Wolf's Clothing* and discover the astounding truth."

—Guy Benson, FOX News contributor and author

"A great story well told. It has everything: a Russian 'agent' hawking gun rights and palling around with the NRA, bungling and bullying prosecutors, and a young, devoted defense lawyer not sure what was coming next. If not for the serious consequences, the story of Maria Butina could be a parody. If you watched *The Americans*—all the while thinking about 'the Russians are Coming, the Russians are Coming'—you must read this book."

—Abbe Smith, Georgetown law professor and author
of *Case of a Lifetime* and *Guilty People*

"Few people understand what it's like to stand in another person's shoes. Fewer still can imagine what defense attorney Alfred Carry and his client Maria Butina experienced after she was charged by the United States with a crime that thrust her into the center of political conflict. In *In Wolf's Clothing*, Carry offers an insider's view, exposing society's dangerous willingness to accept accusations as fact and allow prejudice to masquerade as justice. With quiet wit and keen observation, the book shows why defense attorneys must pull back the veil to strip away media caricatures and governmental overreach that can turn ordinary mistakes into acts of treachery. More than a courtroom narrative, *In Wolf's Clothing* is a powerful reminder why zealous advocacy isn't just about defending clients—it's about defending proportionality and truth itself. In an age when political theater is valued over the rule of law, and public outrage drowns out constitutional protections, the book drives home a sobering truth: sometimes the most dangerous actors aren't the accused at all."

—Moses Cook, former president of FAMM,
national nonprofit for criminal justice reform

IN WOLF'S CLOTHING

IN WOLF'S CLOTHING

MY STORY REPRESENTING
MARIA BUTINA
THE MOST FAMOUS
WOMAN IN MOSCOW

ALFRED CARRY
with Brendan Snow
Foreword by James Bamford

Skyhorse Publishing

Skyhorse Publishing books may be purchased in bulk at special discounts for
sales promotion, corporate gifts, fund-raising, or educational purposes. Special
editions can also be created to specifications. For details, contact the Special Sales
Department, Skyhorse Publishing, 307 West 36th Street, 11th Floor, New York,
NY 10018 or info@skyhorsepublishing.com.

Skyhorse® and Skyhorse Publishing® are registered trademarks of Skyhorse
Publishing, Inc.®, a Delaware corporation.

Visit our website at www.skyhorsepublishing.com.
Please follow our publisher Tony Lyons on Instagram @tonylyonsisuncertain.

10 9 8 7 6 5 4 3 2 1

Library of Congress Cataloging-in-Publication Data is available on file.

Hardcover ISBN: 978-1-5107-7044-7
eBook ISBN: 978-1-5107-7045-4

Cover design by David Ter-Avanesyan

Printed in the United States of America

Contents

Foreword
by James Bamford

About a dozen blocks down Connecticut Avenue from the White House, there used to be a very fine Russian restaurant called Mari Vanna. Spidery houseplants hung from the ceiling, family photos dotted the "shabby chic" walls, and its dacha-inspired interior was cluttered with Soviet-era bric-a-brac, like colorful tchotchkes and nesting dolls that crammed the shelves. I had been out of the country for some time, and I was looking forward to getting together there with a friend, Maria Butina, and catching up. What I didn't realize until much later was that among the other customers enjoying bowls of sushki, black bread, and pelmeni were a pair of FBI agents at a nearby table.

I first met Maria about a year and a half earlier at a lecture on peace prospects in the Middle East. At the time I was the national security columnist for *Foreign Policy* magazine and Maria was a graduate student from Russia at American University in Washington. At the lecture, I told a friend that I was planning to take a trip across Russia on the Trans-Siberian Railroad, and he pointed his finger at a woman in her late twenties with very long red hair and said I should talk to her, she was born in Siberia. And since I had never met anyone from Siberia, and since I was about to cross Siberia by train, I thought it was a perfect opportunity to have a lot of questions answered.

It was an enjoyable meeting, and we had a fair amount in common. I had been to Moscow many times, both as a tourist and for work. Including as the Washington investigative producer for ABC News, a filmmaker for PBS, and a writer for *Wired* magazine, when I interviewed and spent three days with newly arrived fugitive and NSA whistleblower Edward Snowden. So there was a lot to talk about, and we would occasionally get together and bump into each other at lectures and other functions. But even though I had spent my career writing about US intelligence, including three bestselling books on the NSA, Maria never seemed very interested in the topic. Nor did she ever ask me a single question about NSA or intelligence, or ask me to introduce her to anyone in intelligence. Not once.

Which was why I was so surprised when she told me during our lunch at Mari Vanna that the FBI had been questioning her, and that there had been news articles alleging that she was some sort of spy or "red sparrow" seductress. Because I had been overseas when much of that was taking place, I thought at first that she was joking. I certainly knew that Maria was not a spy, but a sincere grad student studying international relations and hoping the United States and Russia could move closer together. And much later I saw an official FBI report that confirmed that agents had followed Maria to our lunch. Afterward, we would instead meet at a private club in Washington where it would be much easier to speak without being overheard. As someone who has written about the government for decades, it was a very scary time.

By August 2016, when Maria stepped off the plane from Moscow to begin her two-year grad school course at American University, Russiagate was in full steam. Slim and attractive, with the figure of a dancer and long rose-colored hair that spiraled gently down her back, Butina fit the stereotype of a seductive Russian spy, like Anna Chapman, the redheaded Russian sleeper agent arrested in New York City in 2010; Jennifer Lawrence, who played the redheaded Russian spy-seductress in the film *Red Sparrow*; and Keri Russell, who starred in the popular television show *The Americans* as a dedicated Soviet spy posing as a typical US citizen.

It was a very hazardous time to be Russian in the city. "Washington's young émigré crowd is beginning to feel like they're living in a spy novel. And they're the bad guys," noted Politico's Ben Schreckinger in an article about being young and Russian in Washington during Russiagate. "Now, more so than ever, the capital's young Russiantonians find themselves living in a battlefield of the new Cold War. Their Tinder dates keep asking them if they're spies. Their landlords are interrogating them. Their résumés are getting tossed in the trash, and when they do get the job, their boss might warn them not to mention their nationality to people at the office. . . . And for Russians who do get the job, office life in Washington can be awkward. Dmitry Sivaev, an urban development specialist at the World Bank, recalled his annoyance when a former boss told him not to mention to colleagues that he was Russian."

Nor was Russia fearmongering limited to Washington. On cable television it became rampant. "The most irredeemable outpost of the national media is cable news," wrote media critic Michael Massing in *The Nation*. "In the past, Fox News stood out for the nakedness of its partisanship and the purity of its ideology; now, both MSNBC and CNN are mirror versions of it, tailoring their programming to the demands of their Trump-loathing audiences. With their noxious talking heads, irritating breaking-news flashes, nonstop commercials (20 or more minutes out of every 60 on CNN), performative White House correspondents, paucity of reporting, and constant drumbeat of Trump, Trump, Trump, Trump, watching these networks is a demoralizing and soul-sapping experience."

As Russiagate exploded, Maria became an easy target since ethnic profiling was nothing new for the FBI. J. Edgar Hoover targeted Black leaders like Martin Luther King Jr. as "communists." Then following the 9/11 attacks more than a thousand Muslims were quickly rounded up, mostly in secret, and deprived of their rights. "The decision of whom to question often appeared to be haphazard, at times prompted by law enforcement agents' random encounters with foreign male Muslims or neighbors' suspicions," said a 2002 Human Rights Watch report. "The Department of Justice has subjected them to arbitrary detention, violated due process in legal proceedings against them, and run roughshod over the presumption of innocence."

Nevertheless, I thought that what had taken place was simply an overzealous new agent out to win points by going after Hollywood's stereotypical spy/seductress, an attractive woman from Russia with red hair. But I was wrong. A realization I came to when I heard that she had actually been arrested and taken away in handcuffs. I was shocked and astounded, as well as angry and frustrated that I couldn't do anything about it. Eventually I wrote a long article about the case for *The New Republic* magazine, and appropriately titled it, "The Spy Who Wasn't." I also wrote several chapters that examined the case and the people behind it in my most recent book, *Spyfail.*

But the one bright note was that Maria's arrest brought me in contact with her attorneys, Robert Driscoll and Alfred Carry. Over the months and eventually years that we would discuss the case and the miscarriage of justice, we became friends, and I greatly admired not just their professionalism, but their passion and dedication in fighting for justice on behalf of Maria. And it was a view she often shared with me. Following her arrest, I would frequently visit her in jail and later prison, and we would exchange letters and phone calls, and she would never stop telling me how grateful she was that Bob and Alfred had agreed to take her case, and at no expense. And yet work at it as if she was paying them a fortune.

So, I was very happy when Alfred told me he was writing a book about the case—reading it brought back many memories, some bad but mostly good. And I also appreciate him asking me to write a foreword to it. It's a story that shows what can happen when overambitious prosecutors and the FBI follow the political hysteria rather than follow the evidence and the law.

A Note on Quotations

What follows is the true account of the Maria Butina case. Throughout the story you'll find two types of quotations. If a quotation comes from my cocounsel, Maria, my friends, family, etc., the quotations may not be exact. While the quotations are close to what was said, the comments were often recorded after the fact. If the quotation comes from a prosecutor, media personality, judge, or if the quotation comes from an email, television, or court record, the remarks are exact.

Chapter One

It was fall, the kind of autumn day when the Jefferson Memorial is framed in orange leaves, when the spires of Georgetown University reflect off the Potomac in terra-cotta Technicolor. On this particular day, I wasn't tromping through a pumpkin patch with my goldendoodle or driving to a pub in horse country. I was leaving the Alexandria Detention Center, a Virginia jail facility just across the river from our nation's capital. It was a workday, as every day had been for the past few months.

I stepped into the autumn air, behind me the concrete-and-chipped-paint facility where my client, the alleged Russian agent Maria Butina, was being held in administrative segregation. Ad seg is just a euphemism for solitary confinement in the way "they're in a better place" is used for "jackknifed by a tractor-trailer on the beltway." I made it a point to visit Maria to keep her spirits high or if not high then at least not "in a better place." I'd been her attorney for only a few months, but with the media circus and trial by fire, it felt like a lifetime.

On my way out, I noticed something: Special Agents Kevin Helson and Michelle Ball entering the grounds. Helson and Ball, which sounds like a brand of high-end paint, were the FBI agents who had arrested Maria. To the public, to my friends, to cable news, to the guy at the coffee shop, the story sounded like a spy novel: cloak-and-dagger, sex-for-access, high-profile politician kind of stuff. The real story was something else altogether, and at that moment, Helson, Ball, and I were three of only a few who knew the real story.

I said hi to the special agents, whom Maria had been meeting with on a regular basis to parse out how this game would end, but I wondered why they were visiting the detention center. They couldn't speak to Maria outside the presence of me or my cocounsel, so, as every attorney would do when they spot a curiosity, I speculated. They liked me. Most people do even when on the other side of a case, so it was a genial exchange. But soon my spidey-sense tingled.

Special Agent Helson asked if I knew why the guys from the Russian consulate want to visit Maria.

"They come every week," I said.

Helson pointed out they come at the same time every week. This time, they were visiting off schedule. He asked if I knew why.

I didn't, but here's the thing about talking to law enforcement, and any attorney worth his salt will say the same: If you're gonna talk, and in most situations you probably shouldn't without your attorney present, but if you do, you better tell the truth. If you don't, according to 18 U.S.C. § 1001, you've committed a felony. Sure, there are nuances about material facts and whether your false statements were made knowingly, but let's just say this: When you're speaking to federal agents, you're walking along the rim of an active volcano. I was certainly no stranger to this walkabout. Before making the move to a law firm on Pennsylvania Avenue, I was a public defender. I'd represented countless defendants for felony assault, drug possession, and breaking and entering. I knew the hike well.

"I don't know," I said.

And again, I didn't. I could never know why the Russians wanted to visit Maria, but it might have involved a meeting between Vladimir Putin and Donald Trump in Argentina. A meeting that would be publicly canceled, but a meeting that would occur anyway and remain unreported for some time. What was said in Buenos Aires? I don't know, but I have a guess.

Chapter Two

It was 7:30 a.m. on July 16, 2018, and my apartment in Dupont Circle was quiet. My boyfriend and I had a small one-bedroom apartment up the street from the White House, and ever since we adopted Piper, a spirited goldendoodle, we'd been feeling the pinch of the place. Even so, we couldn't afford anything bigger. I had just gotten a new job at McGlinchey, a national law firm on Pennsylvania Avenue, and while my salary got a little bump, my student loans were taking a big chunk out of the nest egg we were trying to squirrel away. We were happy though.

While getting dressed, I listened to *Morning Joe*, the MSNBC news show. The host Joe Scarborough has this folksy charm about him. If you like liberals pretending to be conservative, *Morning Joe* is the perfect way to start your day. During the program, Joe usually reads the newspaper, asks his cohosts and friends what they think, and lets you know what he thinks. At some point he slams a GOP critic for pretending to care about what's at stake for middle or rural America—as if he understands the common man from his lofty perch on a Connecticut estate.

I can't throw stones though. His convictions seem earnest, and I lived in a bubble too.

As far as bubbles go, DC was a perfect liberal bastion, a place where Hillary Clinton got over 90 percent of the vote, where the streets were adorned with rainbow flags, where alt-right was a curse word, and where, after Trump had won the election, tony elementary schools canceled classes. We were angry snowflakes in DC, and except for the new occupant in the White House, who sometimes left town on the weekends, my neighbors operated on the same page. During morning walks with Piper, as I'm picking up her alt-right, it wasn't unusual to hear a stranger complain about the president: *Trump, am I right?*

It was a sticky summer day, but I walked to work, passing a protest outside the White House and another one outside the Trump Hotel. It was tough for Democrats to be reminded of their defeat everywhere they looked, but by mid-2018, the liberal depression had settled into a controlled fury. If there was an election, the Left was coming out. If a cabinet official was eating at a local restaurant, liberals were vocal about it. If a large corporation did business with the administration, progressive wallets were taken elsewhere.

I was less inclined to follow the mob.

Former President Barack Obama criticized callout culture by saying "[t]his idea of purity and you're never compromised and you're always politically woke" is not activism. "The world is messy. There are ambiguities. People who do really good stuff have flaws. People who you are fighting may love their kids and, you know, share certain things with you."

I certainly don't despise Republicans. They contain, as everyone else does, multitudes. This is to say, if you paint someone with only the brush of wickedness or the brush of virtue, rather than examine their individual acts, you compress nuanced human experience to a single digit rather than examine what is righteous and destructive in each of us.

Remember how President Reagan and his press secretary Larry Speakes treated the AIDS epidemic when it was killing thousands of Americans, mostly in the gay community? I don't, but I read history. They treated it as a "great joke" according to White House journalist Lester Kinsolving. Moral criticism of the Reagan White House is justified and unexamined by Republicans. However, the same blinders are firmly latched on liberals. George W. Bush started PEPFAR, the largest relief effort by any nation to address a single disease—an initiative that has contributed more than $110 billion to fight HIV/AIDS. I hear Democrats attack Bush for the Iraq War and for vilifying LGBTQ Americans in his second campaign, but I hear nothing about the 25 million lives he saved through PEPFAR. I should.

I arrived at my office building on Freedom Plaza, commemorating where Martin Luther King Jr. wrote "I Have a Dream," and stepped into the cool air of the lobby. In retrospect, I should have taken an Uber. My boyfriend would have complained about the unnecessary expense, but at the moment, I would have stayed in our tiny apartment for the rest of my life if I could get my shirt unstuck from my back.

I'd been at the job for a couple of months, working in the litigation practice group. A friend of my brother recommended me for the job, and I did stuff like defend parties in various lawsuits in federal court. As for the law firm itself, I was beginning to figure out the politics of the place. Like at most law firms, roughly a third of the lawyers are partners, the ones who scoop up big clients with their subject-matter expertise and sometimes do interviews on television. Robert Driscoll, the partner who worked in the office next to mine, was frequently on Fox News hashing out the legal issues of the day. McGlinchey is a national law firm with a lot of attorneys, so naturally some are Republican—the firm is based out of Louisiana. I tend to like Republicans who are lawyers.

I saw a path for my law firm career, and overall, there were three ways to get ahead. One, you distinguish yourself with competent work, like winning an important case. Two, you have a partner and mentor who invites you to important dinners and introduces you to important people. And three, you find clients with deep pockets. I didn't quite fit the bill on the last two counts, but just a few weeks after taking the job, I scored an important legal victory. Before coming to McGlinchey, I argued an appellate case about an immigrant's criminal trial rights before the District of Columbia Court of Appeals. The published decision of the en banc court—the full bench of judges on the court rather than a usual panel of three—was handed down just as I was settling into my new position. The firm sent out a press release, which to me, a young lawyer, was a big deal. I didn't know a bigger deal was sitting in a jail cell just down the street.

Sitting down to dig into one of my cases, I heard a conversation next door, a phone call between Bob Driscoll and a federal prosecutor.

"That doesn't make sense," Bob said. "You've got a First Amendment problem."

I leaned away from the computer and toward the door to listen closer—not lurking exactly but fact-finding. Lawyers do that.

Bob continued, "I don't know any student who's been arrested for being a foreign agent. Do you?"

Foreign agent, the stuff of spy novels. I stood up and stepped to my door.

"Your interpretation of the law is unreasonably broad," Bob said before finishing the call and hanging up the phone.

When he did, I walked to his doorway and found him sitting at his desk. Bob was a big man. His shirt sometimes fell out of place—something I struggle with as a tall person—but he looked good. Sharp in dress but also in mind, Bob knew the insides of the Republican political machine and was frequently on the news telling it like he sees it. He worked at the Justice Department as a Deputy Assistant Attorney General and Chief of Staff in the Civil Rights Division.

"Interesting case," I said.

"Yeah," Bob said. "Government just arrested this Russian I've been working with. Maria Butina. Gonna be all over the news."

A case that gets news coverage was a surefire way to get attention from the higher-ups. Not only would they think of you when the case was splashed across the paper, they'd talk to you about its status, offer suggestions on strategy, and bring you in on other high-profile matters. Seems silly to say now, but I could imagine five or six of us having steaks at The Palm, tossing constitutional concerns back and forth. That was the lawyer big league, which I had only seen through glass windows when providing counsel as a public defender to those who couldn't afford it. I could think of no better way to get a seat at the table than with a case that was "all over the news."

"Who's the judge?" I asked, hoping for someone I knew or better yet seen in my days representing the underserved.

"Uh, Robinson I think."

"Deborah Robinson?" I said, raising an eyebrow. "She was a professor of mine in law school." She taught a seminar I took on the administration of criminal justice, an interesting course. "When's the hearing?"

"One o'clock," he said, checking his watch.

I stepped into his office. "Presumably we'll pick a date for a preliminary hearing. And if it comes up, she may assess bail conditions, flight risk, danger to the community, etc. to determine whether our client can be released pretrial. Do you know if the government is seeking detention? What's our position?"

Our position. You see how I just insinuated myself onto the defense team? Bob noticed the move as he notices most things, but he also realized I could help. I had experience in criminal work.

"Do you wanna go?"

I burst into my apartment where my boyfriend was working with Piper at his side.

"Grabbing a suit," I said crossing our one-room living room/kitchen/office. "Going to court."

"Someone in trouble?" he asked as Piper leapt to the floor to chase after me.

"A foreign student from Russia was just arrested," I called from the bedroom. "Don't know the details, just that the feds claim she's a foreign agent of the Russian government. Might be on the news. Gotta run back to the office to grab some things, then sprint to the courthouse to meet her before the hearing."

"Meat loaf for dinner?"

"Yes, but put it in the fridge. I'll be home late."

Chapter Three

To some Russians, being named after a family member is unlucky. It's thought that if you share a name, you share a destiny, and since the Slavs believe each person should pursue their own fate, names like Henry VIII would be doomed. So it was especially unfortunate when Maria was born and she was named after not one but two family members: both grandmothers. From her first day, Maria was pulled in two different directions by two very different women.

Maria's paternal grandmother, also Maria Butina, was a communist born after the Bolshevik revolution. In the Stalinist era, her devotion to communist ideology was commonplace, but as she rigidly held to those principles in the twenty-first century, she seemed dated to the next generation and mystifying to the generations after that. Imagine having a grandmother loyal to the Bull Moose Party, with the firm expectation that Teddy Roosevelt's theories would rise again.

This grandmother—Grandma Butina—was the man of the house. She never cleaned, cooked, or performed any of the usual domestic duties, which included giving familial affection to her husband and sons. She was present, but she instilled order in the household and demanded perfection. Grandma Butina gave her sons a good education, but beyond that, they were left to figure things out and find success on their own. A loyal communist, she advocated public service, just not the kind that started at home. As Grandma Butina thought, when true communism came, the kind preached by Lenin and Marx, her family would be dissolved.

For a time in the Soviet Union, there was a push to do that. As far as the Bolsheviks were concerned, the family was a capitalist construct designed to preserve private property and perpetuate class divisions. Once private ownership was abolished, the nuclear family could, in theory, cease to exist. Though the family unit was considered necessary during the transition, the Bolsheviks planned to phase it out. In 1918, the Soviets introduced new rules on marriage and family, which brought domestic life in Russia closer to Marxist theory.

Paradoxically, this revision of social norms ushered in a new era of feminism in Russia. Before 1914, women needed their husband's permission to work or attend university. After the revolution, at least legislatively on paper, women were on equal footing—whereas in the United States, women were still fighting for the right to vote. But these novel ideas didn't last. Stalinism brought a new wave of social and economic policies, and by 1936, there was a stark ideological shift away from the Bolshevik ideals. The revolutionary doctrine was deprecated as quickly as it came. It was during this ideological whiplash of social policy that Grandma Butina was born. And much like the secrecy of the Soviet state, she became a Matryoshka doll of socialist ideology—layered, silent, and sealed shut.

The paternal side of Maria's family was full of fascinating figures. Her great-great-grandfather was a cavalier in World War I. Her great-grandfather was an artillery fighter in World War II. Her great-grandmother was a beekeeper. Her grandfather was a shepherd, and her grandmother, Grandma Butina, was a teacher. She was born in Ukraine and raised near the country of Georgia. But beyond those details, secrecy mostly prevailed. Grandma Butina's husband Victor Butin had been incarcerated, though the younger generations didn't know why. Perhaps Victor himself didn't even know—it was Soviet Russia after all. But nobody on the paternal side discussed those family secrets. Nobody discussed anything but patriotism and politics through a socialist lens.

Grandma Butina and Victor Butin's son Valery had known Irina, his future wife, for about five years before they married. Yet they dated only a few months before he proposed. Following custom, Valery traveled to Irina's native village to ask her father for her hand in marriage, a tradition still followed today. Just as customary, the wedding took place in Gornyak, Grandma Butina and Victor Butin's village. It was there that Grandma Butina saw Irina's mother. But as it turned out, it wasn't their first meeting. By a strange twist of fate, they had met many years before.

Irina's mother, also named Maria—Grandma Shapovalova—was a city girl who grew up near Moscow. Well-educated in Stalin's Russia, she went on class trips across the Soviet Union to explore communist history, or at least the version the state wanted her and her fellow students to see. At university, Grandma Shapovalova traveled to the Caucasus Mountains in Georgia on a geological expedition, which sounds much more adventurous than my own college field trips. While on the school trip to the Soviet satellite state, Grandma Shapovalova met a gaggle of young women, one of whom shared her name. It was a brief meeting, and the odds of the two women ever crossing paths again—let alone being brought together decades later by the marriage of their children, among hundreds of millions across the Soviet Union—were extraordinary. Though they were young women when they first met, when they saw each other again years later, they instantly recognized each other.

Grandma Shapovalova's life was winding. In the Soviet days, it wasn't uncommon to be sent to some far-flung corner of the Soviet Union after finishing school, and she was no exception. The government took her passport, gave her a train ticket, and exiled her from the only home she had ever known. Able to return only once a year to visit her parents, she was forced to settle in the far western town of Lokot, a small village of a few hundred people. The grim circumstances of this banishment could have been ruinous if not for a chance encounter with Vladimir Shapovalov, an electrical engineer working in the town.

After a brief courtship, Vladimir proposed on a beautiful black horse in the white winter snow. Maria had been dating another man in Moscow, but the sight of Vladimir overtook her, and she felt compelled to follow her heart, another twist in her young life. In the beginning of their marriage, life was difficult. The young couple raised two children under extreme circumstances, trekking miles each day just to get water and food. Still, they were happy. They never argued. They teased each other, sure, but they loved one another deeply and openly. It was a relationship that stood in perfect contrast to Maria's paternal grandparents.

Without a doubt, the Butins and the Shapovalovs were different. The Butins were cold and closed off. The Shapovalovs were warm and accessible. Vladimir's family was an open book. He possessed a genealogical account, going back seven generations, that noted the heroism of his brother in World War II among other details of the family. These two polar tributaries, the Butins and the Shapovalovs, would eventually meet to create a wellspring of contradiction in their granddaughter on the eve of the Soviet collapse.

In the late 1980s, Gorbachev was leader of the USSR, and the Soviet republics were crumbling. Amid this collapse and among the spiraling unemployment and social unrest, Irina and Valery Butin had their first child. Maria was born in Barnaul, Siberia, on November 10, 1988. In the cold winter months that followed, when the high temperatures could peak at 40 degrees below freezing, Maria contracted pneumonia, a dire condition for an infant. Given the uncertainty of the time and the young couple's own difficult circumstances, Irina and Valery settled on a desperate remedy. Together, they traveled with Maria on a train to Kulunda, a village on the southern edge of Russia. There, Irina and Valery said goodbye to their new daughter before boarding a train back home.

Only an infant, unaware of what had happened, Maria spent the first six years of her life in an orphanage, an early turn of events that could have shattered her future. Yet, though her parents had left her, they had not abandoned her. Maria had not been given up for adoption. She had been placed in the care of her doting grandmother Maria Shapovalova, who worked at the orphanage.

It is Grandma Shapovalova along with her loving husband Grandpa Vladimir who raised Maria. In her earliest memories, Maria can recall the sights and smells of her beloved babushka: pancakes and mayflowers, pearls and fine clothing. And so it was, Maria followed in the literal footsteps of her grandmother, each day accompanying her to the orphanage where she taught and raised young children. Sometimes acting as a dorm mother and sometimes as a warden, Shapovalova raised both the abandoned children as well as her granddaughter from eight in the morning until nine at night. Some evenings, Maria would sleep in the orphanage with her grandmother, but usually, when her grandmother worked late, Maria would meet her grandfather halfway between the orphanage and the electric utility where he worked. In the summer months, Maria would race across the hot concrete street and leap into his arms. With great pomp, he would lift her into the air before embracing her. Carrying

Maria, Grandpa Vladimir would stop for a newspaper on the way home as they chatted about this and that.

On the weekends, Maria would work in the garden with her grandfather, whom she saw as an optimistic and strong leader. She loved burning leaves when autumn came. During lovely spring days, Vladimir taught his granddaughter chess, a game they would play for decades to come. Vladimir instilled in Maria a deep passion for reading. He read her mysteries and told her stories about the famous spies of the Soviet Union. He read her Jules Verne and described in great detail the *Nautilus*, the submarine helmed by the fictional Captain Nemo. At age six, when most Russians were just learning their letters, Maria was already a fluent reader, having been at it for years.

Maria's early life was unusual, but it was nothing if not ideal. Though she seldom saw her parents, who missed her dearly, the years spent with her grandparents were full of warmth, curiosity, and growth. Never once did she hear her grandparents quarrel. Never was she denied kindness. Yet, when Maria turned six, it was time to return to a home she barely knew to attend an elementary school she didn't know at all.

On August 25, 1995, Maria's parents Irina and Valery arrived at the only home Maria had ever known and loaded her into a white Volga, an expensive car for the time. Valery's business had been doing well, and the moment had come to begin again, properly this time. Shortly after returning to her parents' home, Maria started school.

In Russia, the first day of September is Knowledge Day, the beginning of the academic year for every school, college, and university in the country. At age six, Maria was taken by her mother to her first convocation, a bewildering experience for a child. Then, on September 2, the first day of class, instead of being brought to school like so many other children, Maria had to walk on her own. Maria's father had left for a business trip, and her mother had stayed home to care for Maria's little sister. Maria was afraid of the unknown, but as they say, you must face it eventually. No longer did Maria live with the parental figures who literally lit her path. Now she had to venture into darkness alone.

While the first school year was a frightening baptism and a tough integration into a new social order, her summer was spent with her grandparents. Along with her sister and their two cousins, the grandchildren would always spend each summer in Kulunda.

The four of them, all close in age, devoted most of each day to a single game. Not chess, which Maria still played with her grandfather on the weekends, but a game that undermined the very underpinnings of their communist past. They called it The Market. In the game, which was more of a social experiment, their grandparents' home was a society where capitalism ruled. The garden, the sauna, and the guesthouse were different shops and restaurants that did business to those who could afford their products and services. Maria's older cousin was often a banker, a customs agent, and a civil servant. For anything financial or governmental, he could help you—for a price. Maria published a newspaper, *Our Daily News*, which at its peak reached as many as six people. Maria also owned a casino to supplement her bottom line because the journalism racket was tough. Then again, times were frequently lean in the rat race, but at least you could blow off steam at the bar. The children would mix jam with water—they had no lemonade—and the cocktail would do the trick. The younger cousin usually did grunt work, cleaning and doing grandmother's chores. Maria's sister was in even worse shape. Often homeless, she received social welfare, a nod to a previous era in Russia. Throughout the day, the kids exchanged books, made fake money, and provided shoddy services. Inflation was a bear, but they soldiered through the difficult cycles because it was the spirit of the time. Capitalism was on the rise in Russia in the 1990s, so even children had financial empires, if only in their imaginations.

This was Maria's beginning: a newborn raised in Arcadia, transferred back to confront the real world alone, and then for the rest of her childhood, alternating between the fantasy of one and the grimness of the other. In some ways, this cycle reflected the two Marias from which the girl came. During the school year, she followed the dictates of Russian tradition, studied properly, and made few friends. Indeed, she was ordered and pragmatic like Grandma Butina. But during the summers, Maria indulged in her capitalist fantasies. She was curious about new things and met them with a warm and loving disposition like her Grandma Shapovalova. Ultimately, this passion would lead Maria on a path to another country.

When the children made their fake currency, they drew American dollar signs across the tender. Without fully realizing it, they were promoting the greatest antagonist to their motherland, the greatest proponent of capitalism in the world: the United States of America.

Chapter Four

Maria was arrested on a Sunday after a convoy of unmarked FBI vans sped toward her apartment a few blocks from American University. To the FBI, the timing was critical. They hadn't intercepted incriminating intelligence about past or upcoming criminal activity, but they had gotten wind that Maria was planning to possibly flee the country. In the legal world, we call that an indicator of consciousness of guilt. In truth, her possessions had been packed in boxes, and there was a U-Haul truck parked outside her apartment.

Special agents in bulletproof vests flooded the building. She was just one person, but they had to be ready in case she had firearms or explosive devices. Russian spies even have access to radioactive materials, biological weapons, and nerve agents—two assassins used such things in England on Sergei and Yulia Skripal a few months earlier. A young redhead posing as a graduate student may seem harmless, but caution can save lives.

With special agents in place, lead investigator Kevin Helson knocked on Maria's apartment. Her boyfriend answered. Helson called out for her, and she came to the door, setting down her strawberries and stepping away from the Wimbledon match that was on TV. When Helson asked her to step into the hallway, she complied. There, she was placed in handcuffs.

The FBI agents soon confirmed Maria's possessions were packed in boxes, but also discovered she wasn't fleeing to Russia. Naturally, U-Haul trucks have trouble driving across the ocean. She was moving to South Dakota with her boyfriend Paul Erickson, which would be a curious move for a Russian agent supposedly intent on infiltrating American politics. South Dakota certainly has its strengths, but political gravitas isn't one of them.

In hindsight, the idea that Maria was attempting to flee appeared specious at best. Before getting handcuffed, she had actually cooperated with the government. In April 2018, she spent eight hours testifying before the Senate Intelligence Committee. Just nine days later, federal agents searched her apartment, grabbing her computer and phone while she was baking banana bread. She voluntarily turned over her passwords to her electronics and answered every question. When she was arrested three months later, agents seized all her stuff and asked again for her passwords. She hadn't changed them. At no point during the FBI's investigation was Maria evasive, misleading, or hostile. And yet, on Sunday, July 15, 2018, she was taken into FBI custody.

Bob pleaded with the agents to let Maria spend the night at the FBI's Washington Field Office because Sunday was the worst possible day to get arrested. If you're picked up then, you end up waiting in the city's Central Cell Block (CCB) until Monday.

"It was a metal shelf for a bed, literally," said Reverend Graylan Hagler, who had recently been arrested for praying on the steps of the Supreme Court and taken to CCB. "Roaches were walking all over . . . as well as the ceilings and up the walls and on the floors" Hagler told local news. "For 28 hours we were kept in filth. I sat up all night and killed roaches."

And it's not just the roaches. Day and night, you're surrounded by desperate cries, the stench of urine and feces, and other sights of human decay. At CCB, everyone is packed together, whether they are detoxing addicts, violent offenders, or the mentally unhinged. Even if you arrive without a psychiatric disorder, anyone held in those conditions could easily express suicidal ideation after a single night's stay.

If you believe we live in a civilized society, I recommend you visit Washington's CCB. You may change your mind after you witness, as Pastor Hagler did, how we treat the most dispossessed and debilitated among us.

While Central Cell Block wasn't far from Bedlam, the sanctuary of the US District Court wasn't far from my office. Bob and I arrived that afternoon with little time before Maria's initial appearance in front of Magistrate Judge Robinson. The case was still sealed, so the media hadn't learned a suspected Russian agent was sitting downstairs. As we hastened across the polished stone floor, I could almost feel the tremors prefacing the earthquake to come.

Bob has mostly represented white-collar defendants who frequently have the privilege of self-surrender. I, on the other hand, met virtually all my indigent clients for the first time behind bars, so I knew the US Marshals cell block well.

The system is not the same for the rich and the poor.

The US Marshals Service protects federal courts and inmates, and when a defendant goes to a courthouse, it is the marshals who transport them. When Harrison Ford in *The Fugitive* escaped from prison custody, it was the marshals who hunted him down. Fun fact: Ford's character was inspired by a real-life doctor who was wrongly accused of murdering his wife.

I pushed a call button, and after the door clicked open, Bob and I stepped inside. We identified ourselves and handed over our bar cards. The marshal told us Maria was still being processed, which was just as well since Bob and I hadn't discussed what we'd say to the judge.

Though he didn't show it, Bob must have been nervous. Everything he said upstairs would be parsed by every major news outlet and every important lawyer in Washington. And with little understanding of the underlying evidence for the government's claims in the criminal complaint, it was a bit like tandem skydiving with Maria but at night. He had all the right gear and knew the kinds of spots he'd like to land, but he didn't know exactly where we were headed. I suppose I was the pilot in this metaphor because my job was to avoid turbulence along the way and help Bob and Maria land safely.

But I wasn't anxious. If anything, I was excited. I loved criminal defense work, and this was the first time in years I could represent someone at the criminal trial court level. In a way, it felt like returning home from a travel abroad. I remembered the sights and smells of those hallways and waiting rooms.

Bob and I were walking through some of the typical exchanges in an initial appearance when the door clicked open and a marshal waved us ahead. We passed through a little office where the marshals worked—copy machine, cubicles, desks—before turning toward the cell block. A door with thick steel bars was unlocked, and we stepped inside.

In the cell block, defense attorneys triage their clients like trauma nurses after a car crash. Sometimes you find them just after they've been picked up—bewildered, frightened, and overwhelmed—but you always need to figure out quickly whether it was just a fender bender or something worse. That bruised elbow might have to wait. Even a shattered leg now and then might get sidelined because sometimes they are bleeding out (figuratively) with a fractured skull and crushed spine, and the only thing that matters is keeping them alive.

I've met clients for the first time in holding who immediately dive into the weeds about what happened, who said what, why they did it, and other details. I stop them. Usually, there are other people nearby listening, which isn't ideal for protecting privileged conversations. My job at that moment is to get them out on pretrial release, arrange for any medical necessities, and contact worried family members. Everything else can wait.

Maria sat on one side of a small table. She wore khaki pants, a black-and-white-striped, long-sleeved shirt, and flats. Her bright red hair was limp. She was twenty-nine years old.

"Hi, Maria," Bob said. "This is Alfred, another lawyer working with us."

Her eyes were red. She'd been crying. She needed to lift both hands to wipe her face because her legs and wrists were chained. She was either in distress or very good at pretending to be.

After we exchanged greetings, Bob sat across from Maria, and I had a choice: sit next to him or next to her. Bob had worked with her on the Senate Intelligence Committee interview, but I was a brand-new face. I didn't want her to think I was judging her. That was not my job. Lawyers represent their clients, so I sat beside her. When I did, I noticed blood on her ankles and plastic sleeves wedged between the shackles and her skin. They had cuffed her too tightly and the metal had been digging into her Achilles tendon.

"Were you injured?" I asked.

"I cannot go back to that place. I cannot go back to that place."

I made a note to talk to Bob about Maria's need for medical attention for her ankles, and to flag a possible mental health concern given this was her first time in custody. If we didn't secure her release, she could—and likely would—be held under close observation. I'm not saying she was suicidal. But I knew a widow whose husband, overwhelmed by the stress of his sudden incarceration, killed himself by slashing his jugular vein in the DC jail where Maria might be headed.

"We're gonna get you out if we can," Bob said, "but the government is making a request that you be held until Wednesday. It'll probably be granted."

"I cannot go back to that place," she said in repeated succession, pulling against her chains. "You don't know what it's like. It's terrible. I cannot sleep!"

I didn't know it at the time, but there was a misunderstanding. She thought she would be sent back to CCB, though she'd actually be sent to the Correctional Treatment Facility—a local jail that, while far from ideal, is much nicer than CCB as far as lockups go within the DC Department of Corrections. If I had realized this, I could have eased some of her concerns, but I missed it.

"Do you want me to call your parents?" I asked.

She gave me the name of a friend to contact so I could reach her family. Then she said she was thirsty—she hadn't had water since her arrest—and like that, we were out of time. We told Maria we'd see her upstairs, and as we were headed out, I asked the marshal if he could give her something to drink. I overheard the marshal offer her some apple juice as we stepped through the office and heavy doors to make our way out of the US Marshals cell block and back upstairs to the courtroom.

The courtroom should have been sparsely populated since it was still a sealed case. It couldn't be searched in any databases. The government didn't issue any press releases. Any private citizen wouldn't have a clue about what was going on unless they were the client's lawyer or a family member.

The government, on the other hand, knew everything that was happening. When we stepped into the courtroom, their side was filled with FBI agents, colleagues from the US Attorney's Office, maybe even an intern or two. The government seems to love to fill these hearings with supporters, and as if they had rehearsed it, they acted with pitch-perfect condescension. I didn't know their case yet, so it might have been justified. Meanwhile, on our side—apart from Bob, Maria, and me—there was one *Washington Post* reporter, Tom Jackman, who somehow got the hot scoop. How did he find out about a case that had been sealed right up until it was called? I can tell you this: it didn't come from us, or from anyone on our side.

"All rise," the courtroom deputy called.

We stood as Judge Robinson entered the courtroom. It had been nearly a decade since I saw her in law school, where she taught my small seminar class. Once a deliberate, firm professor who clearly knew the nuts and bolts of criminal matters, she sat before us, still deliberate and firm, but with shorter, slightly greying hair. This was the same judge who oversaw the initial court appearances of many high-profile criminal defendants including Paul Manafort, the former campaign chair for Donald Trump.

Federal magistrate judges sign arrest warrants, authorize wire taps, conduct initial appearances, make bail determinations, and arraign defendants—the basic judicial housekeeping of criminal procedure. The next five minutes were pro forma and routine.

Judge Robinson granted the government's requests to unseal the case, hold Maria, and delay the bail hearing for two days. Bob previewed why Maria should be released pretrial, though we knew the judge would wait to rule until after a full hearing.

The whole thing lasted about ten minutes.

The government's side shook hands with each other—kind of a lawyer's high-five. To me, taking someone's liberty, whether just or not, is never something to celebrate. I know there is a certain segment of society that is thrilled when criminals are locked up, but while the incarceration of criminals can be just and fair, it is never good. It is sometimes the last punctuation on a human life gone horribly wrong, the clearest indication of failure.

I turned to Maria and saw panic. Perhaps it was the fear of returning to CCB that caused the desperation I saw in her eyes. Perhaps this was simply what happens when you're an immigrant detained in a foreign country. Or perhaps the banal formality of the process was the cause. If the government could imprison someone with such indifference, what chance did Maria have moving forward?

I walked with her to the rear courtroom door as the marshals escorted her away. "I know where you're going," I said, "and I'll see you tonight—I promise."

A criminal complaint outlines the charges someone has been accused of, and an affidavit presents the investigator's evidence in support of those charges. For Maria's case, you can read both the complaint and affidavit in the appendix, and if you do read them, like I did that afternoon after I got back from the courthouse, your jaw may drop like mine did as I sat at my desk.

Even though I had represented clients accused of a wide range of charges—from financial crimes to drug world and violent offenses—never have I read in a court document the broad strokes of the relationship between the United States and Russia, our most sustaining historical antagonist. The affidavit explained the history of Russian influence operations to degrade our democracy, a startling foreword to the key pieces of evidence that would be used against Maria if this case went to trial. I've seen Tom Hanks represent a Russian spy in a Spielberg movie. I've seen TV shows about Soviet sleeper agents here in DC. I've read fiction about red sparrows, Russian agents who use "sexpionage" to trap their prey. Never have I ever seen that fiction written in an affidavit for a client that I am representing.

Maria was charged with Title 18 of the United States Code, section 951 (Agents of Foreign Governments) and section 371 (Conspiracy to Commit Offense or to Defraud United States). I'll explain what those are in a moment, but in short, they're felonies—the more serious side of the felony/misdemeanor divide. So much more serious that not only do employers usually ask about the graver of the two designations, but even the Supreme Court draws the line there: felonies and other serious offenses, as opposed to petty ones, are the kinds that invoke our Sixth Amendment right to a jury trial. Felonies are the types of charges you don't want to screw up—not just because they carry longer sentences, but also because for visa holders or permanent residents, a felony conviction can mean automatic removal from the country once their sentence is complete.

In this case, the charge of acting as an agent of a foreign government carried a maximum of ten years in federal prison, and the conspiracy charge added another five. Maria was looking at a maximum sentence of fifteen years behind bars.

What did she do? That would take time for us to fully understand. But according to the affidavit, Special Agent Helson alleged that she conspired with "Russian Official," "U.S. Person 1," and "U.S. Person 2" to carry out a kind of shadow diplomacy. The details were unusual—"friendship dinners," "prayer breakfasts," and outreach to politically connected groups like "Gun Rights Organization" (understood to be the National Rifle Association, or NRA), all designed to put her in the orbit of Washington's movers and shakers, including US politicians. It was all framed as an effort to influence American power brokers for the benefit of the Russian Federation.

In court documents, the government will use pseudonyms like "Russian Official" or "U.S. Person 1" to protect a person's identity. Sometimes this is because the individual is an undercover agent or FBI informant— typically labeled a "Confidential Informant" (though our case didn't have one). Other times, it's to avoid dragging someone's name into a sordid story when they haven't been charged with a crime.

As I sat in my office reading the affidavit, I didn't yet know who those three anonymous men were. Soon enough, I'd learn that one was an alleged Russian mafia kingpin turned politician, another a longtime Republican operative, and the third a Rockefeller heir.

I read through the most damning quotations scattered through the affidavit as the plots of Russian spy novels flitted through my head:

All that is needed is for your friends to provide you with the financial resources to spend the time in America to TAKE ALL OF THESE MEETINGS.

* * *

[You] ha[ve] the responsibility of a serious mission – restoration of relations between countries.

* * *

We made our bet. I am following our game. . . . I am just starting in this field. I still have to learn and learn from you! . . . By your recommendation, I am setting up the groundwork here but I am really in need of mentoring.

* * *

[T]he risk of provocation is too high and the 'media hype' which comes after it. . . . Only incognito! Right now everything has to be quiet and careful.

* * *

I'm going to sleep. It's 3 am here. I am ready for further orders.

* * *

[A]ll our phones are being listened to!

I glanced at the two iPhones sitting on my desk—one personal, and the other for work—and wondered if they were being tapped by the Russians, the FBI, or both.

The charges against Maria, as laid out by Helson, were stark. But I was broken from the narrative he was building by a line near the end of his affidavit:

At no time did BUTINA notify the Attorney General . . . that she would and did act in the United States as an agent of a foreign government.

Then I remembered that section 951 isn't really about covert sabotage. It's a failure-to-notify law, a process crime, like not registering for military service or failing to file your taxes. You can legally work for a foreign government or official in the United States. There are hundreds of people doing that right now. But unless you're working for a diplomat, an embassy, or fall under a few other carve-outs, you need to notify the Attorney General. The statute doesn't specify how exactly to notify the Attorney General. But sending a letter that identifies yourself, the foreign government or official you're working with, the nature of the proposed activities, and the antici- pated duration would keep you in the clear. If Maria had done that simple act, there would be no charges against her, which was a curious truth from the way the affidavit read.

I also clocked that even though the affidavit read like a spy novel, Maria wasn't charged under the Espionage Act, the law reserved for actual spies and far more serious offenses, carrying penalties of up to twenty years behind bars. Helson didn't accuse her of anything spy-worthy either— not stealing trade secrets, passing classified info, hacking, obstruction of justice, or making false statements to investigators or Congress. That last omission was especially intriguing since I knew she had testified before Congress, answering questions from a Senate committee. A lie there could've easily triggered charges. She told the truth.

However, affidavits aren't meant to reveal everything. They mostly lay out just enough to warrant an arrest and bring criminal charges, not the full scope of the government's case. And for a matter like this, with national security interests at play, much of that evidence could be classified, under seal, or simply not available to us yet. Perhaps this might be just the tip of the iceberg. Still, I knew something else. I'm a defense attorney. I started as a public defender, then volunteered for a legal aid organization that rep- resented the indigent accused for free. I've seen prosecutors delay turning over exculpatory information. I've seen them obfuscate, stall, and muddle. I've seen them offer spin in court. So while I didn't yet know the full extent of where we stood, I knew to be cautious and reasonably skeptical.

"I just read the affidavit," I said to Bob after walking to his office.

He slouched forward. "Yeah, I don't buy it."

"Why?" I asked.

"I've been working with her for months. Something isn't right here. Talk to her."

In Washington, DC, pretrial detainees and those serving short-term sen- tences are held at the Correctional Treatment Facility (CTF) if female, or the Central Detention Facility (CDF) if male. When I arrived, Maria was still being processed, which was done on the male side of the complex, so they told me to go there to find her.

A guard at the front desk wouldn't let me inside, even though lawyers normally have 24/7 access to their clients. I asked if he could help me locate Maria to find out when she might be available for a legal visit, but he declined. I explained that Maria didn't have my contact information, had no funds in her commissary account to reach me, and that it was late—likely too late for an inmate services counselor to assist, as they had probably gone for the day. Fortunately, another officer beginning her shift overheard our conversation, understood the situation, and offered to take my business card. Maria would call me.

"That's very kind. Thank you."

She said it wasn't a problem because she'd need to walk her and any other female inmates over when they're finished being processed anyway. She told me to write Maria's full name on the back of my business card, and she'd have Maria call me.

I returned to my car and texted my boyfriend to see if Piper, our fifteen-pound puppy, had given him any trouble.

She viciously attacked the St. Bernard down the hallway, he texted.

His name is Bismarck, and he's a Bernese Mountain Dog, I wrote back.

Same diff. I heard about your client. Russian spy?

Before I could respond, my phone rang.

"This is Alfred," I said.

"It's Maria," she said. "Thank you. I want to apologize for being mean earlier."

"Don't apologize," I said. "Are you feeling better?"

"Yes, I've had a shower now. This place is much nicer."

"Glad to hear it. Will you ask the officer when you're going over to CTF?"

"One minute," she said before conferring with the officer. "We're going over now."

"Okay, great. I know where you're going, and I'll see you in ten minutes."

I waited a bit and then walked the path to CTF, a four-story, sand-colored institutional building that looks like a library built in the 1970s for a university with anemic funding. Neither welcoming nor intimidating, it's a structure that only does one thing: houses inmates. After I cleared security and stepped into the frigid facility, the interior, which I knew well, was like any jail on a cable television program about local lock-ups: large grey metal doors, faded paint, chipped concrete floors.

I took the elevator up and stepped into a space with two double doors with a window slit. After they buzzed me in, I pushed through the double doors. In the middle of the room was the family visiting area with a few attorney rooms. There's a vending machine and a security booth where the guard sits. I found Maria in the visitation area, where she smiled and greeted me with a hug and wet hair. Even though she had just been locked up and had just met me, she was happy to see me merely because I kept my promise.

We walked into a little office, a four-by-eight-foot room with a table, a couple chairs, a clock, and a TV. After Maria stepped inside and sat down, I closed the solid steel door, cutting off the feint hum from the other side. Before I sat, I stepped to the TV and unplugged it. This was not something I normally did. In fact, I've never done it before or since. But it indicated the paranoia I felt in that moment—my concerns about what the government might do in a case like this. To secretly monitor a conversation between a client and her attorney would violate a host of rules, but there I was unsure of where I was in a place where I've been many times before.

Maria noticed the curious behavior, but I made no mention of it as I sat down.

"I haven't properly introduced myself," I said.

I was exhausted and hungry. I ate meat loaf standing over the kitchen sink while my boyfriend and Piper slept in the next room. After washing up and taking out my contacts, I slipped into bed and sighed.

Brendan shifted.

"I heard about your client. A Russian spy?"

I didn't answer because I didn't know.

There's a risk to pushing your client's innocence right out of the gate. Maybe not a risk with the person sleeping next to you, but you can lose credibility in my professional world. You might be seen as tricked by your client, easily misled, or simply gullible. Embracing their innocence too readily can also do harm. The more committed a lawyer becomes to a particular narrative, the more constrained the client feels, which makes it harder for the lawyer to get, and the client to share, a full, unedited account of what actually happened.

A spy?

No, I didn't think so. I saw no evidence to support that. I also trusted Bob, who had known Maria for longer. Russian agent or not though, the fact wouldn't make me work any less hard to get the best possible result.

Chapter Five

In-N-Out Burger is a chain of fast-food restaurants with a widely known "secret" menu that appears on no official bill of fare. Ask for "spread" on the side, and you'll get a soufflé cup of secret sauce. If Russian jurisdictions were In-N-Out items, federal districts would be spread. They don't appear in the Russian constitution or any principal document, but everyone knows how to order the sauce. The whole point of these jurisdictions is to allow the federal government to organize its constituent parts. In Russia, there are eight federal districts, and if you ask me which of them most resides in that place where reality and myth collide, my answer would be unequivocal: Siberia.

Both the frozen hinterland of legend and the banal territory of fact, Siberia possesses a mythology that lies closer to truth than you might expect. Discussions surrounding this geographic Frigidaire can quickly reach superlative heights, and you might believe the discourse that surrounds the five million square miles of land is cresting into hyperbole, until, when you dig down into the nitty gritty of Eurasian history, you learn that vodka doesn't top out at 100 proof and can, in certain regions of the world—e.g., Siberia—approach the alcoholic ratios of jet fuel. Usually then, with a bit more research, the hyperbolic stratosphere appears fitting for this teratoidal tundra, perhaps even diminutive for a region called the "Sleeping Land," which to me evokes a monster resting for the past several eons like a jack-in-the-box on the eve of tectonic catastrophe.

Case in points:

Exhibit A: The Trans-Siberian Railway, the longest train line in the world, stretching from Moscow to Vladivostok, a span more than double the width of the continental United States. The expanse of track was literally built by emperors. Or supervised by them anyway.

Exhibit B: The Siberian tiger, the largest cat in the world weighing nearly seven hundred pounds and sporting fur striped in either orange and black or a chic chiffon white.

Exhibit C: The village of Oymyakon, which has the cruel distinction of being the coldest municipality in the world with winters that plunge to −90 degrees Fahrenheit.

Exhibit D: Lake Baikal, the planet's largest body of fresh water and a lake that puts the "Great" ones to shame. Lake Baikal accounts for 20 percent of all unfrozen fresh water in the *world*.

Exhibit E: The Gulag. The cruelest and most extensive network of labor camps, where political dissidents were worked to death. This collection of detention centers was dismantled after the fall of Stalin, but brutal penitentiaries still exist in the Sleeping Land though we don't call it the Gulag anymore. Branding matters. While the prison system no longer works you to death, sometimes death is a preferable outcome.

Stark, snowy, and sizable, Siberia endures as an ideal synecdoche for Russia. Americans can think of it in distant, vague terms—like stark, snowy, and sizable—but while that image isn't wrong, it's incomplete. The region is also home to massive cities surpassing a million inhabitants. The northernmost border of Siberia may kiss the frozen Arctic, but the territory runs the entire height of Russia, all the way down to its southern bits. Likely larger than you imagined, Siberia accounts for 70 percent of Russia's landmass. If Siberia were to secede from the motherland and stitch together its own flag, it would still be the largest country on Earth. Not bad for a place where I bet rubles to pishkis you can't name a single city, even allowing for the one I mentioned above.

Within Siberia, we have ten federal subjects, which come in a variety of flavors: oblasts, republics, krais, okrugs, cities, and one single autonomous oblast, which is Jewish and basically the Boca Raton of the federal subject scene. The Russian Federation, the proper moniker for Russia, is so named because the state is a collection of eighty-five federal subjects, which are like American states, or perhaps the countries in the United Kingdom are a better analogy. Let's put it this way, I won't return to fast-food metaphors if you're willing to accept my thesis that federal subjects are their own thing.

But where were we? Right, unnesting these Russian dolls.

Within the Siberian district, there's one particular federal subject called Altai Krai. Remember, "krai" is just one kind of federal subject—not the Boca type—but a kind that means "edge" or "on the border."

Altai Krai runs along the southern part of the Russian Federation on the border with Kazakhstan. It's kind of like calling North Dakota "Dakota Border," to make sure Winnipeg knows it doesn't belong to the United States. If you take anything away from this geography lesson, it's that Altai Krai is not the Altai Republic. That's a *different* kind of federal subject—though still not the Jewish kind. Unlike the Altai Republic, which gets the definite article, Altai Krai is compared to the Swiss Alps by Russian travel agents everywhere. AK, an acronym no one uses, has dense pine forests, soaring mountains, and crystalline lakes and rivers. If anything, it stands closest in natural beauty to the more temperate Alaskan wilderness. Altai Krai also boasts large cities. One such city buried in this nesting doll of government groupings is Barnaul, which vastly dwarfs cities like Anchorage, Alaska. Situated on the western banks of the Ob River in the Altai Krai region of Siberia, Barnaul boasts over 600,000 people, roughly the population of Washington, DC, and in many ways, Barnaul is a microcosm for the transitions of Russian history from feudalism to the empire to the Soviet era.

I'll skip the SparkNotes on the noble family who founded this town, the Russian serfs who worked the mines, the Grand Duchess who helped abolish serfdom, and the munitions manufactured to fight the Nazis, and I'll jump right to today.

Barnaul is an industrial town with diesel and carbon processing, heavy machinery, tires, furniture, and footwear. But in the early 1990s, one particular product of Barnaul was developed and manufactured by an electrical engineer and furniture salesmen, then shipped overseas. In the Russian Federation, in the district of Siberia, in the subject of Altai Krai, in the city of Barnaul was the place where Maria Butina grew up.

On an overnight train at the age of six, Maria left the semipermanent care of her grandparents in Kulunda to return to Barnaul. Both Kulunda and Barnaul are nestled in Altai Krai with similar cold and dry winters and hot, equally dry summers, but to a little girl, they were sister cities on distant planets. Maria's parents Valery and Irina met her at the train station with a bouquet of flowers picked from their garden—a tradition the Butins still practice when a visitor arrives by train or plane—and for the next decade, Maria would be Barnaulian. She'd continue spending each vacation with her grandparents in their village, but now Maria was a big-city girl in a metropolis falling to ruin.

Only a couple years before Maria's return, before the collapse of the Soviet Union and the crumbling of the Berlin Wall, lines of fatalistic customers were a permanent fixture outside shops with poorly stocked shelves. Living standards had been declining in Russia, one of the fifteen national republics in the USSR, but the decline was for a curious reason: suppressed inflation. Basically, while incomes were rising, supply couldn't match demand, and so the Soviets perfected a complicated ballet to maintain their lives. "*To, schro ne videsh v magazinakh, videsh na stok.*" What you don't find in the store, you find in the home, which describes the flowers that Valery and Irina plucked from their garden. In 1991, when the Soviet Union was finally dissolved, the music stopped, and the dancers found themselves without partners. The dismantling of the Berlin Wall stood as an inspiring symbol for pro-democracy advocates, but for Russians it symbolized the disintegration of economic ties that led to a crippling economic crisis and a catastrophic decline in living standards worse than the Great Depression.

While Maria's family had once lived a charmed life taking their white Volga down the streets of Barnaul, Valery's furniture business collapsed. However, despite the lack of finer things, the family, including Maria's younger sister Marina, were content with the untamed charm of the Russian alps. Maria spent cherished time with her father in the pristine rolling foothills, grasslands, lakes, rivers, and mountains of the region while also enjoying the many museums, arboretums, and amusement parks with her mother. For a child, GDP is not the metric of your living standard. It is the strength of family bonds, and for Maria, the forecast was looking fair.

Because the larger economy was in shambles, so too was the struggling downtown, but as Maria aged into adolescence, fine dining and fine shopping were the furthest things from her mind. A tomboy from the time she could walk, Maria always drifted toward the masculine. Besides playing sports like volleyball with her father, she spent most of her leisure hours with her spirited group of friends—all boys. These comrades were the crazy ones. The misfits. The rebels. The troublemakers. In school, if somebody had scratched a bad word on a desk, you could be sure it was her crew. They weren't exactly the criminal masterminds of Barnaul, but you could bet a scheme was cooking if it got a little too quiet. You might think, after extrapolating her trifling indiscretions, that we have a felon in the making, but if childhood peccadillos mean a lifetime of hard time, then roughly one-third of my doctor, lawyer, and teacher friends would be away for life.

In Russia, there's a saying about the closest of companions: you cannot separate them even with water. For Maria, her other half was Oleg. Certainly, water carved the very mountains of Altai Krai, but to continue the judicial themes, perhaps a better English idiom to describe Maria and Oleg would be thick as thieves. Arm in arm and partners in crime, they were and still are best friends, soulmates really in the most metaphysical sense. Growing up, he had a girlfriend, and she had a boyfriend, and never was there ever an inkling of romance between them. Rather, it was a spiritual bond like between the inseparable twins Lada and Lado of Slavic mythology. Maria and Oleg's souls were stitched so tightly that no light could shine between them.

When they were young, Maria, Oleg, and the gang would play games in the streets. Tag and capture the flag from time to time, but their absolute favorite was Cossacks-Robbers (*Kazaki-razboyniki*). A bit like the American Cops and Robbers yet far more interesting and with a touch of the sinister, this Eastern European game dates to the Russian empire when the Cossacks were the people's champions. In some ways, they still are. The Cossacks are a group of mostly East Slavic Orthodox Christians that escaped serfdom centuries ago and became known as members of semi-military communities originating in the steppes of Eastern Europe. "Semi-military" is the operative word for the games Maria played on the streets. These Cossacks, still an important ethnic group in Russia, Ukraine, and Belarus, were fighters. Across their breast they wore gazyrs, which were clothing for bullets and gun powder, so they were always ready for ambush. Maria, Oleg, and the boys were the freedom fighters of their little realm.

To begin the game, players are divided into Cossacks and robbers, usually by lot, though sometimes by team captains. Rules are made and boundaries are drawn. The Cossacks then scout and prepare a hidden dungeon, while the robbers hold a private meeting to come up with a secret code. Once set, the robbers flee. During their decampment, the Cossacks aren't allowed to peek. Instead, the robbers split up and leave a trail, drawing arrows in chalk on asphalt, walls, or fences, to give the Cossacks clues about where to search. The faster the robbers scurry about and the more baffling their arrows, the better their chances of hiding without getting caught. After waiting around fifteen minutes, the Cossacks begin their hunt. If they catch a robber, he's taken to the dungeon. Another robber can free him—if they manage to find it. But it's in the dungeon where this game takes a grim turn. That's where robbers are tortured. After all, this is the land of the Gulag. Torment is always in the cards.

Torture—in a children's game!

Surely, it's just name calling.

Not entirely. Captured robbers might face downright miseries ranging from merciless tickles, crawling insects, and prickling nettles. But there's a method to the madness. The Cossacks are after something: the secret code. At the start of the game, before the robbers fled, their cabal devised two or more secret codes, only one of which was real. Under pressure, a captured robber could either hold out or crack by spilling the beans. It's up to the Cossacks to determine whether the beans are true. If they guess correctly, or capture all of the robbers, they win. If not, the robbers can regroup, strike back, and claim the Cossacks' headquarters as their own.

Sometimes in these games, you'll need swift help from a compatriot, so fast feet are essential. Sometimes you must draw confusing directions to throw off the other team, making deception key. Sometimes, clever interrogation and a knack for theater or lying are crucial. And sometimes, coercive methods are the only way to extract the truth.

Is Cossacks-Robbers the perfect training ground for a budding spy? Without a doubt. But if you think Maria's path was so easily foretold, you'll find yourself wide of the mark.

The Russian equivalent of the baby-delivering stork is that infants are found in cabbage patches. Valery, Maria's father, always teased his darling girl that he discovered her not in a patch of cabbages but in a patch of poisoned mushrooms. In many ways, no perfect metaphor could be found for Maria's lot in life. Among her associates, she was definitely the poison mushroom, which is to say among her lot of ne'er-do-wells, she was the negative of negatives: the only exemplary one in the bunch. She was the academic star who never got in trouble. Not once in Maria's life would she ever earn anything less than an A, and as a stellar student with shifty friends, she was the perfect front to launder their minor misdeeds.

Case in points:

Exhibit A: In school, the gang had computer class, but since Russia's economy had recently collapsed and finances were stretched thin, they didn't have computers to use. Instead, the teacher Kutlan Sergei gave them pieces of paper with little printed keyboards, and they'd practice typing commands until their PCs arrived. When they finally were blessed with tech from the gods, it was a magical transformation for the young students. Suddenly, they were computer programmers being led by Mr. Sergei and the giant projector situated on a desk. If you were once a scamp, you may already know what was cooking in the minds of Maria's gang, and it wasn't long before an illicit image was projected onto the screen. A matter of weeks, and good old Mr. Sergei was hacked by his budding black hats. Was the image of a woman in a swimsuit, or was she completely naked? I imagine the latter, but after the pic was excised from public consumption, the objective became to find the culprit. The poor, blushing Mr. Sergei demanded to know who was responsible, but in Russia, just as it is in the United States, there's an old phrase that translates to "snitches get stitches." The guilty party? Why, the best student in the course: Maria, the poison mushroom.

Exhibit B: In school, they held elections for the student council led by the school president. Maria, the competitive fireball in preadolescent business, indoor volleyball, or playful torture, very much wished to win that presidency. So her campaign team—her crew—cooked up a scheme. They printed posters of Vladimir Putin, a popular politician at the time, and augmented the "P" and added an "A" to reflect the hopeful future president of the school: Butina. At night, they broke onto campus and pasted the posters in the hallways, ruining the walls in the process. The next day there was electricity in the air when people marveled at the crackerjack campaign move from a political neophyte that was sure to garner the support of the proletariat.

She lost.

To this day, Maria believes the election was rigged as many votes had been on the national stage. Welcome to Russian democracy, I suppose. She ran an election that skirted the rules but was beaten by a rigged system likely because of the company she keeps.

Exhibit C: Militarism was an integral part of Russian life, and citizens of the motherland must conscript for one year. In high school, the Russians still practice for nuclear war, presumably in a battle with the Americans, and basic military training was mandatory for all children. They were taught how to shoot and given some basic self-defense training, but when Maria was in school, those combative lessons were available only to the boys. The girls were shuttled off to learn first aid. As you might imagine for the tomboy bound by her hips to her brothers-in-arms, this exclusion made Maria furious. Why not her? She was certainly stronger, faster, and smarter than most of her male classmates. Inequality had always bothered her, and now it felt personal—so she stomped down the hallway to her teacher Captain Andrei to demand an explanation.

An American first encountering a furious Russian can be startled. The Russian might not smile even in a friendly conversation. When McDonald's first came to the Soviet Union in 1990, they had to teach their Moscow employees how to plaster on a grin, fake or not, which the populace found suspicious at first. And of course it is, but it is also comforting to an American. Anyway, a Russian scowl can be a hammer and sickle. A Russian scowl from a fiery redhead might make you consider when you last updated your will. Captain Andrei, however, was a Russian man, and a brisk dismissal of his discontented student came naturally to him. In America, several parent-teacher conferences would be on the books. In Russia, you get a curt dismissal.

Of course, Maria is not the type of mushroom you dismiss, so every day, she stood outside her teacher's office. For months on end, she stood there, not to wear him down in some Gandhian protest or civil rights sit-in. No, she stood there each day because Captain Andrei was a smoker, and it was strictly forbidden to smoke inside school buildings. If there was a drug narc standing outside his office every day for months, eventually he might crack. And crack he did. He didn't like folding to a teenage girl, but the alternative to folding was much worse: nicotine withdrawal. Pressure applied at just the right spot can reap rewards.

Maria was allowed to join the boys in their fantasy combat training but under one condition: she would be treated as a boy. No special allowances for feminine pursuits. No gendered objectives for their missions. Which is all just as well. Maria wouldn't have it any other way. Pleased, she succeeded in all the various disciplines, surpassing most of her peers in the same activities. When a government official visited the school to check the readiness of the Youth Army, the fat frog in military paraphernalia carefully adjudicated each recruit and how they might assimilate into the military. This one an infantryman. That one a comms guy. As he went down the line giving checks to his new draftees, he reached Butina and did the Russian equivalent of a spit take.

"Butin . . . *a*? What the hell is going on!"

Captain Andrei shrugged. He had his cigarettes, and all was right in the world. Sometimes when Russian indifference is dispatched on your side, it feels good. Needless to say, Maria never served in the army like her compatriots, but that was just as well. She had other interests.

Chapter Six

"I'm Alfred. I'm thirty-five. I've been practicing law for nearly eight years, some of that time as a public defender. Before we begin, I want you to know two important things. First, whatever you tell me is confidential. Other than Bob and the other lawyers at McGlinchey on your team, I won't and can't share what you tell me to anyone else in the world without your consent. Second, I'll never judge you for anything you tell me. I'm not a judge. I'm not a jury. My job is to represent your interests to the best of my abilities. Now, there will be times when I question you, and you might feel like I'm against you. I'm not. I'm always on your side, but it's important for me to ask you tough questions to get an understanding of what happened to best prepare your defense. I'll usually give you a heads-up when I'm doing this so you don't feel attacked, but remember: in this case, I work for you and only you."

It's an important speech I give to new defendants because sometimes I'm the only one in their corner, and the idea that your corner man might seem to be rooting for the big bruiser on the other side can shatter you. For some, it does. Under the weight of prosecution, isolation, and everything at stake, some defendants come undone. In the justice system, suicide watch is a real thing—and I've represented people who know the cost of that despair, having lost family members to it. I've also had the unsettling experience of feeling attacked by my own side.

When I was a public defender in Boston, I represented a man charged with violating a restraining order from jail. That might sound like a paradox, but restraining orders also cover phone calls and my client definitely made one. He called his ex-girlfriend to apologize for past wrongs and left a voicemail that began, "I know I shouldn't be calling you." The problem with the prosecution's case was that he didn't know his ex had gotten a new restraining order against him. There had been an old no-contact order, but it had already expired. The new one hadn't been served, and jail records showed he didn't receive it until after the call. I pointed all this out to the prosecutor on the case, but she didn't seem to care—which was strange, considering they were missing a pretty essential element of the charge.

Sometimes prosecutors and police officers get so locked into their belief that someone is guilty that they try to force a conviction regardless of the evidence. These are the Judge Dredd types and they're dangerous to any justice system.

In my restraining order case, the prosecutor refused to drop the charge and instead gave me a plea offer that included jail time. She was convinced his voicemail—"I know I shouldn't be calling you"—was enough, even though that's how apologetic people sometimes talk. And since he was already in jail, she insisted, what difference did it make? Take the deal. And it almost worked. My client came close to pleading guilty, just to get it over with, but couldn't stomach admitting to something he didn't do. So we went to trial. That isn't always the outcome. Plenty of people plead guilty because the risk of losing at trial is too great. It's a problem, and it frankly shows how flawed plea negotiation can be because it can have no regard for innocence. Refusing to accept that kind of unjust fate, no matter the consequences, has always made sense to me. And to be fair, sometimes taking the deal does too.

But here's where the story became a learning lesson about how a team should operate, and how a client can see her lawyer once he starts questioning her case. My supervisor in Boston was a skilled lawyer and seasoned public defender, and she vetted my defense theory, which is a necessary part of the process. I'm fine with the back-and-forth of asking tough questions to make sure everything has been considered—the dotting and crossing that comes with supervision. The problem was, she wasn't critiquing my argument, offering insights, or helping me tease out weaknesses. From my perspective, she was criticizing *me*. I get that there's a subtle shading between critique and criticism. But we've all had teachers or mentors who've provoked those kinds of feelings. I don't have a particularly fragile ego, and I'm able to dodge the usual family baiting at a Thanksgiving table, so when my supervisor pushed me to get a better deal or press the client harder on taking a plea, despite his being manifestly innocent of a crime, know that my agitation was deserved. It almost seemed like she was working for the prosecution.

There's a competing dichotomy about what makes the best public defender and criminal defense attorney: those who are your friends or those who are your lawyers. The way I phrased the choice makes it seem like I'm leading the witness—because, of course, you'd want a lawyer when you need one. But in truth, as with most things, neither end of the spectrum is ideal.

It's possible that in my restraining order case, I was just a fresh-faced and idealistic greenhorn willing to go to the mat for each injustice I saw. But perhaps my supervisor was at the other end, nearing the burned-out, jaded stage that public defenders and defense attorneys know all too well. Maybe she was once like me, which can lead to a faster burn out. As for me, I was a lawyer, yes, but also a friend. And any attack on mine felt like an attack on me. Incidentally, that supervisor would leave the public defender's office soon after to become a judge, and I would take my case to trial and win.

Back in DC jail, Maria appeared reassured by my little speech. But one can never be certain—she came from a different country, with a different culture and justice system. In Moscow, lies might flow a bit more freely in the Russian courts. Not here in the United States.

That's worth pausing on. Despite all the commonly riffed lawyer jokes, here in this country, lying to clients, judges, or even third parties (yes, even misleading TV ads are a no-no) is a swift way to get yourself a bar complaint. A couple years ago, Rudy Giuliani, a.k.a. "America's Mayor" to those with long memories, had his ability to practice law in New York suspended because, according to a five-judge appellate panel, he had made "demonstrably false and misleading statements to courts, lawmakers and the public at large."

Though some may believe otherwise, law is an honest profession. And we have organizations in place to investigate malpractice, adjudicate misconduct, and when necessary, remove lawyers from practice. Does your profession have that? Not even doctors have such weight on their shoulders—prohibited from lying only in matters of medical malpractice and patient safety. Outside of that, they're welcome to spin whole tales of fiction. Indeed, not too long ago, this deception was part of the job. A patient diagnosed with cancer? Tell the spouse but lie to the patient.

Hold up, you might say before offering an anecdote about your ex-wife's lawyer who lied in court about all sorts of things. First, you're not a great witness. Second, lawyers are held accountable for *deliberate* false statements. That means we have to know something is false when we say it to get into trouble. Yet, the rule goes further: we're also not allowed to say things we *think* are false either. I've had clients confess to crime, so I didn't go to court and claim otherwise. I've also had clients claim they were innocent, even when I had real doubts, and in those cases, I didn't say something I didn't believe.

But I'll admit there's a reason why lawyers have the reputations we do. I think it mainly comes down to two things. We represent both sides of every case, so if you see courtrooms as battlegrounds of good versus evil—which is a shallow view—then lawyers cancel each other out in the moral fight. In addition, we often have both good and bad evidence, but then make strategic decisions on what to present in court. Our duty is to pursue the best outcome for the client. Still, I get why a layperson might look at me with suspicion. Even some in my family have raised the occasional eyebrow, though I also know I'm the one they call when something falls apart. To practiced attorneys, we all know the feints and jukes our colleagues make. We know where the Red Queen will land, and we know how to draw our own inferences rather than the ones opposing counsel wishes us to draw.

Unsure of her present conditioning, I asked Maria where she grew up, about her family, her education, the kinds of topics you might broach over a cocktail on a first date. It's important to lay these foundational stones—not just for the information they yield, but because trust and truth are both paramount to having a good working relationship. It also helps me get a sense about how best to communicate with a client. Code-switching is part of the work—maybe because I'm a lawyer whose white clients may think I'm one of them and whose Black or Latino clients may think the same—and I've been code-switching since I was little.

Through chatting with Maria, I soon discovered she spoke in the patois of the academic world. She'd read Hegel and Kant. She knew politics and prose. This kind of communication works fine for me, but I'd need to make sure she wasn't using an armor to deflect a truth that she doesn't want shared. I could also tell how sharp she was. Aside from the elevated topics of academia, which can be used as a camouflage for idiocy, she was talking in a second language. Though she needed a word defined or something reexplained every now and then, I could tell how quickly she was able to grasp complex topics. This would be helpful as we dove into complicated issues.

As we progressed through our strange first date, I told Maria about myself. I explained that while Bob was the paradigmatic Republican, I was the die-hard liberal. She appreciated the appeal of the yin-yang duality. Especially in the legal world, it's effective. If you're talking to a bunch of liberal attorneys, it helps if they know we have something in common. A liberal gives the client some credibility. Likewise, if we're before a conservative audience, Bob can wave the elephant flag with his mere presence. Much of our work in the legal tapestry can be on the fringes of things, the little ruffles that mean the difference between a deal you want or a sentence you don't.

A perfect example of when the fringe work of the legal profession is instrumental to a case's outcome would come a few years after Maria's case. Bob and I were representing a young defendant being targeted by an aggressive assistant state prosecutor in Virginia. Since we could read the political headwinds, we knew the prosecutor's office was on the verge of a leadership change due to an upcoming election, and we hoped that a new Commonwealth's Attorney might approach the case with fresh eyes and a more proportionate sense of justice. Thankfully, the strategy paid off. When the new Commonwealth's Attorney was sworn in, the office engaged with us, reviewed the case with care, and ultimately recommended a resolution that was fair and measured—one that acknowledged the seriousness of the conduct without allowing a mistake from our client's youth to define his future. That client would go on to graduate with high marks from a top university, and I remain grateful to that Commonwealth's Attorney for helping make that possible.

Prosecutors have awesome power. As Attorney General and later Supreme Court Justice Robert Jackson said, "The prosecutor has more control over life, liberty, and reputation than any other person in America.

His discretion is tremendous. . . . While the prosecutor at his best is one of the most beneficent forces in our society, when he acts from malice or other base motives, he is one of the worst. . . . [The] citizen's safety lies in the prosecutor who tempers zeal with human kindness, who seeks truth and not victims, who serves the law and not factional purposes, and who approaches his task with humility."

Back to Maria. After our tête-à-tête, the hour was growing late, so I asked her if there were items she'd like to see right away. She asked for the direct messages she sent on Twitter. I knew the complete evidence file would be about a terabyte, so I made a note to ask the warden at CTF if Maria could get a computer instead of boxes of paper. They'd refuse this request, as they'd refuse many other requests, but I didn't know it at the time. Maria also requested her glasses because she couldn't see. They'd refuse that request as well. Normally, if you're arrested wearing glasses, you're allowed to continue wearing them. However, she came to the door of her apartment without them.

I'd say our first date went well. She certainly presented differently than most of my low-level street offenders. Smart, clever, charming, but all those qualities can be liabilities. Especially when accusations of spycraft and sexpionage are swirling about. Our job was to prepare for a detention hearing, but fortunately, I wasn't working alone.

When I first met Bob, I didn't think we had much in common. Though his legal advice is sought across the political spectrum by outlets like CNN, PBS, NPR, *The New York Times*, *The Washington Post*, and *The Wall Street Journal*, at his core, he's an old-school Republican and a Fox News talking head. He's also a member of the Federalist Society, the conservative legal group from which every Republican president in the past thirty years has drawn their judicial nominees.

As a Republican insider, Bob has offered insight into conservative thinking. When Mayor Pete Buttigieg was running for president, his campaign publicly rejected political donations from longtime Democrats and top Washington lawyers Alexandra Walsh and Beth Wilkinson because they represented then Judge Brett Kavanaugh in his controversial Senate confirmation hearings. Bob criticized the move as shortsighted. As a candidate with crossover appeal, Bob thought Buttigieg could have used it as an opportunity to appeal to everyone.

"Politicians should be looking for converts, not identifying heretics," he said.

At first glance, you'd never confuse Bob for anything but a conservative. As with all people, however, Bob was much more than just one thing.

Under George W. Bush, he worked as a Deputy Assistant Attorney General in the Civil Rights Division of the Justice Department and was the Chief of Staff to Ralph F. Boyd, who led the division. It was Bob's job to fight for the most vulnerable members of our society by enforcing federal statutes prohibiting discrimination on the basis of race, color, sex, disability, religion, familial status, national origin, and citizenship status. If you ask me, the Civil Rights Division is the most liberal part of the Justice Department, though Bob would say justice is neither liberal nor conservative.

Bob got his undergrad degree from Georgetown University—my boyfriend's alma mater—and he falls squarely into one of my favorite buckets: the Catholic Bostonian. And there we have overlap. I was confirmed in the Catholic church and spent the early years of my legal career in greater Boston, working for the statewide public defender's office called the Committee for Public Counsel Services. This fact impressed him, though he wasn't at all surprised that I had trouble fitting into the Boston social scene. Bostonians can be standoffish. And as an over-six-foot-tall lawyer from the Midwest who moved a lot growing up because of my parents' jobs, attending three different high schools before settling in DC, I was a tough sell.

As a father of two daughters and as the husband of a vigorously kind and whip-smart woman, Bob also has a temperament forged in a household of strong women. He nods to this sometimes. When on television, Bob might ingratiate himself by saying things like, "I hope my daughters aren't watching," implying they'd be embarrassed by his conservative viewpoints. But to his credit, while Bob is quick to point out when the Left gets it wrong, he's just as willing to call out the Right.

Now, while I was a cornerman for Bob, we had one more fighter in the ring. For a case as important as this one, we could call up any heavy we wanted, and so we drew Daniel Plunkett. With his salt-and-pepper beard, kind smile, and Louisiana drawl, he's the avuncular lawyer everyone needs. With our team assembled, our first job was to get Maria out of detention. We had to convince Judge Robinson that Maria wasn't a flight risk. Easier said than done.

In the United States, we don't deprive people of life, liberty, or property without due process. That means, if the government has a hunch that someone is a bad dude, they can't just throw them in the slammer, or worse, execute them on the spot.

Sadly, this prospect has been pitched too often in recent years by both conservatives and liberals. I've heard we should "lock *him* up"—a ghastly play on the equally ghastly chant that came before it—even more regularly because I'm almost always surrounded by left-wingers or Never Trumpers in Washington. There are countries that absolutely "lock 'em up" by the way—North Korea, Saudi Arabia, and Russia spring to mind. But thankfully, in our country, we seek to preserve something besides an autocrat's whims: our precious oligarchy. No, I'm kidding (kind of). It's our democracy.

You might say, *Yeah, but Trump committed a bunch of felonies.*

Here's the point: Justice is far more important than the fate of one person you don't like. If you had the opportunity to throw away the key, and just this once, for this one particular person, what do you think happens next? It's always surprising to hear how careless and thoughtless people can be about the justice system. It's like someone who's never attended a day of medical school handing out a complex diagnosis. That's what some people sound like to attorneys when they confidently prognosticate about a difficult case.

But if you're looking to be the resident smartypants at your next potluck, the one casually dropping light constitutional law between bites of potato salad, here's your moment. We can't just lock someone up and throw away the key, even if we wanted to, because of the Fifth Amendment. If you're charged with a crime, you're presumed innocent because you cannot "be deprived of life, liberty, or property without due process of law." Equally important is the Eighth Amendment which says bail can't be excessive. Together, these two amendments lay the groundwork for how pretrial release works. If you're arrested, you get a bond hearing where a judge has to decide whether to keep you in or let you out, and if you're let out, under what conditions. Basically, it all comes down to a few options:

1. A judge can release the defendant on "personal recognizance," meaning they're trusted to return to court on their own. This is the default. Conversely, if a cash bond is required, the defendant would have to deposit it with the court, and once the case has concluded that money would be returned. Obviously if you're wealthy, posting bail can be fairly easy. If you're poor, you may have to hire a bail bondsman or bail bond agent to post the money for you. Sadly, money can keep you out of jail in some parts of the United States. I should tip my hat to New Jersey and Alaska, who had noticed this injustice and abolished cash bonds altogether. Good on them. If you're like a lot of states, however, you bend to big bail and punish poor people with the law.

2. A judge can release the defendant under the "least restrictive further condition, or combination of conditions," that the judge believes will reasonably assure the defendant's appearance in court and the safety of the community. Now that's where the justice system overlaps a bit with being a teenager who just got grounded. Aside from posting a cash bond, defendants may be subject to other release conditions—such as maintaining a job, attending school, surrendering a passport, avoiding certain people or streets, observing a curfew, abstaining from drugs or alcohol, or checking in regularly with a pretrial probation officer. But the key phrase in the federal bail statute quoted above is worth emphasizing: "least restrictive." That means if a judge reasonably believes the defendant will show up in court and pose no danger to others, the judge must choose the least burdensome way to ensure that. If the judge can't reach that conclusion, there's still one more option.

3. A judge may detain the defendant. This one is rare and the worst option. The other two are manageable. Even a panoply of conditions for pretrial release can be navigated. But incarcerating

someone, even for a few weeks, well, that basically blows up their life. Jobs are lost, people are evicted, and families are broken up—all consequences given to someone guilty of no crime. For these reasons, this option should truly remain a last resort.

Part of the judge's responsibility is to look at all the possible conditions for release. Some charges will get you held no matter what. In the federal system, certain offenses like murder, kidnapping, child sex trafficking, and similarly heinous crimes trigger automatic detention. (That's not a complete list, but you get the idea.) If you don't fall into one of those categories, a judge can only hold you if no conditions or combination of conditions would reasonably assure your future appearance in court or the safety of others. That's it. Reasonable assurance that the defendant will show up and the defendant won't harm anyone.

How does a judge make up her mind? Not by trusting her gut. Not by reading the op-ed section of *The Washington Post*. Like everything in the law, we love our guidelines. So, judges look at the nature and circumstances of the offense—was it violent? How strong is the evidence? They also assess the defendant's character, physical and mental health, family ties, job status, finances, and how long they've lived in the community. Past conduct matters too, like any prior drug or alcohol abuse, criminal history, missed court dates, or probation violations. Finally, they weigh any potential dangers the defendant might pose to an individual or the community. That's basically the bucket list of bail factors a judge needs to consider.

As far as we were concerned, Maria had a strong claim to be released.

There was nothing in Maria's past to suggest she was a danger to anyone. Similarly, when tested, her prior record showed she would show up. She'd been showing up and talking with the federal government in various ways for some time. To suggest she'd suddenly skip town now would be weaving a story that didn't exist. Maria was a model student, having just graduated from a master's program at American University. She had a long-term boyfriend, and she had recently applied for work authorization status in the United States. She'd never been charged with a crime. Her alleged crime was nonviolent, and so was she. When it came to the nature and extent of the evidence against her, things were less certain, though that's always the case. The defense rarely knows the full picture early on.

Conveniently, we were about to get a taste of the government's case through the prosecutor's detention memo. Full discovery would come later, once the case was in motion. But these early materials offer little flickers—like a flashlight sweeping through a dark room—into the government's case and its supposed evidence of guilt. Sometimes, the glimpses are horrifying: a ghoulish visage on the edge of the dim light. But other times, when the lights are completely turned on, that ghoul turns out to be nothing more than an ugly doll in a lovely tea party panorama. And so the thrust of our team's focus would be on the government's pretrial detention brief, which it would hand over before Maria's hearing on the issue. Generally, you get these briefs in advance of the detention hearing so you can review it and prepare. A couple hours in advance is hardly enough time to do that. Yet that's how much time we got.

Chapter Seven

Maria's favorite movie was Christopher Nolan's 2010 big-budget, sci-fi, mind-bending blockbuster *Inception*. In it, Leonardo DiCaprio plays an "extractor" who enters people's dreams to steal top secrets, but things get topsy-turvy when he and his crew are hired to—instead of *steal* an idea *from* someone—*implant* an idea *into* someone. With this act of embedding the queen in a corporate three-card monte, the business world would never know where the life-altering idea originated. Or something.

The concept of "incepting" thoughts, the ability to manipulate somebody's ambitions without them realizing it, fascinated Maria, and she wished to find the path to access those extraordinary levers of power that can control the human condition. Where did she look? Law school. And in terms of prime movers, lawyers are as close as humans get. Not only do we wield laws like epees, but we've also created those laws in the legal foundries of elected office. In the United States today, roughly one-third of House members and more than half of Senators have law degrees. To change things to how they should be, to create lasting justice, Maria needed facility with the tools of law, so fittingly she wished to be in the profession that would ultimately both doom and save her.

In Russia, all universities are public, and they're free if you get a certain score on the EGE, Russia's Unified State Exam—kind of like the SAT in the United States. The more the government believes a certain profession needs practitioners, the more seats they'll hand out. Unfortunately, while Maria's board scores were excellent, they were a few points shy of the requirement to receive a free legal education. It's possible to purchase a seat yourself, but in post-Soviet Russia, Maria's family had little money, and those limited resources could not be spared. Maria understood that not only could her parents not afford to help her achieve the thing she most wanted, but she also knew her father would feel great shame at not being able to provide for his daughter.

And so, she lied.

She told her parents that she never actually wanted to become a lawyer. Waving her fingers at her dad, she said it just wasn't the profession she was looking for. Political science, she assured him, was her true passion—and conveniently, it came with a tuition-free seat. Squint just right, and political science might look like it offered something similar. If you're not the one who wields the law, it's better to be the one who makes it—or at least be close to those who do. Maybe political scientists were the real prime movers, whispering in the ears of the public to change for good. Perhaps lawyers were just automatons following scripts written by others. And maybe that was the mind trick she was playing on herself—and on her father.

With that, she received an offer to attend Altai State University to study political science. Even if Valery bought into her excitement, he wasn't exactly pleased. Practical then as now, his concern was her job prospects. In political science, he saw none. But Maria insisted, Valery agreed, and she enrolled. Before college commenced, there was one important piece of advice Valery gave his budding scion. He sat Maria on a blue velvet couch in their apartment in Barnaul and issued a warning.

"Remember, kid. It doesn't matter what school you're in or what you study. You must never be an ordinary student."

Maria was smart and had always been a great student—top grades, a diploma with excellence, but that wasn't really what her father was talking about. What he meant, and what she didn't need explained, was that the time for indulgence had passed. She could no longer be a child whose indiscretions could be overlooked. She could no longer follow a path lit by the flickering flames of dire straits. It was time to grow up, and she did. She packed her things and moved into an apartment near campus, where she would live for the next few years. Just like that, she was an adult. Her father, ever practical, cast what enchantment he could to disguise his poison mushroom in the cloak of the impeccable. But like all spells, it would not hold forever.

At Altai State, Maria continued her track record of academic dominance. The only difference is that she avoided the swirls and whirls of ancillary interests—the traditional time-sinking relationships of college when you stay up all night eating questionable food, chatting about slightly esoteric music, and pretending to be knowledgeable on some half-heard topic in a survey course.

Maria practically lived in the library with the other worker bees. She had no friends to meet, no parties to attend, no drinks to slam. In short, she was a square. But lumping Maria in with the other drones might undersell her activities in college because, besides her academic studies, she worked four jobs. She served as a press secretary for a businessman overseeing human rights programs and youth initiatives. She worked as an executive director in the Barnaul Project Lab where she managed grants to create twenty-four sports fields across the city. She handled PR for a waste management company, and she volunteered as head of the press service for the Altai Civic Chamber. Oh—and did I mention that during her junior year, she also applied for a separate teaching profession that was basically a second major? No? Did she have a better résumé than I did in college? Mind your own business.

With two majors, stellar grades, and a CV fit for a forty-five-year-old professional reaching midlife crisis, Maria had little time for anything else. When did she stop being so serious? She never was. Sure, she skipped the parties, but she was energetic and cheerful—qualities she credits to her parents. In prison, she would later tell me that other inmates often asked her, "Why are you so darn happy all the time?" I can confirm that she is fairly smiley, and while she surely has her down days, the answer is simple: she likes people. She sees the good in them. That openness makes her friendly and trusting, but it also left her exposed in ways she wouldn't fully understand until later.

In college, she genuinely loved working and studying. That chapter of her life made her feel purposeful, relevant, and useful—like everything she did went toward something that mattered. Yes, she had little time for socializing beyond small kindnesses and fleeting pleasantries, but she did what she set out to: live like an impeccable college student. For prioritizing productivity over building allies and tending to relationships, she would eventually pay a price.

In a liberal arts education, most students will at some point encounter Machiavelli's *The Prince*, whether as a required text in some history or political science class, or perhaps clutched by some wannabe eccentric. You know the type: some guy—and it's always a guy—who lives down the hall and can't wait to tell you about libertarian philosophy and why *Atlas Shrugged* might be the single best literary achievement of the twentieth century.

These days, we use "Machiavellian" to describe the power-hungry, but the life of the sixteenth-century Italian thinker was more than a mere quest for power. In fact, when he was stripped of his authority, he got to see most of the cogs and wheels that fed into sovereignty. Sometimes a great loss lets you see the full picture.

Maria's favorite subject was political philosophy, not for the intricacies of culture, ecology, or economics. Her intrigue was power. How it's accumulated, used, and lost. Essentially, Maria was the Machiavelli of Altai State—in the most positive sense. She was a certain type of political scientist who studied authority and control. Maria consumed absolutely anything that discussed the fundamentals of dominance, influence, or privilege, and while never interested in the biographies of great historical leaders, those who began influential wars and those who ended them, she was fascinated by the ideas they propagated and how they managed to inculcate those ideas in others. Sound familiar?

For Maria, the perfect articulation of this model came from Plato, and for me, the perfect metaphor for Maria's pursuit of higher education is the philosopher's cave of shadows. Basically, Plato's alter ego Socrates describes a group of cave dwellers who spend their lives watching shadows projected against a stone wall by the true objects that are unseen behind them. The dwellers give names to these shadows. That one is a tree. This one a Mercedes S-Class. That one is true love. But the shadows are a prisoner's reality, not accurate representations of the true world. In a self-aggrandizing salute, Socrates explains that only a philosopher can turn from the fakery to know they are merely fuzzy representations of reality. In his paradigm, a philosopher aims to perceive, understand, and explain the higher levels of truth even though other inmates of the cave do not wish to leave the prison of their mind. Of course, if a philosopher were wicked and were able to manipulate the play being performed for the masses, well then you have *Inception*, and now we have Maria's attention.

Throughout her education, Maria learned that these real-life shadow plays are told with different tools—television, nationalism, religion—and Maria was interested in all of them. The state was an excellent prime mover. "In country we trust" might be a better fit in the twenty-first century for most centers of power, but Maria noted that religious systems possessed the quintessential prime mover. She learned how this once ancient paradigm can even today direct significant change. Slogging into the weeds, she studied Islam, Christianity, pagan cults, and various regional religions across Russia and Kazakhstan, really any ideology that brought people together and moved them as one. For the most part, this was the thrust of her educational pursuits.

As a straight-A student and the youngest member of the national Russian Social Channel—a political organization across the country—Maria was a rising star able to brush elbows with those creating laws. However, despite her status in the collegiate set, her bona fides amounted to a hill of beans in the college lecture hall because there, in that particular solar system, there was a single governing star: the professor.

At Altai State, professors ran the gamut. There were brilliant ones like the faculty luminary who rarely worked with students yet still wanted to work with Maria. (One of her biggest regrets was not accepting his offer, a load she deemed too heavy.) There were lousy ones like the humdrum academics who, while never dissuading you from the topics they taught, never inspired you to pursue them either. Then, beyond the genial instructors and the pedantic pedagogues, the easy graders and the strict rule followers, there was Professor Kolupaev.

A constitutional law professor by trade, Kolupaev was the kind of teacher, according to Maria, who insisted on dominating his students. She said he'd snatch things off her table just to prove he could, or march her to the front of the class to try to humiliate her. But having seen that kind of behavior from other men before, Maria's initial reaction was to ignore him. She had expensive real estate in her head with limited allotments reserved for academics and work. She had little time to perseverate over an irksome professor. Besides, Maria found that starving gestures for attention always did the trick. And with that attitude, the months floated by with only minor humiliations and annoyances. At the end of the semester, Maria looked forward to finishing her final exam and being done with the course. For the final, she would be given fifteen minutes to review two questions and then answer those questions in an oral format. She claims to have prepared with consistent and thorough study. Maria said that Kolupaev forced her to go last, and so she waited. The hours ticked by, and after the last student had shuffled away, it was finally her turn. She entered Kolupaev's office, and he closed the door behind her, and here's when their stories diverge significantly.

Professor Kolupaev claims he caught Maria with a cheat sheet tucked into her skirt. He says he told Maria that, because of the cheating and excessive absences from class, she would have to retake the exam. Maria has a different account: she says Kolupaev told her she didn't have to worry about the exam. Instead, she would meet him the next day at a hotel. She would bring liquor and be dressed in the way he preferred. In Maria's telling of events, she gathered her papers with a flushed face and an unsteady gait and went straight to the dean's office. After hearing what happened, the dean gave Maria a choice: she could keep the story quiet or make a formal complaint by submitting what she called "a record of her experiences." Maria chose to report the professor, which initiated an investigation. Two other women would later report similar allegations against the same professor. Kolupaev denied Maria's version of events and the stories of the other women and added one of his own about Maria flirting with him at a faculty party. Denials aside, he was fired from his position.

These days in the United States, following the #MeToo movement, a woman can hopefully feel like a champion on her college campus for standing up against sexual harassment, but for Maria—perhaps because it was Russia or an earlier era—her story was different. And here's the cost of years of seclusion in the library or at work. While others were building alliances over questionable food and niche music, Maria was alone. She had no close relationships with any classmates and was too removed from the student community to appeal to any peers. The jealousy her academic success may have stirred suddenly became a liability. Though she wasn't the only young woman put in this position, her classmates supported Kolupaev, called Maria a prostitute, and alienated her. She assumed they had been paid off with A's from Kolupaev for their services.

As a lawyer, I know that few rulings are inviolable, so it brought me no surprise to learn that Kolupaev later challenged the firing decision and had his position reinstated. In his telling, the stories of all three women were false and collapsed like a house of cards.

Chapter Eight

The timing of the release of the government's pretrial detention memo, crafted by assistant US attorney Erik Kenerson, could only be described as inopportune. The brief was submitted at 10:50 a.m. on the same day of our hearing at 1:30 p.m., which means less than three hours to dissect, fact-check, and rebut a document that, despite its nickname, was not brief.

In fairness, we could have asked the judge to set a briefing schedule—a procedural move that would have required the prosecution to submit their memo with sufficient time for us to review and perhaps even file a written opposition. But having assumed the government would operate as it had in other cases, we instead found ourselves largely in the dark and over a barrel.

I know that many malcontents, liberal and conservative alike, take pleasure in seeing defense attorneys over the proverbial barrel, as long as we're representing an unpopular client. However, a barrel-bound defense team, in a country founded mostly by lawyers, is both unusual and unjust. Fair notice helps secure a defendant's right to due process. The Constitution guarantees every person a meaningful opportunity to confront their accusers and present a complete defense. Yes, it's an adversarial system, but these and other important principles exist to give our side a sporting chance. Remember, we are the ones defending a human being, sometimes even protecting an innocent person from conviction for a crime they did not commit.

To put aside any shade, I doubt Kenerson was making life difficult for us. I'd later come to see him as decent, and at times in the unenviable position of enforcing decisions he didn't agree with, but had to follow. More likely, he just had time management issues. Whatever the reason, if we were unable to convince Judge Robinson to release Maria while her case played out, we could try again with our district judge, whoever that turned out to be. Given the circumstances, instead of requesting a brief continuance to review the government's rather explosive claims, we put on our speed-reading glasses and read the brief.

Based on the text, you'd think I was defending an honest-to-goodness Russian spy. Picture me reading these assertions for the first time:

- Maria's role as a student was a "cover occupation" for her secret work on behalf of a Russian official. The FBI found "text messages and emails" between U.S. Person 1 and Maria showing her "routinely ask U.S. Person 1 to help complete" her schoolwork.

- Maria's "closest tie to the United States" was U.S. Person 1, but she viewed him and that relationship as merely instrumental in her broader mission.

- Maria "engaged in a years-long conspiracy to" operate "covertly in the United States." She was "calculated, patient, and directed by" the Russian official, and her "covert influence campaign involved substantial planning, international coordination, and preparation."

- She used "deceit" to move to the United States. Maria swore on her student visa application "that she was no longer" working for the Russian official, but that was a "premeditated" lie and "consistent with" her role "and part [in] a Russian operation."

- The FBI found an FSB-affiliated email address in her contact list and a handwritten note contemplating a job offer from the FSB: "How to respond to FSB offer of employment?"

- Maria remained in contact with the FSB "throughout her stay in the United States."

- Additionally, "FBI surveillance observed" Maria "sharing a private meal" with an individual "suspected by the United States Government of being a Russian intelligence officer."

- Her chats, emails, and tweets referenced a billionaire Russian businessman with close ties to the Kremlin—who was described as her "funder."

- Maria was preparing to leave Washington and had taken steps suggesting plans to flee the area, possibly the country.

- And then there was this: Maria had "offered an individual . . . sex in exchange" for a job at a special interest organization.

That's what Bob, Dan, and I read just hours before walking into court—a black-and-white document from the United States government claiming our client was a Russian agent and possibly a full-blown spy.

Put plainly, they claimed Maria wasn't an earnest student—that was her cover. U.S. Person 1 was doing her schoolwork, and she was using and manipulating him to advance her illicit interests for the Russian government. They said she acted covertly. She lied on her visa application, concealing her ongoing ties to a Russian official. Apparently, she was also offered a job by the FSB, the Russian spy organization and successor to the KGB, and Maria had been considering the offer. Further, according to the FBI, her electronic devices showed ties to Russian intelligence services, and surveillance captured her meeting privately with a suspected Russian operative. A cherry on top: she was funded by a Kremlin-linked oligarch. She even offered sex in exchange for access—the stuff of spy novels.

I had met with Maria a handful of times, but just before the detention hearing, I saw her again with Dan, who was meeting her for the first time. The seconds were ticking, so we didn't have an opportunity for anything but the task at hand.

We handed her the government's detention memo.

Her initial reaction mirrored ours.

"What do we do now?" she asked.

Dan was keen on finding out about the sex-for-access allegation because it made her look like a honeypot, a spy who used sex as a tool, and we knew the courtroom would be filled with journalists interested in spilling ink on such a claim.

When questioned by Dan, Maria said, "I don't know what this is about. This is not true."

Dan told her that we believed her—and perhaps he did—but he added that the whole thing looked bad.

Being a criminal defense attorney isn't easy. If your client doesn't trust you, you may never get the full story, and if your client is a trained liar, the full truth may never come. At that stage of the proceedings, we had little concrete proof to push back on the government's claims because they hadn't turned over their evidence. And as I'm sure you've heard, it's hard to prove a negative, which is why the burden is on the government to prove its claims.

Unlike our first court appearance when only a single, enterprising reporter showed up, the place was now crowded with the usual suspects for a case of international importance: print and TV reporters, courtroom sketch artists, government employees hoping to catch a peak of a real-life red sparrow. The government's brief had already been released to the public and read by everyone like a grocery store tabloid.

Bob, Dan, Maria, and I were positioned on one side, and at the other table was a trio of government lawyers including Erik Kenerson. Kenerson, trim and balding, wore a dark suit, glasses, and a short beard. He appeared restless, like a rabbit in the brush. This posture is unusual for a prosecutor, who holds all the cards at this point, which meant one of three things. Kenerson always appeared as if stepping to a guillotine. He was understandably nervous about the high-profile nature of the case and immense media presence. Or he was not prepared. I *hoped* he was prepared because judges are a notoriously cranky bunch. In a few days, Judge T. S. Ellis, the federal district judge presiding over the Paul Manafort trial in Alexandria, Virginia, would possibly make a seasoned prosecutor cry in open court. "I understand how frustrated you are," Judge Ellis told Greg Andres, a member of the prosecution's team. "In fact, there's tears in your eyes right now." Andres denied that he was crying, to which Judge Ellis responded: "Well, they're watery." And that lawyer was *winning*.

At a detention hearing, the judge has one major order of business: to determine whether the defendant should be released pretrial, and if so, under what conditions. There are a few reasons why a defendant may be denied bail entirely. Is she a danger to the public? Is she a flight risk? Maria had never offended before and showed no danger to anyone, so the government's entire argument turned on whether she was a flight risk.

What makes someone a flight risk? Again, a few things: the nature of the crime (a potential death sentence can make someone wanna hop a plane to Shanghai), ties to the community (if you have family, children, a job, or other local commitments, you are considered less likely to abandon those ties), previous record of appearance (if you've shown up before, you are more likely to do so in the future), previous instances of flight (if you've skipped bail in a previous case, you're likely to do it again), and financial standing (wealthy persons can pose a risk of flight because they arguably have the means to flee).

We thought Maria had a good case for pretrial release. The government disagreed.

"Good afternoon," Kenerson began. "As the Court knows, the government can proceed by a proffer on a detention hearing[.]" (A proffer is an offer of proof—a way to explain what the evidence would show without presenting it. It's a good-faith representation of what a party expects the evidence to prove, and proffers are usually given to save time.) "There are no conditions," Kenerson continued, "or combinations of conditions that the Court can set in this matter that will assure Maria Butina's return to court. . . . Furthermore, even if the Court orders her to surrender her passports and even if she is left without a passport, after all of that, and if she requests a new one, the Russian embassy can issue her a new one. If she gets into a diplomatic car, that car can drive her to the border and she can get across the border and get back to Russia. We do not have an extradition treaty with Russia.

"Any order the Court might fashion restricting her ability to go to any sort of diplomatic location is essentially unenforceable. And once she is in a diplomatic location, there is nothing that the Court or law enforcement can do to assure her appearance back before this Court."

Everything Kenerson said was true. The problem is that it was true of all foreign nationals. In other words, Kenerson was saying that foreign citizens should be held because they could easily flee to their embassy. Even if this claim only applied to countries without an extradition treaty with the United States, we're talking about half of the world's population. There are dozens of countries without extradition treaties with the United States, some of them our allies. If a Ukrainian were arrested for an unlawful demonstration at the Capitol, the government's position was that he should be denied bail because Ukraine holds no extradition treaty with the United States.

This is both wrong and imprudent. It's important to consider that other countries watch the ways the United States treats its foreign nationals and often reciprocate in kind. If you are wrongly arrested on suspicion of smuggling drugs out of Morocco, you might be placed in jail until trial because the United States argues for just that. Additionally, beyond the diplomatic headaches caused by the government's position, locking up people only because of their citizenship is a frightening if not constitutionally problematic result. If you're a foreign national from, say, Vietnam, you should not be held in jail simply because Vietnam has an embassy in Washington but no extradition treaty with the United States.

The command of the Eighth Amendment that "Excessive bail shall not be required" at the very least requires that bail be denied only for the strongest of reasons. Being a citizen of a country without an extradition treaty with the United States may suggest an opportunity for flight, but opportunity is not the same as inclination to flee. A passport to a non-extraditing country is hardly sufficient to establish a disposition for flight—least of all when, as in Maria's case, the remaining evidence of past behavior indicates no inclination to flee.

While the government provided an explanation of how Maria *could* escape, they failed to prove that Maria was *inclined* to escape. But here was the strange thing, the government never emphasized or explained some of the more salacious claims in their memo: trading sex for access, working for the FSB, lunching with suspected intelligence operatives, and being well-connected with a Russian oligarch.

We noticed the omissions but didn't know why they had happened.

And now it was our turn. Bob approached the podium.

"The government got into a lot of things that have nothing to do with this; but what I found remarkable was, most of the government's argument would apply to any Russian in America. Russia does not have an extradition treaty with the U.S. Does that mean any Russian detained for any reason has the same ability to go to a consulate, to go to an embassy, to get a new passport, to possibly get out of the country? But that is not the rules of the courts of this country. The rules are, there has to be an individual determination for each defendant as to what . . . the minimum conditions are to assure her return."

Bob continued, "In this instance, we have a timeline, some of which the government laid out. And we know how Ms. Butina would react, knowing she's under criminal investigation. She is not a private person; she's a public person. She was famous in Russia before she came to the U.S. She founded a gun rights organization in Russia which received lots of publicity. She was featured in the Russian *GQ* magazine, posing with guns and talking about her Russian gun rights organization. That is how she became aware of the NRA and that is how she and the NRA developed a relationship, which resulted in mutual travel back and forth. So there's a completely innocent explanation for trips to the United States periodically by Ms. Butina. Conversations on email with her prospective and then boyfriend about what visa status to apply under are perfectly normal. There's obviously a concern when two people are in a relationship to get the appropriate visa status. The tourist visas are only temporary. You can get other visas to make speeches at gun rights conventions. But looking at something longer term is not nefarious, nor is applying to the school of international relations.

"And in terms of her risk of flight, your Honor, in May of 2016, she started at American University in a graduate program in international relations. On November 22nd, 2017, she got a letter from the Senate requesting cooperation with one of their investigations. . . . [They] inquired about her relationship with Mr. Torshin. They asked for all documents related to Mr. Torshin. They asked for lots of documents related to her contacts with various Americans and various Russian people. When she got that letter, did she flee the country? She did not. She retained counsel and she ended up cooperating with the Senate Intel Committee to provide eight hours of closed testimony, helping the United States government understand the issues surrounding her communications with various American and Russian officials.

"On March 12, 2018, Ms. Butina through counsel responded to the Federal Election Commission, which had inquired about whether or not certain donations had been made to political campaigns. Again, an indication of government interest. Did she flee? She did not. On April 2nd, 2018, *Rolling Stone* published an article, a gigantic article, suggesting that she was part of a large scandal to fund the NRA through Russia through Person 1 as described in the government's indictment. And it was one of the bigger political scandals of modern times. What did she do? She put on her backpack, and she went back to class. She didn't flee the country. She didn't go to an embassy.

"In early April 2018, she turned over 8,000 pages of documents to the Senate Intelligence Committee through counsel, including almost all of the communications the government relies on in their filing. April 17, 2018, she voluntarily met with Senate Intelligence Committee staff to answer questions under oath for eight hours. She explained many of the documents that the government relies on in their affidavits in this case. Again, we don't have to guess as to how she reacted when confronted with government accusations and knowing she's under government scrutiny. If that weren't enough, your Honor, on April 25th, 2018, over a dozen FBI agents wearing tactical gear with guns drawn appeared at Ms. Butina's front door in Washington, DC. Did she flee the country? Did she call her embassy? Did a Russian car with diplomatic plates roll up and get her out of there? No. She called her attorney. We stood there and let the government go through the entire apartment for a full day. She didn't flee the country.

"She's been around under surveillance and made no moves to leave, even after a very interested search of her apartment; after providing testimony to the Senate Intelligence Committee; after being subject to massive speculation in the media that she was a spy, essentially; after her connections with Person 1; connections with the Russian government official, alleged by the government. All have been public. There's been numerous media articles about all of it. If she were truly a risk or she truly felt at risk, she could have left at any of those times. And she didn't. And here stands the government today saying there are no conditions, no combination of conditions, that could assure her return. I submit to you that she's entitled to leave on her own recognizance and that, at worst, there could be other conditions that could be set that could give the Court assurance of her return.

"But certainly keeping her in jail, for what is—and let's look at the merits of this case—this is not an espionage case. This is not a spying case. This is a regulatory filing case. There is nothing that has been alleged that Maria did that is illegal or unlawful but for the government saying that there was a filing required [to] the Attorney General.

"There [are] tensions between the two countries. This has nothing to do with that. This has to do with a student who attended class, who got a 4.0, who applied for a work visa, which indicates she wants to stay in the country, and who deserves at least the ability to be free while we resolve this case with the government. Your Honor, that's all I have right now. And I think that she should be released on her own recognizance."

Judge Robinson asked, "Do you wish to respond to Mr. Kenerson's proffer concerning the inability of any U.S. law enforcement official to preclude Ms. Butina's entry into an embassy or consulate, for example?"

"My only response," Bob replied, "is that it's an argument that proves too much, your Honor. It would apply to anyone from any country we do not have an extradition agreement with. It would mean that every Russian who appeared before you, there would be no conditions of release that could satisfy the Court. . . . There are all kinds of countries in the world we don't have an extradition agreement with. Anyone charged with a crime from one of those countries would conceivably walk to an embassy and gain protection. I mean, it's certainly true that that's a theoretical possibility. . . . But it's up to the Court to make a specific finding on Ms. Butina. And she's in the unique position of—you can see evidence of how she's reacted to what I think to any reasonable person are credible threats of government action in a criminal way."

She did not flee.

"Thank you," Judge Robinson said.

"The Court, having very carefully considered the evidence offered and proffered during the course of this hearing, finds that the government has demonstrated by a preponderance of the evidence that no condition of release or combination of conditions would reasonably assure Ms. Butina's appearance. And accordingly, the Court will order Ms. Butina held without bond pending trial."

And that was it.

For a defendant with no prior record, our argument was as good as it got when it came to assessing flight risk, but our magistrate could not be reasonably assured Maria would appear, even after months of good evidence of her doing just that. She showed up before Congress for questioning when required. She didn't pack her bags or buy a one-way ticket home after federal investigators searched her apartment. She retained a lawyer to help and defend her, not a diplomat from her embassy. I suppose Judge Robinson just felt differently. Perhaps the mere opportunity to abscond was simply too great. As succinctly put by American author James Bamford, Maria is "the only Russian arrested to date in the government's investigation into the Kremlin's efforts to interfere with the 2016 presidential election."

It wasn't enough in our view. And for Maria, it meant more weeks in jail despite being convicted of no crime.

No matter how you feel about criminal defendants, or this particular one—and put aside Russia and your feelings about politics for a moment—know that a lawyer's job is to vigorously represent and help their clients, and when you fail it hurts. The weight of that loss is immediate. You see it on your client's face, and then you have to bury your own disappointment—not just for yourself, but for them. It hurt that day when we couldn't help Maria. As we walked to the back of the courtroom to meet with her, we carried our disappointment, doing our best to mask what we could because whatever we were feeling, for her, it was much worse.

Bob, Dan, and I met Maria in the holding area behind the courtroom, an enclosure where defendants can meet with their lawyers on the other side of a metal screen with tiny tight holes, not quite mesh, but small enough that you can get dizzy if you look through it too long. A scared defendant will often pace in those holding areas like an agitated animal trapped in a cramped cage, and you can't really close the distance to settle them. That's how we found Maria, alone and distraught, not like an ice-cold spy, not like a hardened professional expecting a prisoner swap, but like a young woman in a land she didn't know.

"I'm never gonna get out of here. I'm never gonna see my grandmother again."

"We can try again in front of a different judge," I said. "We'll file a motion."

"How long could I be here?"

"Hopefully, not too much longer. Our next court date is on the calendar, and we'll be with you every step of the way."

"But how long? How long can I be imprisoned?"

"The maximum sentence is fifteen years."

Fifteen years. I could feel the weight of the sentence as it left my lips, but it was too late. Informing a client of the maximum possible sentence is essential. Saying it without context can be a grave mistake. Lawyers toss these years around as shorthand for the severity of a crime, but actual penalties require consultation of sentencing guidelines.

Maria wasn't going to get fifteen years in prison even if everything went as badly as it had gone that day. Federal judges are obligated to avoid unwarranted disparities in sentencing outcomes among defendants with similar records and offense conduct. And Maria had no record. She wasn't dangerous. Her offense conduct wasn't violent. Even for the worst federal crimes—those carrying life as the maximum penalty—actual life sentences are rare and imposed in only a small fraction of cases. From 2016 to 2021, there were 709 federal offenders sentenced to life imprisonment, which accounted for 0.2 percent of the total offender population. Maximum sentences are typically given to repeat or dangerous offenders, those who commit crimes with aggravating factors, those who show no remorse. Sentences for substantive or conspiracy violations of section 951, varied greatly but generally fell between ten and sixty months. If Maria rejected a plea offer and lost at trial, she'd probably get a single-digit sentence in years—and with good behavior, even less.

These were the facts that Dan, Bob, and I had, but Maria did not, and before I could explain it, before I could continue to my next sentence, she had panicked.

"Oh my god, fifteen years! I'm going to be here for fifteen years!" she said, oscillating between the cage and the wall.

I set down my bag and stepped closer to sit on the table in front of me, sliding right up to the cage between us.

"Maria, you're not going to get fifteen years," I said calmly. "Listen, okay, fifteen years is the statutory maximum sentence you could get. But there are sentencing factors and sentencing guidelines that judges must consider. You don't have any prior convictions. You would be a first-time offender. You've lived a law-abiding life. It would be exceedingly unlikely for someone like you to get the maximum sentence."

She focused on me and listened. She stopped rocking. Bob and Dan chimed in.

"We'll run the guidelines to let you know what kinds of sentences you might face," Dan said over my shoulder.

Bob added, "You're not going to be here for fifteen years."

She nodded. She understood.

"I'll see you later today," I said, "and we'll be back here in court next week. And we'll be working on a motion for bond review. We'll be appealing the magistrate's decision to try to get you released. Okay?"

"Okay."

With that, she exhaled. She knew things were serious, but she also knew she had a team of lawyers willing to fight for her.

We stumbled out of the gate, but it was hard to shake the feeling the race might have been fixed. You get a sense of what's fair when you've been working as a lawyer for long enough. Most of our cases are just hearings and are given impartial decisions but sometimes you get a sense that something besides justice entered the court. A Russian national arrested for being an undocumented agent can give you that sense.

After we lost our hearing, Bob and I started writing a motion for bond review to revisit the magistrate's decision.

Bob tries associates out. He's kind, but he doesn't keep working with them if they don't pass muster. He had this reputation of flying solo on important matters because he trusted his work product the most. I get it. If you can't trust the guy you're working with, you might as well do the job yourself. But as we started putting words to the page, he began to trust me.

Lawyers have different attributes. Some are good researchers. They know how to turn all the stones. Other lawyers are good at seeing the forest for the trees. They can craft broad strategies without getting lost in the details. I'm strong in those two categories. I can also think quickly on my feet. But my greatest talent is my pen. I can write a brief. Reading a sentence should require no effort. The thought should pull you along and reward you every step of the way. To achieve this clarity and concision requires great attention to detail and time, but to me, there's no other way to write because in the end, if you do it properly, the judge has no choice but to see the case the way you do. And if your argument is truly heard and understood, you're halfway there. Bob noticed this talent of mine right away.

Bob is an excellent writer as well—truly, he's strong across the board—and it was fun to read his writing, his pith, his clever metaphors. We didn't know what our future held at the time, but it was exciting to find the yin to my yang, like an alley-oop when everything goes right, and on a case for a client for whom everything had gone wrong.

In the days following the detention hearing, we dug into the government's brief together, talked things over with Maria, and quickly saw why some of the government's more extraordinary claims were never pressed in court.

They weren't true.

Chapter Nine

We say the Soviet Union collapsed in 1991, but that makes it seem like a rickety tree fort built on a windy afternoon. The country didn't collapse from any divine misfortune; it was demolished by a collection of failures over many years. In the late 1980s and early 1990s, steadying the Soviet Union was a bit like steadying a hostile nation in Asia after its insurgents were gifted five hundred Stinger missiles. Or maybe a better analogy for steadying the Soviet collective is steadying a drunken head of state as he stumbled down Pennsylvania Avenue shouting for a slice of pizza. Or better yet, steadying the Soviet Union was like steadying a Ukrainian RBMK-type power plant after its reactor core had ruptured. Sure, firefighters would hear the explosion, and yes, they'd ride to the power station to put out the flames. Three would even climb to the roof. But they'd all die. Yes, the collapse of the USSR was certainly akin to the collapse of the Chernobyl nuclear reactor, but in truth, it was partially caused by it, and by President Boris Yeltsin, the Soviet–Afghan War, and many other problems at the time.

First elected president in the summer of 1991, Boris Yeltsin would, by year's end, agree to the dissolution of the Soviet Union. The country quickly became privatized including the transfer of natural resources to powerful businessmen. Despite Yeltsin's reforms, the economy hit the skids through most of the 1990s, losing almost 40 percent of its GDP. By 1997, however, Russia managed growth though the gains were short-lived. A financial crisis spread across Asia that summer and oil prices fell, causing Russia to default. This confluence of events, ironically, laid the groundwork for a decade of rapid economic expansion. But because of his failing health, it wasn't Yeltsin who oversaw this renaissance. It was his appointed successor: former shoe salesman Vladimir Putin.

I'm kind of joking about Putin's prior experience as a shoe salesman—but only a bit. Many know about his past as a KGB operative, and some could probably even recite trivia about his time in East Germany where he coordinated with groups responsible for bombings, assassinations, kidnappings, bank robberies, and shoot-outs. Or perhaps you've heard about his dealings with the neo-Nazi Rainer Sonntag, or his support for research about deadly, undetectable poisons. But did you know that before his escapades along the Berlin Wall, Putin was stationed in New Zealand as a shoe salesman?

We all start somewhere.

Anyway, this Kiwi connoisseur of the Brannock device stepped up to the political craps table at the perfect time. GDP surged because of the depreciated ruble, and Putin's well-timed rise to power earned him wild popularity. He simplified and lowered taxes, eased business registration, and privatized agricultural land. Then in 2003, he snatched up the Yukos Oil Company, the most successful company in the nation, which would presage a string of government takeovers.

While Putin was given a lot of credit for the economic turnaround, the coincidental rise in the price of natural resources such as oil accounted for more than a third of Russia's GDP growth. In turn, this dependence on the natural resource sector would create headaches—first during the 2008 global financial crisis, then under the West's sanctions that were imposed following Russia's initial conflict with Ukraine, and again when oil prices collapsed in the middle of 2014. The cracks in the soft shale of Russia's undiversified economy became manifest.

By the time Maria was bartering in her invented childhood game, The Market, she had witnessed the early success of capitalism in Russia. She came of age in the era of McDonald's in Moscow. She saw the French grocery store Auchan stocked with international brands and regional specialties. She watched Ford establish the first Western assembly plant to make the Ford Focus the best-selling foreign-branded car in the country. And because of these experiences, she felt more closely aligned with Western economic thinking than the communist past of older generations. Maria was eager for Russia's continued push into Western ideology.

In her last year at university, she took on a part-time job at her father's furniture company. There, she would help fill out government forms and do minor tasks, somewhat like an executive assistant to her beloved father Valery, who came from the pre-collapse generation. Valery knew wood-working and Maria knew modern bureaucracy, so for a robust regional manufacturing enterprise, the cooperative was nearly perfect. Yet in pursuit of that, disaster would follow.

After a year gaining insight into the workings of a successful business, Maria had seen how the kolbasa was made—and in her fresh post-undergrad mind, things could use some improvement. Her pitches to improve the company, however, could devolve into petty disputes over everything from the minutiae of daily operations to the broader economic philosophies rattling around Russia. Things then came to head when it was time to hire an accountant. Their spat boiled down to whether they should bring someone in-house or outsource the work. Maria argued that an in-house hire would spot more levers to pull and savings to find. Valery balked at the added cost. Maria shouted that the world had changed, and Valery was content to be left behind. This conflict could have blown over like so many others, but this time, their disagreement crescendoed until an arbiter had to be called: Irina, Maria's mother and Valery's wife. After hearing both sides, Irina agreed with her daughter, wounding Valery's pride. And with that blow, a fissure became a fault line, and the earthquake that followed shook the foundations of not just Valery's company but his family too.

In retrospect, Maria sees the absurdity of a twenty-two-year-old making demands of a veteran business owner about how to run his own company, but at the time, she was both certain and an immovable object. That obstinance came from somewhere: her father, Valery. And since he was an irresistible force himself, they stopped speaking to each other. Days passed. Then weeks. Then months. And the once-inseparable pair were suddenly estranged.

One thing the US media machine got right about Maria was that she was ambitious in the same way American mythology likes our immigrants: entrepreneurial, modern, creative, and undeterred. When she graduated from Altai State, she set out to start her own business. Her idea was simple: follow in her father's footsteps and build her own furniture chain.

In her daydreams, she and her father worked in perfect sync: he built, she sold. But with those dreams dashed, Maria left her father's company to strike out on her own. It was a hard road—made harder by her deep feelings for her father—but she was determined to prove herself relying on nothing but grit. After designing a business plan for Home Comfort, her domestically named furniture store, the next step was to find startup cash. With only a "brilliant idea," Maria scheduled meetings at several banks, asking for half-a-million rubles, which was around $30,000, give or take. This was a lot of money for a twenty-two-year-old Russian. And after each of her sober pitches about furniture commerce, every bank said no. Every bank except one. To her fortune, literally and figuratively, one institution agreed to give her a deal with a yearly interest of absurd proportions that was well into predatory lending territory. But Maria had little choice.

In Russia, as in life, sometimes it's better to be lucky than smart. Vladimir Putin may be the poster child for this idea, having risen to power and influence because global oil prices had surged, and Maria may have inadvertently followed in his footsteps. At the time Maria secured her loan, the Russian economy had been on a tear thanks to those high oil prices. Combining this wellspring of national wealth with the advent of the consumer credit and loan market, Russia became a place where everyone and their dog was borrowing rubles from the bank. And some of those people were also buying furniture.

Within a year under these conditions, Home Comfort had grown to seven stores, and Maria had paid off the loan. Everything was working out, not because Maria was a genius, as she might admit, but because of good timing. Maria didn't have a business degree but was making five times what her peers were making. While they were just trying to get some work experience, she was managing a team of twenty people working under her. Maria was independent, running her own show, needing nothing from anyone—except for one thing.

It always comes back to insurance, they say.

It's not really a Russian phrase exactly, though perhaps it's a Butin family saying. You see, with all of Maria's success, she still needed to jump through certain bureaucratic hoops like renewing her driver's license. Yes, the Russian DMV fell neatly into the government bureaucracy bucket of simple tasks, but the wrinkle in her tunic was that her car insurance was still listed under her father's name. Like in the United States, such an adjustment to a government document requires forms in triplicate and multiple signatures. As such, she needed her father for one last thing. So after some mediating with dear mother, a final date was set to end things once and for all between her and her erstwhile beloved.

Perhaps all breakups should be scheduled at the DMV, the ultimate purgatory. There, couples have time to reflect and consider the paths they've taken.

Maria arrived at the government building like she was all business, ready to rid herself of an inconvenience. She parked in the parking lot, walked into the building, and spotted her father there. A stout man with a fine mustache and a strong bearing.

Maria cried. But like—a business cry. Efficient. Productive.

Resembling a Russian soldier, Maria marched toward her father and stood beside him, tears in her eyes. And there they waited in perdition for a few quiet minutes.

"The weather is good today," Valery said.

"Yes," Maria replied.

The first word she had spoken to her father in a year. A few minutes passed. No movement in the line.

"What did you have for lunch?" he asked.

A question. An open-ended question, the poison to all wallflowers and misanthropes, and Maria had no choice but to answer it. She did. But then something strange happened in that something so ordinary happened: they continued to chat. About what? Nothing. They simply talked in the purgatory of that DMV, and like that, with simple exchanges and the need for a signature on a transfer form, their relationship was repaired in full.

Later in prison, Maria would tell her father how stupid she was during that year. She had wasted it when they were so close. Maybe. Or maybe she was just the prodigal daughter who needed her year abroad to learn who she was.

Chapter Ten

"You're a traitor! I have a traitor in my home!" my friend Jack said as he poured me a drink.

While Jack was a committed liberal, he was also a Russophile. He had studied Russian in college, traveled to the Bolshoi, and could recite every tsar from the House of Romanov, and while his interests seemed more geared to the grandeur of the imperial age, I knew he held no ill will. That said, his humor was often tinged with inconvenient truths, and Jack, more than any of my friends, was attuned to the vague crosswinds of the Democratic party.

"And you can forget running for office," he added. "No Democrat will vote for the man who defended a Russian."

As I scooped Thai food onto my plate, I considered his warning. Jack knew I had considered returning to public service. I'd gone to some DNC meetings, networked, and talked to my friends in politics. I had even met my favorite politician Pete Buttigieg, a.k.a. "Mayor Pete," the future Secretary of Transportation. Once Brendan and I moved to Northern Virginia, the plan was to throw my hat in the ring for a part-time, local elected office position or perhaps the Virginia General Assembly.

"You have to understand the political climate right now," Jack said. "A few decades ago, it would have been the Republicans burning you at the stake. Today, it's Democrats."

"John Adams represented the redcoats at the Boston Massacre trial," I said.

"They were all British back then. We all had the same insane king. This is a Russian we're talking about. The enemy in all our favorite eighties films."

"Nowhere does the Constitution say criminal trial rights are only for American citizens. They protect everyone."

"As a lawyer, I appreciate that, but I'm telling you how the unwashed will view it. Have you entered an appearance?"

"Yes," I said.

"You're doomed!"

"If it matters, the government has things wrong about her. She might be innocent."

"Of course that doesn't matter," he said with a playful grin. "I can't imagine you winning this."

"What about that Tom Hanks movie?" I said, snapping to Brendan.

"*Bridge of Spies*," he said, his mouth full of pad thai.

"*Bridge of Spies*," I said to Jack. "That guy represented a Russian spy. And my client isn't even a spy! She's basically accused of not filling out some paperwork."

"I liked that movie," Brendan said to himself.

"Yes, Brendan, we all liked that movie," Jack said, "but we like Alfie more, and this case could change his political future. Kings have fallen for less."

"What kings?" Brendan said.

"Kings!"

"Let's see what happens," I said. "Maybe discovery and briefing will help."

"Da nyet, navernoye," Jack said. "Probably not."

Defense attorneys are often blind when a client is first arrested. If the defendant committed the crime he's accused of, he usually hasn't informed his lawyers about where the guns are stashed. If the defendant is innocent, the whole process begins as a guessing game with serious stakes.

For Maria's case, my cocounsel Bob had some insight because he had worked with her on her testimony to the Senate, so we started with an ounce of understanding of her recent history and the legal landscape. That broad knowledge was what made the indictment so perplexing. Bob had combed through her emails, documents, social media posts, and Twitter DMs, and still couldn't make sense of why the feds brought this case, or how they planned to prove their many claims. On the other hand, the FBI had reportedly put her under surveillance and seized her phone, computer, notes, calendar, and diary, which all could have been chock full of incriminating stuff—because secret agents often write their crimes down in journals. We'd know soon enough.

As a criminal case proceeds, the government must turn over discovery. The government must also turn over evidence that exonerates or helps a defendant. This evidence is called *Brady* material, named after an alleged murderer who was denied a letter that may have proved his innocence. Sometimes prosecutors fail to turn over this kind of exculpatory evidence, which is illegal. Fabricating inculpatory evidence—the kind that makes a defendant look guilty—is equally bad. Unfortunately, both are all too common. Moses Cook, a former supervisor and mentor from my legal aid days, recently told me about a defendant exonerated after such prosecutorial misconduct. Defense attorneys trade these stories like baseball cards.

In our case, the government had made such sweeping assertions that Bob and I expected them to turn over reams of inculpatory photos, messages, reports, FD-302s (the form federal agents use to summarize interviews), and other records to support their accusation that Maria was a covert Kremlin agent. This was, let's not forget, their claim. That evidence never came. But even if it had, even if a mountain of incriminating evidence had shown up, our job would remain the same: to defend our client by mounting a vigorous defense in court.

I think this is where some people get uncomfortable: the idea of defending someone they assume is "guilty." Here's the thing—just because a defendant has committed a terrible act doesn't mean they're guilty under the law. Guilt is a legal conclusion, and it can only be made by a judge or jury. Sometimes, prosecutors fall short and can't prove guilt beyond a reasonable doubt. Other times, they technically can but the case still falls apart because of a coerced confession, false testimony, or inadmissible evidence. You can even have a defendant who confesses to a crime and still walks free. That's why framing a case as a binary—*guilty* or *not guilty*—misses the point. I prefer the approach used in Scotland, where jurors have three options for a verdict: *guilty, not guilty,* or *not proven.* That third option matters. It gives society a kind of moral permission, allowing jurors to acknowledge any lingering suspicion while still acquitting a defendant. It recognizes that some people didn't do what they were accused of, while others may go free not because they're innocent, but because the government couldn't meet its burden. Our system doesn't offer that nuance, and as a result it tends to conflate "not guilty" with "didn't do it" when really, it just means the prosecution didn't prove their case.

Some people find the notion of a truly guilty man walking free reprehensible. And I agree, that can be maddening. But here's the problem: the alternative is far worse. The laws that get evidence thrown out are much more important than the verdict in any single case.

If the police were allowed to beat confessions out of people, we'd be living in one of those countries our State Department strongly urges us not to visit. We don't want cops planting false evidence to frame suspects they *think* are guilty. This was the state of affairs in the Philippines, where police officers were murdering people they *thought* were drug pushers or users. Some in our country praised that Filipino system of raw "justice" and longed for a return to the literal Wild West of jurisprudence. If you were a racial minority or an unprivileged person, you'd be in trouble. I mean, you're already in trouble now if you fall into those groups—just for different reasons.

The government bears the burden, and a high one at that, because we don't want innocent people going to jail. The English judge Sir William Blackstone put it like this: "It is better that ten guilty persons escape than that one innocent suffer." His ratio, known as Blackstone's formulation, is better than a 10-to-1 proportion of freed criminals to wrongfully convicted innocents. This BF scale is a good metric of where you are on the authoritarian spectrum. At one end, you have Pol Pot, the genocidal murderer of millions, whose brutal philosophy justified the suffering of ten innocent men to ensure one guilty man didn't escape (that's a 1-to-10 ratio on the BF scale). Closer to this extreme are figures like Vice President Dick Cheney, who defended harsh interrogation techniques, including waterboarding, despite the risk of innocent people being caught in the net. When asked about Gul Rahman, a 9/11–era detainee with no known ties to terrorism, who was taken in a case of mistaken identity and left to die of hypothermia after being chained to the floor of a CIA black site in Afghanistan, Cheney said, "I have no problem as long as we achieve our objective." At the opposite end stands Benjamin Franklin, who said, "That it is better 100 guilty Persons should escape than that one innocent Person should suffer."

When it comes to criminal justice, I place myself closer to Franklin than to Cheney. Why? Because it prioritizes the protection of the innocent—including those in the *maybe they did it, but you didn't prove it* crowd.

Bob, a former civil rights attorney from the Justice Department, had a firm understanding we were defending a client whose actual innocence was unknown but whose ultimate culpability was irrelevant. Defense attorneys are integral to every functioning criminal justice system. If we did not exist as staunch defenders, we would be in Putin's Russia or Duterte's Philippines. Given this, Bob and I hunted for any details the government may be interested in, and as we did, we began collecting strange facts. Strange facts are the bread and butter of defense work, and defense attorneys are very good at sniffing them out. Sometimes they're nothing but a curious coincidence. Other times, they're the very things that may set your client free. At the time, these were the strangest facts we had collected:

1. Federal investigators arrested Maria because they thought she was fleeing the country. She was actually moving to South Dakota, but the scramble to cuff her was curious. Why now?

2. Robert Mueller and his special counsel's office, hired in May 2017 to investigate allegations of Russian interference in the 2016 presidential election, wasn't handling the case. Why? It had all the hallmarks of their investigation: Russians, election interference, political skullduggery. Bob had a colleague who might know the answer to this question, so he reached out.

3. The National Security Division of the Justice Department was handling the case, and the lead prosecutor was Erik Kenerson, a guy in his thirties. I wouldn't say he was inexperienced. But for a big case like this, you'd expect to see a much larger team and a more senior prosecutor speaking for the government, someone of the stature of my cocounsel.

While we waited for the government to produce discovery and for her seized materials to be returned, Bob and I talked to Maria's longtime boyfriend Paul Erickson and others to better understand what Maria had been doing in the United States. What we learned could best be described as underwhelming.

She liked guns, the NRA, church, and networking. After moving to Washington in August 2016, Maria helped the Rockefeller heir George O'Neill Jr. set up "friendship dinners" between Americans and Russians, but there were no politicians on the invite lists. She schmoozed with Republican presidential candidates, became a supporter of Donald Trump, and was once invited by J. D. Gordon, one of his campaign aides, to a Styx rock band concert. There was nothing romantic about any of these interactions.

The indictment accused Maria of acting as a Russian agent, but we hadn't seen any evidence that she was a typical one. For example, Gordon—a former naval officer and Pentagon spokesman under President George W. Bush, who later served as the Trump campaign's director of national security before being offered a role in the early Trump transition effort—would have been a perfect target for cultivation by a Russian operative if that's what Maria was about. But she wasn't. Gordon said all of his interactions with Maria were innocuous.

"From everything I've read since her arrest last month, it seems the Maria Butina saga is basically a sensationalized clickbait story meant to smear a steady stream of Republicans and NRA members she reportedly encountered over the past few years," he told *The Washington Times* and *The Washington Post*. Maria simply networked extensively, the way many ambitious professionals do.

"I wonder which prominent Republican political figures she hasn't come across?" Gordon added.

As far as we knew, Maria held no position in Russian intelligence, no role in the Russian government, and received no paycheck from the Kremlin, a Russian national, or any organization for that matter. We couldn't find evidence of her ever following or receiving any "operations" or directives from anyone acting as a Russian official. And to our knowledge, she never engaged in any "secret" communications apart from texting on WhatsApp, the world's most popular encrypted messaging application, owned by Meta (formerly Facebook). Yes, Maria had completed a few tasks at the request of her friend and mentor, Aleksandr Torshin, an official at the Russian Central Bank. But none of this banker's tasks amounted to a mission or operation to justify criminal prosecution in our view. There was simply no evidence that Maria was ever under orders, direction, or control of Torshin or the Russian government. Torshin wielded no authority over her. He couldn't give her "orders," and she wasn't bound to follow any.

Again though, we didn't have all the government's evidence at the time.

The government also wished to prove that Maria was attempting to travel freely between the United States and Russia by getting a travel visa. "First, Butina applied for a B1/B2 visa, which would allow her to travel to and from the United States," Kenerson wrote in his briefing. Yet, as far as we could tell, Maria never applied for a B1/B2 visa. The government would have known this because they possess the paperwork. "Despite that," Kenerson argued, "she neither applied for nor obtained a work visa." This also wasn't true. Maria requested and received OPT status, which is work authorization for recent graduates to apply their studies for twelve months in the United States.

Most concerning of all, however, was the accusation that Maria traded sex to get a job. That claim was stunning and carried by every major news organization and TV news outlet, including the program playing on Maria's parents' television back in Russia. We could only wait for the evidence because Maria firmly denied the accusation.

So that's where we were: staring at a gold and white dress that everyone said was black and blue. In the 1944 film *Gaslight*, a young wife is driven insane by a manipulative husband who distorts her perception of reality. When the facts before you don't line up, it can send you into existential doubt, a crisis of confidence in the very underpinnings of life. In those days, we felt we were being gaslit, though by whom, we weren't sure. Fortunately, the legal process of discovery would be the clear antidote to our condition.

In federal courts, judges are randomly assigned to cases according to a written plan or system. Basically, courts use some variation of a random drawing. The US District Court for the Southern District of New York, for instance, uses a spinning wheel that looks like it could be used to call out bingo numbers, and finding out who your judge is can be a bit like opening a Christmas present from a great-aunt of questionable taste. Will it be the new iPhone Apple+ Pro in Rose Gold, or a wooden spoon with Nicholas Cage's face etched on it? Only fate knows.

For our case, the system shot out Judge Tanya S. Chutkan, a Jamaican-born, UPenn Law grad who had worked for the Public Defender's Service in Washington, DC, and also spent time in private practice. From our perspective, she appeared an excellent draw, a jurist with a full understanding of the kind of tricks and overreach prosecutors can engage in. Then again, there's a kind of institutional wisdom in the legal profession: judges who were once public defenders can be tougher on the defense, just as former prosecutors can be tougher on the prosecution. They've seen how the sausage is made and can spot a hinky argument from a mile away.

As the new lead in our federal case, Judge Chutkan kicked off discovery, which would eventually involve the production of multiple external hard drives. The first thing we did, though, was ask the government to hand over the evidence supporting their claims in the pretrial detention memo. It would take weeks to get it. But when we finally had our paws on those documents, images, text messages, and emails, we could finally see the depth of the government's case against the young woman sitting in jail. And when the floodgates opened, imagine our surprise to find ourselves standing in the shallowest of puddles—a damp patch of grass, really.

"Seriously?" a journalist from *The Wall Street Journal* texted Bob about the government's lack of evidence supporting their claims. "This can't be. This is pretty bad."

"Yup," Bob replied.

Beyond withholding *Brady* material, a prosecutor can also commit misconduct by making claims that aren't true. Not every inaccuracy amounts to misconduct—facts can be misinterpreted, or a witness might lie. These things happen. It can be tough to be a prosecutor. But when the government's filing is littered with unsupported claims, the court is using a bad map to traverse inhospitable terrain because judges rely on the government to provide the truth. In one of the most cited law review articles published, Bill Stunz says that prosecutors—not judges, legisla-tors, or police—"are the criminal justice system's real lawmakers." They are the decision-makers. And if I were to highlight every false, incomplete, or misleading statement in our prosecutor's pretrial detention brief, its pages would be more yellow than black and white.

Let's take the government's claims, one at a time.

The FBI has uncovered electronic communications revealing Butina's involvement in the planning of the covert influence operation with U.S. Person 1. This series of communications included a discussion about how Butina could best enter and remain in the United States. Butina chose a student visa from a range of options for her ultimate application, but not before a lengthy discussion of the risks associated with traveling to the United States repeatedly on a tourist visa. The FBI has discovered text messages and emails between U.S. Person 1 and Butina in which Butina would routinely ask U.S. Person 1 to help complete her academic assignments, by editing papers and answering exam questions. In other words, although she attended classes and com-pleted coursework with outside help, attending American University was Butina's cover while she continued to work on behalf of the Russian Official.

Maria's boyfriend Paul Erickson (U.S. Person 1) wasn't doing her assign-ments. She was a straight-A student, as she had always been. Paul merely answered questions or would help edit certain work because English was not her first language.

The defendant's legal status in the United States is predicated on decep-tion. She not only has deep ties to her country (with which the United States has no extradition treaty) but actually works on behalf of the Russian government. FBI surveillance over the past week has confirmed that Butina has access to funds and an intention to move money outside of the United States. Butina's closest tie to the United States is the indi-vidual identified as U.S. Person 1 in the Indictment, but she appears to treat that relationship as simply a necessary aspect of her activities.

Maria was deeply in love with Paul and had been for some time. They had dated well before she traveled and later moved to the United States. They'd gone on romantic vacations. They'd accumulated hundreds of little moments of intimacy that would make anyone not deeply in love gag a little bit. Paul had met Maria's parents and sister. They'd quarreled over dishes, argued about finances, and battled over the remote control. Basically, they were in a relationship despite the inconvenience it might have been for the federal investigators who may have read one too many spy novels.

[T]he defendant engaged in a years-long conspiracy to work covertly in the United States.

There was nothing covert about Maria's actions in the United States. Putting aside that she was a public figure—the former leader of a national gun rights organization in Russia—she had turned over all her passwords and accounts to the federal government when they asked for them. No decoder rings, no secret knocks. She traveled freely, networked for entrepreneurial gain, and chronicled her life on social media, like countless other foreign students and twentysomethings in DC. The only reason the government had her WhatsApp and Twitter messages to turn over to us is because *she* had turned them over to them. Covert? Hardly. Try wildly open.

The plan for Butina also required, and she demonstrated, a willingness to use deceit in a visa application to move to the United States and bring the plan to fruition. . . . It is notable that Butina stated, under penalty of perjury, that she was no longer employed by the Russian Official at the time she applied for her student visa. Butina likely only admitted her affiliation with the Russian Official at all because she had been previously publicly linked with that Russian Official in media reports. Her false attestation on the visa application was premeditated and consistent with her actions being part of a Russian operation.

The government never charged Maria with lying on her visa application. She never did work in any official capacity for Aleksandr Torshin or the Russian government. She never had an interview with them, never received a paycheck from them, and never got employee benefits or any of the other normal sorts of things that employed people can expect.

When checking into a hotel while traveling on a trip with Torshin to the United States for an NRA event, the front desk asked them, "One room or two?" This made Maria uncomfortable. She wanted to be appreciated for her intellect, not her gender, so she asked Torshin if she could make fake business cards that listed her as "special assistant" to Torshin. The title was made-up. The card and phony title were to keep anyone from mistaking her relationship with him for a romantic one. Did it work? Probably not.

The FBI has uncovered evidence during the course of executing several search warrants that, during the course of her deployment to the United States, Butina was in contact with officials believed to be Russian intelligence operatives. First, the defendant maintained contact information for individuals identified as employees of the Russian FSB . . . the main successor agency to the USSR's Committee of State Security, the KGB. For example, in the defendant's electronic contact list, there was an email account listed at an FSB-associated domain. Another document uncovered during the execution of a search warrant contained a hand-written note, entitled "Maria's 'Russian Patriots In-Waiting' Organization," and asking "How to respond to FSB offer of employment?"

There was no offer of employment by the FSB and the handwritten note wasn't even written by Maria. It was written by Paul, an important bit of context the prosecutor left out of his argument. As for the email contact found on her devices from "an FSB-associated domain," that was a single reply communication to Maria as the founder of her gun rights group, the Right to Bear Arms. Her organization had made submissions to numerous Kremlin departments and state agencies, including the FSB, to lobby for better gun laws and rights in Russia. The FSB provided a standard reply, noting it would take the matter under advisement.

Based on this and other evidence, the FBI believes that the defendant was likely in contact with the FSB throughout her stay in the United

States. Additionally, FBI surveillance observed Butina in the company of a Russian diplomat . . . . That Russian diplomat, with whom Butina was sharing a private meal, was suspected by the United States Government of being a Russian intelligence officer.

The government would never substantiate the claim that she was "likely" in recurring or sustained "contact with the FSB" over the entire period of "her stay in the United States." Nor did it ever revisit the throwaway claim that she dined with a suspected Russian intelligence officer.

Her Twitter messages, chat logs, and emails refer to a known Russian businessman with deep ties to the Russian Presidential Administration. This person often travels to the United States and has also been referred to as her 'funder' throughout her correspondence; he was listed in Forbes as having a real-time net worth of $1.2 billion as of 2018.

The government was referencing Konstantin Nikolayev. His wife had a gun company, and he helped fund Maria's gun rights group in Russia. But Maria never got money from him for anything she did in the United States, and he wasn't involved in any of her activities here. In a statement to CNN, he said he'd "not been in contact with her since 2014." The only financial support she received came from U.S. Person 2—George O'Neill Jr.—an American who helped cover some of her graduate school tuition, purely as a friend and with no strings attached.

Her last tie to the District of Columbia—her apartment lease—ends on July 31, 2018, and there were boxes packed in her apartment consistent with a move at the time of her arrest on July 15, 2018. . . . Finally, in the days leading up to her arrest, Butina was observed by the FBI taking steps consistent with a plan to leave the Washington, DC, area and possibly the United States.

Again, she was headed to South Dakota to live with her longtime boyfriend, you know, the boyfriend the government said was fake.

[O]n at least one occasion, Butina offered an individual other than U.S. Person 1 sex in exchange for a position within a special interest organization.

Just read what Judge Chutkan had to say to the prosecution about this claim. But before you do, imagine being Maria's father or mother. Just for a second, imagine raising and loving your daughter only to watch the news back home in Russia report that she'd been caught by United States authorities offering sex for access.

Here's how NPR put it:

"[Judge Chutkan] had a warning for prosecutors in the case, who recently acknowledged they had misinterpreted messages between Butina and a friend to make the false claim that she was trying to trade sex for a job. Actually, . . . it was a lighthearted exchange. 'It took me approximately five minutes to read those emails and tell that they were jokes,' Chutkan said. 'It was apparent on its face.' Chutkan said she was 'concerned' that officials at the US Attorney's Office in Washington, DC, and the Justice Department would read the exchanges and somehow find otherwise. Those allegations generated sensational headlines, spikes of traffic online and comparisons between Butina and the recent film 'Red Sparrow,' in which Russian operatives exploit their feminine wiles to get information."

Prosecutors would walk back the libelous statements they released to the entire world, for every newspaper and media organization to report on. The judge also publicly castigated the government for what it wrote in its detention memo. But it was too late.

A lie gets halfway around the world before the truth has a chance to get its pants on. Our pants were certainly down, and now it was our job, our ethical mandate, to hoist them up and get onto TV to try to fix the travesty the government caused. The problem was that in the world of media, there is no judge to make someone eat their words.

Chapter Eleven

In May 2015, at a home in Southhampton, England, thirty-six-year-old Alex Chapman was found dead of a drug overdose. His untimely end was not terrifically unusual in the English port town, and yet the circumstances of his death would be closely scrutinized because of another incident three years later in Salisbury, England, just twenty miles up the road. There, an attack happened that featured a terrifically unusual weapon: a military-grade nerve agent. The connection between Alex Chapman and a banned chemical weapon, administered by a banned foreign agent, would, at first blush, appear unlikely because, when you get down to it, Alex's life had been terrifically English. With one exception.

Growing up in the 1980s and 1990s, Alex attended English public schools and lived a typical British life until his early twenties. That changed one night at an underground rave in London's Docklands, where he met a young student named Anna. Among flashing lights, designer drugs, and heavy bass, their connection exploded off the blocks to become something of a whirlwind rave itself. Though Anna held positions at Barclays and another company that managed private jets, her pantsuits and buttoned-up business demeanor masked a very different flair behind closed doors. An attractive brunette with Disney-princess cheeks and an innocent smile, her interests in the bedroom veered toward whips and bondage—Alex's fantasy come true. Five months later, Alex and Anna Chapman were married. It could have been the end of some early-aughts storybook romance. Except it wasn't. The problem was, Anna's given name was Anna Kushchenko, and she worked for Russian Intelligence. A tale as old as time: the sultry Russian raver of your dreams, your idealized honey bunny, turns out to be more of a honeypot working for the SVR, Russia's Foreign Intelligence Service. I guess true love blinds more hot-blooded mammals than the guy from *Equus*.

But was Alex really unaware of any red flags in his cyclone of hasty decisions and mile-high impulses? Because there was enough hammer-and-sickle fabric in this story to outfit a Soviet military parade.

Case in points:

Exhibit A: Anna Kushchenko's father worked in the Russian Embassy, located in Nairobi, Kenya. Embassies often double as the command posts for local intelligence operations. In fact, Russia's top spy in any given country—the *rezident*—works out of the *rezidentura*, which is typically within the embassy itself. American top spies within a country are called station chiefs and work the same way—out of their station—just like Stephen Holmes, a.k.a. Steven Hall, who led our operations at the American embassy in Moscow until Russia revealed his identity and expelled him in retaliation for trying to recruit a Kremlin agent to work for the CIA. Tit for tat is always better when there are no nerve agents involved. But getting back to it, if a friend works for an embassy, I'm not saying he or she is definitely a spook, but I *am* saying there may be reason to clear your internet cookies before they come over. Weak circumstantial evidence but a red flag all the same.

Exhibit B: At the start of their marriage, Anna wasn't materialistic or showy. She was lovely, with plain brown hair and the typical style of a young woman her age. She possessed nothing that drew much attention beyond her Russian accent, which wasn't rare in London. But seemingly overnight, she transformed into someone else, someone with access to a lot of money and influential people. Sure, she worked for jet-setters who flew on private planes, but when she dyed her hair red and began to dress like a runway model—which she later became—Alex felt like she was having a midlife crisis in her twenties. A sudden change in behavior is circumstantial evidence, but anyone who's dealt with juries knows that red flags are additive. Pile up enough of them, and people start drawing conclusions.

Exhibit C: Alex and Anna were young, hip socialites who enjoyed a fine underground rave, and perhaps indulged in the stills and pills of the young partygoer scene. Early in their marriage, they frequented London's nightlife together. But over time, Anna began making plans on her own, often without her beau. Alex, always interested to be with his alluring wife, expected to tag along, but she would tell him, again and again, not to bother because they would all be speaking Russian. Maybe she was right or maybe it was a convenient excuse for someone diving into the dark caves of clandestine spelunking. Whatever the case, when I'm out with my Spanish-speaking friends, my other half is always invited and quite content to not understand a lick of what we're saying. He is easy to please though.

Exhibit D: In legal exhibits, there is no hierarchy in the naming convention, so D-001 is no more important than D-002, which is to say, you might start your exhibits with a notarized note saying the defendant prefers oysters to snails, and the next exhibit might be the murder weapon with clear prints for each finger. In this mock trial, Exhibit D makes Exhibits A through C seem like passing curiosities because Exhibit D shows Anna told Alex that her very controlling father Vasily Kushchenko was an agent in "old Russia," high in the ranks of the KGB, and that she would do anything for him. In the United States, this fact borders so closely to the felony Maria Butina was charged with (doing something for a foreign official without registering) that red flags just became air-raid sirens to any investigator. Ready to accept marching orders from a foreign spy would be problematic for law enforcement.

I rest my case.

For those not hip to my tongue-in-cheek legal patter, the case above is anything but rested. If I presented that kind of anemic evidence in court, my case would surely lose. Unfortunately, the anecdotes I've described above are still sufficient for some to issue a life-altering verdict without batting an eye. Lock-her-up-and-throw-away-the-key kind of justice, which legal experts call "injustice." Weird, I know, how stripping someone of their freedom based on a hunch can be seen as a miscarriage of justice by the very people who operate the justice system. But here we are, in a society that loves to render verdicts based on snippets they've accumulated from the mailman, the golfing buddy, or Deb down the street whose daughter's best friend "knows the real story."

People like to feel like they have sureness with facts and truth. But to all those civic-minded citizens who may one day serve on a jury: please don't reach for a clear answer just because right and wrong feels simple and clean. Your gut feeling and your good guess are not enough. Even when we think we're absolutely sure about something, we're often wrong because humans are spectacularly bad at certainty. We're just not as good at being right as we think we are.

Take eyewitness cases, for example. If someone points to the defendant and says, "That's the guy," it feels like a sure thing. Right? Not exactly. According to the Innocence Project, a nonprofit legal organization that helps free people who were wrongly convicted—69 percent of their exoneration cases involved eyewitness testimony. In each of those, someone swore under oath that the defendant was the one who did it, and they were wrong. Why? Because as any defense lawyer will tell you, eyewitnesses are vulnerable to corruption. Not in the palm-a-twenty-into-the-valet's-hand kind of way, but to the limits of human memory. A witness can believe they're telling the truth, but their memory can be distorted like a corrupted computer file missing a few 1s and 0s.

The same is true with forensic evidence. Sure, forensic methods like hair comparison or bullet lead analysis carry weight, but they're not foolproof. The Innocence Project found that 43 percent of its cases involved the misapplication of forensic science. Just ask Duane Deaver, the former forensic analyst at North Carolina's State Bureau of Investigation, who was fired after falsifying evidence in thirty-four criminal cases. As for confessions, they're viewed as surefire proof of guilt, however, 29 percent of the Innocence Project's cases involved false confessions. Before the advent of DNA testing, we made wrongful convictions all the time, and they continue today—often in cases with no DNA evidence at all, but instead "eyewitnesses," some "forensic evidence," or a supposed "confession." If this rankles you, good. Consider not making snap decisions about someone's criminal conduct. If it doesn't, I'm a little concerned.

So how do we measure things if not by whim or hunch? In law, it's called the "standard of proof"—basically, the level of certainty required to measure a case. In civil matters, the plaintiff must typically prove their claim by a preponderance of the evidence, meaning it's more likely true than not. In criminal matters, the government bears a higher burden: it must prove the defendant's guilt beyond a reasonable doubt. Not, *I think he probably did it*, but as Edward Coke (the greatest English jurist and judge of the Elizabethan era) once put it, "proofs clearer than light."

What does that mean? Do you have to be 90 percent sure? Ninety-five percent? Ninety-nine percent? Our legal system won't tell you. But the percentage doesn't really matter because people are pretty lousy at judging how correct they are. This is called the overconfidence effect. Some of us are pretty accurate predictors of confidence—the robots among us. And, of course, you're gonna get some weirdos on both ends: those who think they failed their med-school exam and end up with an A+ (my sister-in-law) and those who are quite sure they'll win the lottery this weekend (everyone's sister-in-law), but if we average all of our overconfidence, we find people are more certain than they deserve to be.

According to research by Adams, P. A., subjects were given a spelling task and on average scored about an 80 percent when they thought they got a 100 percent. If 20 percent of the time, you were dead wrong and didn't know it, and during those times, people go to prison, there's a problem. This is why we have twelve-person juries that must vote unanimously for a conviction. But here's another interesting truth: our overconfidence doesn't happen all the time. It tends to diminish with easier questions and more familiar topics. When we actually know what we're talking about, we're decent at gauging our confidence, and here's what's key to the legal spectacles splashed across the television: many don't know what they're talking about.

Let me give you an example: What was the brand of sugary drink the Jonestown cultists mixed with cyanide? Kool-Aid, of course.

"Don't drink the Kool-Aid." Investigators reported finding packets of "Kool aid" [sic]. Eyewitnesses described "kool aid" or "Cool Aid" [double sic].

Except it wasn't Kool-Aid. It was Flavor Aid, a Kool-Aid competitor. We have footage of Jim Jones opening a large chest of the stuff. But facts get distorted—sometimes intentionally, sometimes not. The media takes those facts and creates a story with clear heroes and villains. The American public internalize these stories. And your friend Dawn across the street may tell you about it. If you're not a subject matter expert, you're welcome to have an opinion. We all do, even impassioned ones. But perhaps we should stop bringing absolute certainty to the conversation.

Anyway, Alex and Anna Chapman—remember the happy couple? With our 20/20 hindsight, we know Anna was up to no good. But let's cut Alex a break. Maybe he was a forgiving man. For the next four years, their marriage stayed on track. Eventually, though, the changes in Anna's behavior caught up with them. They divorced in 2006 but remained in touch.

In 2006, with a new British passport in hand, Anna relocated to New York City to run PropertyFinder LLC, a real estate website. Unbeknownst to her, those activities were already being tracked by American law enforcement officials in an investigation called Operation Ghost Stories. They knew Anna was part of the Illegals Program, a network of Russian sleeper agents working in the United States and abroad, and they were clued-in on their escapades. When it appeared a Russian agent was ready to slip the country, the FBI decided to round everyone up. At a Manhattan coffee shop—a Starbucks, naturally, where most undercover operations go down—an undercover FBI agent handed Anna a phony passport and asked her to pass it along to another spy.

"Are you ready for this step?" the agent asked.

"Of course," Chapman replied.

And *of course*, that was the beginning of the end for the dabbler in spycraft. After accepting the passport, Chapman realized something might be fishy about this total stranger meeting up with her to commit crimes. Given this, she phoned her father back in Russia before turning over the passport to the local cops. Too late though. She was arrested for having accepted the phony passport in the first place. She and nine other individuals would eventually be swapped in a deal with the Russian government.

Upon returning to Russia, Chapman became a media sensation. President Dmitry Medvedev awarded her and the other spies in the Illegals Program the country's highest honors. Job well done. What did they accomplish? Unclear. But in late December 2010, Chapman was appointed to the Public Council of the Young Guard of United Russia. According to the organization, she would engage in educating young people.

One of the group's members was Maria Butina.

Chapter Twelve

Bob and I were ushered into a green room where a few folks sat on couches. Bob was tranquil. For years, he'd been espousing hot takes on legal trends across cable news. This time, the topic was personal—his own case, his own client—but it takes a lot more to rattle him. I, on the other hand, was racked with preshow jitters, even though I wasn't the one going on TV. Still, there I was, like a gazelle suddenly realizing it had wandered into the lion's den: the Fox News Washington Bureau. Bob, with his conservative views, was at home—a lion among his pride. I was just hoping not to be eaten. Anger and outrage are the traditional seasonings in the Fox News opinion stew. But I should add, if you're a liberal who adores MSNBC, the tapenade of condescension is slathered on with Costco-sized drums.

Bob was called around the corner to get his makeup done alongside Leland Vittert, a host of *America's News HQ*, a now-defunct program that ran on weekend afternoons. While I waited on the couch, I overheard Vittert ask Bob about President Trump possibly pardoning Paul Manafort, so I made a note to ask him if that might come up during the interview.

A Republican congressman (now the junior senator from Kansas) walked into the green room and said, "If anyone cares, today is Bob Dole's birthday." He had turned ninety-five. The other two guys in the room didn't seem to care, but I nodded hello and smiled. As the congressman sat and looked at his phone, one of them, a middle-aged man, typed away on his computer. After Bob was done with makeup, the congressman went on the air, and I talked to Bob about the Manafort question. Bob said it was just small talk. We were there for one reason: Butina.

That's when the guy on the computer suddenly looked up as if he'd been paying attention the whole time.

"Fascinating case," he said.

I scanned the room. Was he talking to us? As if on cue, the man introduced himself as Daniel Hoffman, a former CIA station chief in Moscow and one of the officials who arranged the prisoner swap of Anna Chapman.

"I know she's no spy," Hoffman said. "That's clear."

Up until then, his suggestion seemed clear only to us, her attorneys. It certainly wasn't clear to the prosecution, the news media, the Twitterverse, or some in my family. But this diagnosis from a professional in the field, an expert to boot, gave us just the hit of dopamine we needed. Hoffman then said that either Maria was actually working for Russia and *wanted* to be caught, or she was just a naive student trying to make her way in America. Almost definitely the latter. We all exchanged cards because we knew this man could be valuable in the future.

A production assistant stepped into the room and said it was time, so we walked down the hallway, crossed through the newsroom, and stopped at a set door. Cold air blasted beneath the doorway like it led to a walk-in refrigerator, and I wondered if I was properly dressed for the Alaskan cold season. Bob wore a blazer, button-down shirt, a tie, jeans, and flip flops, which he loves to wear in the office even in the dead of winter. He'd be fine. The "on air" light turned off, and we stepped onto set. I took my place in the eaves as Bob took his seat on the stage, which was much smaller than I thought it'd be.

Vittert noticed me and said to Bob, "Who's that guy?"

"He's here to make sure I answer the questions correctly—then report back to the Russians," Bob joked.

Vittert chuckled as I flashed my best Slavic smile (a stone face) to play the part.

While I waited for the segment to start, I spotted the teleprompter with the first question Vittert would ask. Basically, he wanted to know why the Russian government was making such a big deal about Maria's arrest—demanding her release and going so far as to change the Russian Foreign Ministry's Twitter profile image, which had displayed their official logo, to a picture of her—and whether that strong reaction suggested something more. I was too far away to tip off Bob, but I got the sense there was some snark ahead. Luckily, Bob was a born-and-bred Bostonian. Snark is his clam chowder.

"Russians seem to really want their woman back. Why are they so exercised about this?" Vittert asked.

"Well, just to be clear, they don't want her back—they want her out."

After conceding the point, Vittert asked his question again.

"Well," Bob said, "I think that she was known in Russia before she came to the US because of her gun-rights advocacy. And I think it's a young woman who's twenty-nine years-old, who just graduated from American [University] with a master's, and she's being held without bond in a DC jail . . . and so I think that a lot of people look at a young woman like that and think of their own kids, or their sister, or something like that."

"So let's assume your line—that she is an innocent woman who was a grad student and has sort of gotten mixed up by a much older, well-connected Kremlin associate, Aleksandr Torshin, and she's just sort of been railroaded on this. Conceivably, the DOJ knows that. They have access to everything that's happened. I'm sure you've explained that to them. Is this a political prosecution? Is this the DOJ trying to sort of send a message to the Trump administration?"

"I would never accuse the DOJ of that, but . . . you have to segregate Maria's case from the other cases that are out there. Maria has nothing to do with the twelve Russians that were indicted. She has nothing to do with the Mueller probe. The Mueller probe had nothing to do with her."

Two days before Maria's arrest, Special Counsel Robert Mueller indicted twelve Russian intelligence officers from the GRU for hacking the DNC, the Democratic Congressional Campaign Committee, and Hilary Clinton's campaign, then releasing the stolen emails through fake online personas and WikiLeaks. We kept repeating the line about the "Russian twelve" to underscore that Maria had nothing to do with that Russian intelligence hack that dominated the headlines before and after her arrest.

"But the timing is pretty coincidental," Vittert said. "I mean, she got grabbed and arrested as President Trump was landing in Helsinki. We're not trained to believe in coincidences, Bob. . . . [You're] saying that there's no political parts of this prosecution, but you're saying that the prosecution itself is bogus. How can both be true?"

"I think that they're stringing together things out of context and . . . they haven't pointed to anything she did that would be remotely spy-like.

Just to take a few examples: spies don't communicate on Twitter direct message, generally—"

"Because they want their lawyer to be able to say that spies don't communicate on Twitter—"

"Spies generally communicate under assumed names. She's a . . . heavily accented Russian. You can google her, find her Facebook page—most of the pictures you've seen are from her Facebook page."

"And we have those up there," Vittert said, referring to some of the images shown during the live broadcast. "All right, so let's talk about some of these messages. The one that is in the indictment that everyone is pointing to is this: Aleksandr Torshin—'You're a daredevil girl! What can I say!'—in terms of her going to the inauguration. Butina writes back, 'Good teachers!' If this is totally innocent, who are her teachers?"

"She had a relationship with Torshin going back to [her] gun-rights days [in Russia]. She founded the group, Torshin joined the group, and I think he was very interested in her career—wanted to promote her career."

"Answer to a question—just not the one I asked. When she says 'Good teachers' who is she referring to? Torshin? Or to the Russian FSB? Who are the teachers?"

"Oh certainly not the Russian FSB—"

"Of course not," Vittert said sarcastically.

"—because she's not an FSB agent. But Torshin or others in Russia that helped the gun-rights lobby."

"Okay. And they taught her to be brave enough to go to the inauguration?"

"Again, none of this. There's nothing secret about what she did. There's a picture of her in front of the Capitol, which is taken by every foreign student that's ever come here."

I'm not sure how persuasive that point was, but it was true. Maria was doing what plenty of people in Washington, and twentysomething Americans more broadly, do: networking, attending events, and hobnobbing with those in power.

"You've worked with the DOJ," Vittert said, "and in the past on this program you've given them an awful lot of credit for being—number one, fair; number two, nonpolitical. Now, you're arguing, essentially, that they're bumbling idiots who have somehow railroaded this poor grad student and charged her with being a Russian agent. How are those two compatible?"

"Well, I think, importantly, they haven't charged her with being a Russian agent. They haven't charged her with anything espionage. They haven't really said she's a spy. Everything she's done, according to the government itself, would be legal if she had filed a piece of paper with the Attorney General. So they're not accusing her of—"

"Why are they doing all of this over this gun-rights activist?"

"It's hard to know. Probably because they've invested a lot of time in it. They've been tailing her for eighteen months, according to their proffer in court the other day. And after eighteen months, they appear to have one picture of her with a Russian who's the head of The Russian Cultural Centre, who shows Russian movies to Russians that live in Washington. So to me, I think it's an overblown case."

Bob was referring to the photo prosecutors used to accuse Maria of dining with someone they "suspected" was "a Russian intelligence officer."

"So why overblow it, though?" Vittert said. "Why overplay their hand, if that's what they're doing?"

"Well, again, I think that Maria circled among people who were involved in US politics, and I think that people got excited when they saw that. And she's been subject to media scrutiny for over a year—"

"So you give the DOJ a pass here in terms of any kind of ulterior motives—of trying to sort of raise the issue of Russia[n] malfeasance in . . . light of Helsinki?"

Vittert and the Fox News desk were focused on the fallout from the Helsinki summit, held about a week earlier. The backdrop was the US intelligence community's assessment that Russia interfered in the 2016 election. At the summit, Trump said he didn't see why it would be Russia, appearing to question those findings. The backlash was swift and bipartisan. The next day, Trump clarified that he had misspoken and meant to say he saw no reason why it *wouldn't* be Russia. But then he added, "Could be other people also. A lot of people out there." It was this kind of qualified acknowledgment that kept the controversy alive and continued to prompt public debate. The coverage on *America's News HQ* that day reflected a swirl of questions: Was Trump wrong? What should he have said or done? And in Maria's case—why arrest her the same day as the summit? Was it timed to force Trump to publicly confront Russian interference?

"Well, I'll put it this way," Bob said. "I don't think they do things in bad faith. If you asked me, 'If Maria [were] from a different country, would this be happening?' I'd say absolutely not. I think the Russia overlay on this can't be ignored. But she's a separate person from all the rest of this Russia stuff, and she—I firmly believe—is not guilty of what she's been charged with and is simply a Russian national who's been in the US."

"We'll follow the case and have you back to talk about it. Open invitation as it goes on. Thanks, Bob."

> **thisisourcountry** Aug '18
>
> Oh shut the hell up, you dirty Russian vermin...there are real women who suffer from sexism and you don't qualify you disgusting spy. And to her two-bit lawyers - f*** you too for playing the sexism card. I know lawyers are supposed to protect their clients but this is absolute B.S.
>
> This woman should be executed for espionage after she is convicted as a fearsome lesson to any other Russian pigs who dare try and screw with our Democracy.
>
> I for one will never forget Russia is the prime criminal nation in the world and their entire economy and government should be literally burned to the ground for their evil. The Dems had better get this message too. No quarter for Russia.

Bob warned me about online comments, but if someone puts Pandora's box on Wi-Fi, I'll bookmark it without a second thought. And what a horror show it was, scrolling through comment sections. Regarding the frequent demands to *lock her up* and other more disturbing recommendations, you could chalk them up to internet anonymity run amok. From my perspective though, those thoughts could easily be the same ones we'd find in the jury box. Months from now, we could be starting a trial with a guilty verdict already locked in. In conversations with friends and family over the previous months, I'd come to see how little facts seemed to matter. So far, the public had only heard the government's version of events, and they were confident she was guilty—partly because of Russiagate, but also because the media was telling a dramatic story instead of a true one.

I love my prime-time lineups on CNN and MSNBC. Sometimes, I just want to sit with my friends at the circus and laugh. Sometimes, I like to commiserate over the injustices I see every day. But when it comes to actual news, when it comes to the hard facts I trade in, I'm wary of cable news. Setting aside the malicious personalities on TV, I suspect most news organizations get things wrong more often out of misunderstanding, limited expertise, or inexperience than anything else. As a human, it helps to keep Hanlon's razor on the leather strop and ready for use: "Never attribute to malice that which is adequately explained by stupidity." Though I like Goethe's quote more: "[M]isunderstandings and lethargy perhaps produce more wrong in the world than deceit and malice do. At least the latter two are certainly rarer." I've found that adage true with lawyers, friends, family, and even myself. More often than not, we get things wrong because we're inept, lazy, or both.

For cable news, innuendo is the lazy river of journalism. Frequently, media personalities and their guest "experts" say something that isn't true and slap a question mark on the end or add a modifier like "probably" or "could." Should we check it out? Hunt down sources? Crosscheck claims? Nah, let's just pump our copy full of modifiers.

Rachel Maddow said on her program that, "observers have even speculated that Maria Butina might possibly have her case resolved as part of a spy swap with the Russian government." Unnamed "observers" and semantic tap dancing like "speculated" and "might possibly"—what's going on here? It's all verbal squish. Who are these observers?

Speculation is the bedrock of cable news, and I don't mind when experts speculate and offer informed guesses within their field. There's value in mapping out the range of possible futures, but speculators should be identified and questioned, so we can evaluate the strength of their forecasts and the credibility of their reasoning.

"That is why Special Counsel Robert Mueller, who is investigating that interference, is 'likely' to question Butina now that she has agreed to cooperate with the government," Natasha Bertrand wrote in *The Atlantic*. And Bertrand thankfully named this observer: "Barbara McQuade, the former United States attorney for the Eastern District of Michigan."

I don't think Maddow and her ilk are intentionally lying to their audiences, though some cable news personalities do exactly that. But things tend to go off the rails when they're chasing a preconceived narrative. That's when they start to draw false inferences, twist facts to support their narrative, ignore context that undercuts their thesis, and use innuendo when they don't have anything concrete.

"So, look, they also say your client trained as a spy in Russia," Erin Burnett of CNN said to Bob on her show *OutFront*.

Wait—*they*? Who exactly are *they*?

No prosecutor, FBI special agent, or government official ever accused Maria of having "trained as a spy in Russia." Not once. Not in any court document, oral statement to the court, or DOJ press release. And Maria wasn't a spy. Why? Because in the United States, a *spy* is someone who secretly gathers or shares national defense information—like military plans, classified material, or security systems—with the intent to harm the United States or benefit a foreign country. Details are important. Maria was not charged under the Espionage Act. She was never employed by Russia or a Russian official. She never secretly conveyed anything, let alone classified information. And to say she delivered things of strategic importance, well it's difficult to say that with a straight face.

But if she's not a spy, then what was she? you might ask.

An agent.

Not a *secret* agent. Just an agent, someone who does something for someone else. I have a book agent. As an attorney, I often act as an agent. I even have friends who've been agents of foreign governments.

But Maria was doing something bad, right?

If she had registered as an agent with the Attorney General, there would be no crime. Most folks on all sides of the political spectrum prefer to tell the story how they feel it should go. We all do it.

Erin Burnett did apologize for her mistake, and I think that speaks volumes to her character. I expect errors in journalism, especially for news that's breaking. But it's important to correct mistakes. Maddow never apologized for her errors, though she did stop calling Maria a spy. Wolf Blitzer had a harder time making the fix despite being informed by his producer.

What about the pinnacle of journalism? How does *The New York Times* fit into this tapestry? As far as Pulitzer Prizes go, The Gray Lady is the most decorated newspaper in history. It also has the largest online readership in the United States, and despite regular shade from some quarters, the paper is far from failing and generates profits in the tens of millions. Here's what our country's best newspaper had to write about Maria a few days after her arrest: "[She] carried out her campaign through a series of deceptions that began in 2014, if not earlier, prosecutors said. She lied to obtain a student visa to pursue graduate work at American University in 2016. Apparently hoping for a work visa that would grant her a longer stay, she offered one American sex in exchange for a job. She moved in with a Republican political operative nearly twice her age, describing him as her boyfriend. But she privately expressed 'disdain' for him and had him do her homework, prosecutors said."

None of this was true. Yes, the *Times* was reporting the government's claims. But when a reporter bookends a paragraph with "prosecutors said," everything in between can read like established fact. I get that the paper has an important role in covering what prosecutors allege, yet a little healthy skepticism goes a long way. It would help if reporters noted when no supporting evidence has been presented. But that was one paragraph in the *Times*.

I've skipped the nefarious journalists and critiqued the usual ones, but I'd be remiss if I didn't compliment the masters in the field, including scores of journalists from *The New York Times*, *The Washington Post*, *The Wall Street Journal*, and NPR. Esteemed print and radio reporters are looking for one thing: the complete picture. They don't care if someone is a hero or villain, if someone is guilty or innocent. What they want to know is what's accurate.

The Wall Street Journal might have been the only major news source *not* to publish the government's false statement about Maria trading sex for favors. Either the writer, the editor, or both recognized that while they could legally skirt defamation laws by accurately reporting the government's claim, printing something so odious about someone—without a shred of evidence or support offered by the prosecution—was another matter entirely. They turned out to be right.

Matthew Rosenberg of *The New York Times* tells stories faithfully. Rosalind Helderman and Tom Jackman of *The Washington Post* do as well. Carrie Johnson of NPR is fact-driven and reliable. Zoe Tillman, a reporter who worked at BuzzFeed and now works at Bloomberg News, is solid. Betsy Woodruff Swan, who writes for Politico, is an honest reporter. Their reporting was sometimes unpleasant for us, but it was truthful and accurate. I'm fine when something is harsh as long as it's correct.

Those were the reporters who figured out, and seemed to sense, before anyone else what Maria's story was. It was a view we shared: that the government's case, which the Mueller team had rightly avoided, was perhaps built on sincere but ultimately unfounded hopes, and that over time it just fell apart. The problem was that reporters were slow to print, and Bob and I needed to correct the record before Maria was hanged by the mob. Prosecutors would walk back their errors, but they wouldn't do it on cable news or on NPR or wherever "experts" had been repeating the government's false statements for months.

That's where Bob and I came in. We were duty-bound by ethics to correct these mistakes, and the government didn't like it one bit. As Rachel Maddow said on her program on August 31, 2018: "Just tonight . . . after close of business, the US attorney in Washington, DC, filed [a] motion in federal court . . . asking for a gag order to be imposed by the court on the legal defense team that's representing Maria Butina."

The prosecution wanted the judge to keep us off the air.

Chapter Thirteen

A promising young student—maybe a valedictorian or prom queen—leaves the watchful eyes of her loving parents and settles into a college or university filled with endless possibility. Will she become a doctor? A lawyer? Whatever her path, college is a chance to remake herself, to strip away the ersatz costume she built over the past four years to find out who she really is. Our young coed meets a few people in her dorm, not the type-A, always-studying teacher's pets that filled her social circle in high school. No, these students are the funny, exciting friends like those she lost touch with after middle school, the wild childs of sleepaway camp or summer school high jinks. *These* friends know how to get extensions on term papers. *These* friends know how to sweet-talk cafeteria workers into giving extra scoops of ice cream. *These* friends consider rules as mere suggestions. Soon, our apt pupil is taken to a few parties, and there she meets a few more friends of friends. Then suddenly, she begins seeing things she's only ever heard whispered about. Without warning, these once foreign prohibitions are now being offered to her, ever so casually, as if only a neophyte doesn't partake. Our coed decides to dip her toe into this unknown planet. At first, she feels like an imposter, but after more experiences during small get-togethers and late-night kickbacks in dorm rooms and rundown bars, the once whispered activities are now being tossed about with abandon by those she calls her closest friends. Our young honor roll student doesn't tell her parents right away—she's her own woman now—but they suspect something is up when she comes home for the holidays. Perhaps they find incriminating evidence when going through her book bag. Then one night, they catch their precious daughter red-handed at 3:00 a.m.: She's reading *Reason Magazine*. Their sweet little princess has become a libertarian.

At Altai State University, Maria burrowed into that well-worn rabbit hole already lousy with new adults. If you first discover libertarian philosophy at her age—say, after reading *Atlas Shrugged*—you might feel you've discovered a secret instruction manual for life, the code underlying all human interactions great and small. And if the curtain of human experience had recently been pulled back in your introductory liberal arts courses after discovering that Stalin and Mao, two world leaders who helped take down the Axis Powers, killed five times as many people as Adolf Hitler, and that Winston Churchill was an egregious bigot who thought Indians were "the beastliest people in the world next to the Germans," and because of these revelations you found the contours of the world were flooded with shades of gray rather than the stark black and whites of childhood when "truth" was always right and "violence" was always bad, *then* the New Atlantis of a libertarian mindset might have become a warm blanket from yesteryear when you could simply pretend to fall asleep in your parents' car so they might carry you inside as a limp little bundle. This is all to say, the tenets of libertarian philosophy are crisp and clean, the heroes without flaw, and the villains without nuance. It's like a Disney movie for grown-ups, which I suppose is just a Marvel movie. Except instead of Spider-Man, libertarian champions have no genetic alterations. They simply get it.

Maria was the perfect target for the opioid of libertarian thought. She belonged to the first generation of Russians who never knew the Soviet Union and could plainly see the glimmer of capitalism shining like a beacon from the West—the golden arches of McDonald's and the pumpkin spice latte of Starbucks. As a young adult first huffing the vapors of ideological prose, Maria found libertarianism had all the answers. The idea of absolute individual freedom was a rejection of the Soviet Union's belief in allegiance to the state, and true freedom came in the form of laissez-faire capitalism, strong private property rights, and a means to preserve life, liberty, and property. With her recipe in hand, all she needed to do was assemble the ingredients.

In today's Russia, the political spectrum is constricted. But in Maria's early adulthood, the ideas swirling in the civic discourse were both diverse and mixed with new and old thought. Hordes of political managers roamed the nation to run campaigns of all stripes, and while many scrapped and hustled for these positions, they saw political management as a means to be in government itself—if not pulling the levers of power, then at least whispering into the ears of those who did.

Being someone who wished to clutch the reins of power, Maria knew the key to opening the locks of politics was found in developing apt speaking skills. With a naive plan and a will to succeed, Maria began her quest to become the best public speaker in Barnaul. And her first important speech was an absolute failure.

In the early aughts, Russia's political world was an oratorical boot camp for the aspiring politician. Young people were given the chance to wax poetic in front of recreation centers and retirement homes, and when the opportunity arose, Maria snagged a plum speaking spot before a gathering of veterans. Her topic? The Great Patriotic War—World War II by another name. These nationalistic veterans were the kind of sitting ducks that fresh young-faced politicos could really cut their teeth on, much like the Catskills crowds of the 1930s for the aspiring Jewish comedian. If you can't play there, you don't have it.

For Maria's talk, she decided to expound upon the trials of mobilizing an entire nation to fight the evil of Nazism. Maria was poised for great success in her battle to win hearts and minds along the libertarian battlefront. She possessed poise and a deep resonant voice. She raised her chin with conviction and gestured with purpose. You might even say her speech was going about as well as a blitzkrieg in the East. She would soon take Moscow in the fall. That is until winter arrived with full malice. As Maria reached a section about the number of tents the Russians had manufactured during the war, a fact both unimportant but also strangely specific, Maria couldn't remember the figure. She stopped, her mind washing away like the outgoing tide, and stared at the veterans before her.

An experienced public speaker who can see the whole picture might skip over the precise number and ballpark it. Unfortunately, Maria was a rehearsed public speaker, and for those who can't see how the Lego pieces of a speech fit together, taking out a section for a meticulous elocutionist can make the whole thing collapse. After the stutter and obvious stumble, Maria came to a shocked silence. Absolutely flushed, she stood speechless before the group of old men for what felt like an eternity. Albert Einstein said, "When you sit with a nice girl for two hours you think it's only a minute, but when you sit on a hot stove for a minute you think it's two hours. That's relativity." Maria was probably experiencing a bit of relativity herself.

This agonizing moment was a thick stitch sewn into her psyche, a story that still brings back humiliation when she recounts it. But she also recounts it as a vaccine of sorts, one performed with the longest of needles. She's now inoculated against the panic and fear associated with public speaking, and moreover, it changed her approach to the craft by giving her two important rules for any of her speeches. One, she never learns speeches by heart. Without the ability to extemporize, a single missed word or forgotten phrase can leave her stranded under the spotlight. Two, she makes little notes about broad topics and then learns speeches from those notes. This way, if an audience seems eager to hear more about a particular section, she can dig into that content. If not, she can take the exit ramp to the next. At university, Maria decided that in each class, she needed to ask a question. It was her internal obligation to feel comfortable before crowds. And it worked. Over the next few years, Maria gave scores of speeches and became better with both the patter of public speaking and more comfortable with being the center of attention.

As far as branding, Maria's speeches were anything but typical. She used her adoration of Russian poetry to give speeches containing her favorite poems, especially ones about the hard life of Russia, which appears, to me, like a martyr complex that Russians share with Bible Belt Christians except in Russia it's probably earned. Her speeches were basically the slam poetry of political stump speeches, and her tour de force, her greatest hit on the political poetry circuit, was *The Railway* by Nikolai Nekrasov. Written in 1864, the poem is an anti-capitalist diatribe originally banned when published but now regarded as one of the most important anti-capitalist statements of nineteenth-century literature—a Russian genre not light on content. Maria memorized the poem by heart, and her speech was nearly as long as the railroad itself, five pages, which I know doesn't sound like the length of a railroad but remember it's a memorized poem.

And yes, I know I just told you she doesn't memorize speeches, but this was a poem. You shan't lose a word in "Shall I compare thee to a summer's day." Anyway, with her from-the-heart reading, and I mean that phrase with extra metaphorical emphasis, Maria claims her listeners cried from the sheer force of her rhetoric. To me, that sounds a bit romanticized, but my other half recently reminded me of the toast he gave at his sister's wedding, when the groom's grandfather was so moved he shouted from the crowd. So I suppose strong emotion can be invoked with a speech.

Maria had become the gifted orator of all things patriotic, but she also needed to dive into the world of politics proper. Running on a parallel track to her rhetorical training, Maria became ingrained in local civics by serving a term in the Altai Social Chamber, a kind of proto-political group. It wasn't long before Maria grew tired of the group because of the corrupt politicians who took a heavy toll on her revolutionary sensibilities. No one was searching for truth or principle; they were trying to service themselves. Naively, Maria assumed only regional politics possessed such egocentrism and vainglory, and that the national game must be filled with heroes of her ideology. After all, it was on the national scene where Vladimir Putin found success, and at the time, Putin was the champion of the people.

Searching for a path to the main stage, Maria discovered that the Young Guard was holding a competition. A relatively new political group, founded by Putin's United Russia party, the Young Guard ripped its name from the famed World War II underground resistance movement. Today, the Young Guard is a massive association of over 160,000 members.

I don't know about you, but when I hear "Young Guard," my mind goes straight to the Hitler Youth. Any political organization that relies on young people, whose brains are still developing and who are vulnerable to peer pressure, seems like a recipe for indoctrination. Groups like the National Teen Age Republicans and High School Democrats of America also strike me as problematic propaganda machines, not unlike the e-cigarette makers who pushed their once-popular fruit-flavored nicotine products. Then again, I also don't think eighteen-year-olds should have assault rifles, so what do I know?

Anyway, so what did the Young Guard do? That's difficult to answer without first discussing its origins and historical counterpart in the youth propaganda space: Nashi.

In 2005, allies of Vladimir Putin formed two political youth groups: the Young Guard and Nashi (Russian for "Ours"). When Maria was coming of age, both groups were active. They promoted a mix of social programs and political events, but their main purpose was to serve as vehicles for pro-Kremlin propaganda. At their peak, each claimed hundreds of thousands of members, though those figures deserve some skepticism, especially in twenty-first-century Russia. While the Young Guard still exists, Nashi was dissolved in 2019.

If the Young Guard was the polished, buttoned-up careerist wing of youth politics, Nashi was the punk rock, Molotov cocktail cousin—loud, aggressive, and violent. The Young Guard operated from within United Russia's headquarters, projecting professionalism. Nashi, by contrast, gathered in a grungy building with barred windows and an unmarked door. Inside, you might find rabble-rousers with piercings and tattoos and hallways wallpapered with clipped-out photos of their members picketing storefronts or leading massive demonstrations in an effort to get people out to the polls—for Dear Leader, of course. However, Nashi's ideology extended beyond the purely political. Members opposed smoking, drinking, and condoms (a nod to Russia's declining birth rate), while also promoting military service alongside violent tactics. They hurled feces at adversaries, gassed opposition events, and disrupted dissident meetings. You can find photos of Nashi child members posing for pictures barefoot or in socks while toting assault rifles.

This is where the Young Guard came in, Maria's chosen path for political power. For those with political career ambitions, the Young Guard offered a more reliable path. They had a modern office, clean-cut staff members, and professional signage. "We are meant to prepare our young people to become young, professional politicians," said Ivan Demidov, the group's former leader. Their mission was to "fight" opposition movements through less confrontational means and to burnish their image by pretending to be philanthropic, leaving the real brawling to

Nashi. In essence, the Young Guard sought to groom its members to become politicians.

My favorite bit of Young Guard lore involves a video—a slice of propaganda allegedly pushed out by the organization and now hard to find on the internet. In 2010, wildfires spread across the country due to record-high temperatures and a massive drought. Heavy smog blanketed cities and that summer's heat wave caused over 50,000 deaths. Volunteer groups across Russia pitched in to help firefighters battle the blazes, and according to Radio Free Europe (RFE)—a Cold War–era news outlet once funded (and maybe still?) by the CIA to fight communism—the Young Guard posted a video of their members fighting the flames with surgical masks and determined expressions. Ruslan Gattarov, then the leader of the Young Guard, heaped praise on his crack firefighting squad.

"Without us," he said, "I think there would have been a serious blaze, although fire engines and vehicles with water are constantly arriving. If we had not intervened literally seconds after the first flames arose—and these flames were two times higher than us—several minutes, or several dozen minutes more, and several fire brigades would have been unable to control the blaze."

Good thing they were there.

According to RFE, however, the blogosphere was calling the whole thing staged. The event was allegedly faked using computer editing tools and doctored photos. Some viewers and bloggers were said to have noticed pristine leaves, grass, and trees around the supposed fire, leading to speculation that there had never been a blaze there at all. RFE also reported claims that the Young Guard staged the stunt to make up for their lackluster performance in the previous month.

I haven't been able to find the alleged video or any reporting beyond this RFE article. Is it a good news source? While I certainly don't rank it among the journalistic greats like *Cat Fancy*, true or not, the story does track. According to the *Vedemosti*, a business daily newspaper published in Moscow, the firefighter cosplay drew criticism from Kremlin deputy chief of staff Vyacheslav Surkov, who oversaw all pro-Kremlin youth groups. The Young Guard insisted the video was not fake. However, Gattarov, the leader of the group, was sacked.

Coincidentally, this firefighting incident happened in Ryazan—the site of another scandal a decade earlier. In 1999, as Putin was making his first run for the presidency, a wave of deadly bombings struck apartment buildings across Russia. The culprits? Supposedly the Chechens. At the time, Chechnya, a republic within Russia, was full of dissidents who wished for independence from Moscow's control, having already fought a brutal First Chechen War with the Russian state in the mid-1990s. Chechen militants had a reputation for being instigators, so it wasn't much of a leap to pin the apartment bombings on them. Besides, who else could it be?

In a stroke of luck on September 22, 1999, loyal and alert Russian citizens foiled a planned bombing of another residential complex. Alexei Kartofelnikov noticed two men ferrying large sacks from their car to the basement of his apartment building in Ryazan. Perhaps it was the recent bombings that had him on edge, but Alexei decided to take a closer look. He checked the license plate and saw the car was registered in Moscow—about four hours away. Even more suspicious, the last two digits of the plate had been obscured by a piece of paper to make it look like the car was local. Acting fast, Alexei called the police. By the time the city constables arrived, the suspicious men and car were gone. But after searching the apartment basement, they discovered three 110-pound sacks of white powder, each rigged with a detonator and a timing device set to go off at 5:30 a.m.

Close call.

With the city now on high alert, nearly 30,000 residents from that apartment building and neighboring complexes evacuated their homes. Within hours, a bomb squad had dismantled the devices and tested the white powder, detecting the presence of hexogen, a military-grade explosive. Police sketches of the suspects were plastered across the city and broadcast on TV. A total of 1,200 officers were mobilized. Highways and roads leading out of the city were locked down. Train stations and airports were barricaded. A manhunt ensued. Putin, then prime minister, publicly praised the vigilance of Ryazan's residents. He followed that with a call to attack the Chechen capital of Grozny—the would-be kickoff to the Second Chechen War.

But that's when things got weird.

"Leave one at a time, there are patrols everywhere," said a man whose call to Moscow had been tapped by a telephone service employee. That call was traced back to an exchange unit connected to the FSB.

The call was coming from inside the house.

The suspects were arrested. But they flashed FSB IDs and were soon released after a call from Moscow. Suddenly, the official story from the Kremlin shifted. What was initially called a Chechen terrorist plot was now a training exercise. A drill. With real explosives (confirmed by a bomb squad). In a real apartment building. In the early morning hours of that September day. According to FSB Director Nikolai Patrushev, it was all a training simulation meant to test responses following the earlier bombings. But as Edward Lucas recounts in *The New Cold War: Putin's Russia and the Threat to the West*, the local Ryazan FSB "reacted with fury." They issued a statement saying Patrushev's training "announcement came as a surprise to us and appeared" right when they were preparing to detain the suspects. The FSB later issued a public apology and claimed that the "explosives" were actually bags of sugar tied together with wires and a dummy detonator as part of a security exercise.

I mean, either you believe the Russian government planted a bomb for a drill and forgot to tell the local FSB office in Ryazan. Or you believe the FSB was intentionally blowing up apartment buildings across Russia, killing over three hundred people and injuring one thousand more, to stir up anti-Chechen sentiment so that Putin might springboard off the new war and propel him into the presidency.

"I hope no one in the world can bomb their own population," Maria would later say about the war in Ukraine two decades later.

I agree.

When your political system runs on image and illusion, it makes sense to train young people in the art of narrative control to navigate that world—one shaped more by messaging than by truth. The Young Guard became a natural extension of that system and the perfect pipeline for grooming talent in that space.

That's not to say US politics is immune to distortion, or that we've perfected honesty. Far from it. These days, concerns about democratic backsliding and institutional erosion persist. Plenty of members in Congress and other public figures continue to dodge, distort, or outright deny reality. But I don't want to make a false equivalency. The systems are not equal. Ours, for all its flaws, remains more transparent and accountable. Just look at what happened in December 2010, when Russia appointed a new member to the Public Council of the Young Guard. Who? Anna Chapman. Remember her? The same Anna Chapman who had recently been convicted as a Russian spy in the Illegals Program, and the same redheaded media figure Maria was, and still is, frequently and often intentionally confused with, though Maria herself was never a spy.

When a convicted deep-cover agent becomes the public face of the largest and most influential political youth organization in the country, you can bet dollars to dumplings that country doesn't place much value on truth.

In 2011, the Young Guard held a competition for young and aspiring political leaders like Maria. Technically, contestants didn't need to be members of United Russia (Maria wasn't) or even part of the Young Guard to participate. But those who completed certain tasks, like writing a political platform and defending it publicly, were promised a spot on the candidate list for the State Duma, the lower house of the Federal Assembly of Russia.

Maria completed the entire rigamarole, including the public speaking part. Her speech was about gun rights. She advocated for the right of Russians to own and carry concealed pistols and revolvers—a stance that did not sit well with her audience of teachers and old women. Still, she and a few other contestants won the local competition, and were told they'd be added to the State Duma candidate list. According to Maria, however, that never happened. The Young Guard cheated. Despite fulfilling the requirements, none of the winners were included and they basically ended up with nothing. Starting to see a trend? Just another example of empty promises and behind-the-scenes maneuvering in Russian politics.

Despite her disappointment, Maria could often see the silver linings in things. She took away valuable lessons and got a good sense of the politics of it all. She also built a small network of like-minded friends and, with her sister and the rest of her family, formed a strong team that began organizing locally. She collected signatures for a petition urging President Putin to allow concealed carry and delivered it to her representative in Barnaul. And just like that, she was running a small gun rights group. At the moment, it was only local. To grow, she'd need to head to Moscow.

Chapter Fourteen

"We need money," Bob said to me one afternoon.

At the time, I was just an associate—the bottom rung on the attorney ladder. But Bob, a partner with Big Law experience, had a broader understanding of firm operations and the realities of dollars and cents. While publicity from Maria's case might raise our profile, he worried that if we couldn't raise money to plug the financial gap, senior leadership could stop us from representing Maria, ethics permitting. Neither of us wanted to abandon her. With the clock ticking, we reached out to anyone who might be able to help.

Thinking the Russian people may wish to support one of their own, we started a legal defense fund for Maria. We established the fund in the United States, and it may be the reason why we got essentially nothing from the endeavor. US sanctions make it difficult if not impossible for Russian nationals to process US transactions from Russian financial institutions. Consequently, contributions largely came from Americans, presumably people who felt bad for Maria's situation and could see through the bunkum about her being some kind of Russian spy and international honeypot.

Hoping to find more luck among her friends, we called Patrick Byrne, the then CEO of Overstock, the internet retailer based in Utah. Maria thought fondly of Patrick. She knew him to be charitable, and the two had had a brief relationship. To my surprise, Patrick personally took my call.

"But what about that guy Torshin?" he asked. "Wasn't she doing things for him?"

"Yes," I said. "She bought him American toothpaste and clothes for his grandchildren. She also described a presidential campaign event she attended because he asked her about it. But she's not a spy."

The exchange reminded me of another conversation I'd had recently with my mom. She was worried—about me, about my safety—and asked what I thought of Maria. Did I believe she was a spy? Not that it would matter, even if she were, but I told her no. "In my heart of hearts, I don't believe she's a spy, and the government hasn't charged her with espionage."

Patrick told me he'd think about it, but then something curious happened. We got a message from one of Patrick's lawyers suggesting that donating to Maria's legal defense fund might present a conflict because, as the lawyer intimated, Patrick could be a government witness in this case due to his prior work with the FBI. What's more, he believed he had given the government *Brady* material—exculpatory information suggesting that Maria was innocent, or at least more like a graduate student than the secret agent the government made her out to be.

Huh, Bob and I thought.

The government had not turned over any such information, which is required.

We decided to ask the government about it.

In most courtrooms, you'll find a literal bar—a wooden railing that divides the action from the audience. To be a lawyer, you have to study law, but to be an attorney, the kind who stands up in court, you have to pass another type of bar: a grueling two, sometimes three-day exam.

Take me, I'm licensed in Virginia, Washington, DC, and Maryland. I'm also admitted before certain federal district courts and appellate courts, including the Supreme Court. While I haven't argued a case before Chief Justice John Roberts and the other Supremes (though my mom did sneak a picture with Ruth Bader Ginsburg—may she rest in peace—at my swearing-in ceremony), I have worked on a few federal circuit court appeals. Collectively, these courts routinely handle more than 50,000 appellate cases across the country each year. Most of them fail. Fewer than 9 percent result in a reversal of the lower court's ruling.

You might be impressed to learn I presently have a perfect score of winning on appeal. My mom certainly is.

Once upon a time, we called those who studied law but never practiced it "demi-lawyers," a derisive term for those who read the map but never made the journey. James Madison, the Father of the Constitution, was something of a demi-lawyer himself, a label he despised. Kudos to America, by the way, for putting an amateur in charge of the most important legal document we have. This document, both elegant and riddled with issues, is constantly analyzed, debated, and interpreted by our sharpest minds. Our soldiers swear to defend it. Our elected officials and judges swear to follow it. Somehow, it feels uniquely American that the very document that binds us was written by a man who never practiced law but studied it on his own in private.

Madison's claim to fame is his role at the 1787 Constitutional Convention, where he helped steer the difficult negotiations and compromises behind the drafting of our founding document. And that must have been challenging—getting a room full of rich white men, many of whom enslaved people, to agree on the foundation of their nascent country. Madison, too, enslaved people. Why is it that the great Enlightenment and constitutional thinkers of our founding, men who so carefully considered the inalienable rights of man, so often denied those very rights to others? Incidentally, of all the many lawyers in the room where the Constitution was drafted, only three owned slaves. One of them—Richard Bassett of Delaware—would soon become a fervent abolitionist.

In any event, Madison whittled down the long list of proposed amendments and wished to stitch them into the body of the Constitution's text. But Connecticut's Roger Sherman disagreed. He suggested tacking them on at the end. Sherman prevailed, which is why we have a numbered list of ten—our Bill of Rights.

The numbered ranking doesn't indicate importance. This is to say the First Amendment has no special primacy over the others. I can also confirm that the Third Amendment—regarding the nonconsensual quartering of soldiers in private homes—is no more important than the Fourth Amendment, which protects against unreasonable searches and seizures.

Despite this, the First Amendment contains a bunch of goodies for lawyers and nonlawyers alike. Here it is:

Congress shall make no law respecting an establishment of religion, or prohibiting the free exercise thereof; or abridging the freedom of speech, or of the press; or the right of the people peaceably to assemble, and to petition the Government for a redress of grievances.

The religion and freedom of speech clauses get plenty of airtime, so here's a quick plug for the *right to petition the government for a redress of grievances.* This clause doesn't just protect your right to speak out against perceived injustice, it protects your ability to seek change without fear of punishment or retaliation. Bad governments engage in reprisals and retribution all the time. Since the war in Ukraine began, Russia has prosecuted officials, politicians, and even its own soldiers for "discrediting" the government. In September 2022, members of a local council in St. Petersburg were summoned by police after petitioning parliament to remove President Putin, citing the invasion's staggering death toll, the rise in disabled veterans, and the economic fallout. For seeking change and airing those grievances, they were punished. That kind of state retaliation should not be permissible in any true functioning democracy. It's why lèse-majesté laws, or so-called "state insult" laws, don't exist in the United States. Here, by law, you can criticize and defame the government all you want without fear of retribution. Still, some might point to recent uses of executive power and the treatment of law firms like Perkins Coie, Susman Godfrey, and WilmerHale as raising questions about how power is wielded in response to dissent. They might even argue that those actions aren't really so different and are a sign of democratic decline. But these claims and the fears they reflect only underscore why constitutional protections matter.

The freedom of speech clause is the real star of First Amendment discussions—though demi-lawyers make two common errors when citing it. First, many thump the First Amendment drum when asserting a right to bring bigoted speech onto private property. Yet the amendment protects speech from government interference, not consequences imposed by private parties. If you're on your neighbor's lawn chanting "white lives matter" while bearing a repugnant sign that says, "Jews will not replace us," your neighbor can tell you to leave. So can Starbucks. The First Amendment doesn't apply there. Second, your freedom of speech from government interference isn't absolute. There are certain categories of speech that receive no protection under the First Amendment.

Most people know that "shouting *fire* in a crowded theater" is not protected speech. In *Schenck v. United States* (1919), Justice Oliver Wendell Holmes Jr. famously wrote, "The most stringent protection of free speech would not protect a man falsely shouting fire in a theatre and causing a panic." A longer list of unprotected speech includes obscenity, fraud, child pornography, speech integral to illegal conduct like perjury or sedition, speech that incites imminent lawless action, and speech that violates intellectual property laws, among others.

There's another limitation on free speech that's often overlooked: a judicial gag order.

On September 10, 2018, Bob, Maria, and I, along with prosecutors from DOJ, assembled in Judge Chutkan's courtroom for a status hearing. Two issues were before the court: Maria's continued detention and a gag order requested by the government.

Regarding detention, Judge Chutkan said, "I cannot envision a scenario where it is not possible, pardon my double negative, for Ms. Butina to be released from the jail, to be put into a car with diplomatic tags and to be placed on an airplane taking her out of the jurisdiction of this court. High intensity supervision won't stop that, or any other combination or series of conditions that I impose. There's a very real risk of flight, and the fact that her home country has no extradition treaty, and the government of that country has made repeated and vocal demands for her release does not reassure this court that if she's released she will remain within the jurisdiction of this court."

I've made my argument on the issue, and you may be buoyed to learn that our Justice Department eventually found itself showing a change of heart. You cannot target someone based on their nationality, as Russians were in 2018, and then hold that nationality against them in legal proceedings. Years later, the Department of Justice would scrap a program called the China Initiative, which focused on countering economic espionage and trade secret theft linked to Beijing, after a series of failed or dismissed cases and widespread criticism that the effort fueled suspicion and bias against innocent Chinese persons, as well as excessive and abusive prosecutions. "Anything that creates the impression that the Department of Justice applies different standards based on race or ethnicity harms the department and our efforts, and it harms the public," Assistant Attorney General for National Security Matthew Olsen said in 2022 when ending the program.

For Maria, she wouldn't be so lucky in the midst of the Russian scare. The court then moved to the gag order.

Judges sometimes feel compelled to control the flow of information in highly publicized cases to safeguard a defendant's right to a fair trial. One way they do that is by issuing a gag order, which is a court order that bars attorneys, parties, or witnesses from discussing the case publicly.

Don't get me wrong, I understand the instinct to keep certain details out of the press to preserve an unbiased jury pool in a big case. It's just that gag orders limit the free expression of thoughts and ideas on issues that matter—issues that are central to public life and government accountability. That's why I think judges should be cautious and avoid issuing gag orders too readily. When First Amendment rights are on the line, there ought to be a really good reason to restrain someone from speaking out.

True, the Constitution guarantees a criminal defendant the right to a fair trial. But that only justifies a gag order if there's a credible belief the defendant *can't* get a fair trial without it. Publicity alone doesn't cut it. An impartial juror doesn't have to be oblivious to the facts of a case, just willing and able to set aside any early impressions and decide the case based on what's presented in court.

In *Nebraska Press Ass'n v. Stuart* (1976), the Supreme Court recognized that publicity surrounding a defendant's confessions to the police could affect his right to a fair trial. However, the Court still struck down the trial judge's gag order, stating jurors aren't fragile. They can be instructed to ignore outside matters and confine their considerations to what they observed in the courtroom. The Supreme Court was clear: a gag order is justified only if "publicity, unchecked, would so distort the views of potential jurors that [enough] could not be found who would, under proper instructions, fulfill their sworn duty to render a just verdict exclusively on the evidence presented in open court." The test isn't whether the case is high-profile or whether public discourse might risk revealing prejudicial information. The question is whether the judge can seat an impartial jury without the order. If it can, the gag order shouldn't issue.

The idea that Maria, a gun advocate, alleged Russian agent, and criminal defendant facing trial in a politically progressive city hostile to her views, would somehow benefit from a jury pool biased in *her favor*—simply because her lawyer might push back against the overwhelming onslaught of misinformation and prevailing Russophobic sentiment that fostered distrust toward anything Russian—was not a credible concern.

The District of Columbia Bar, which oversees attorneys practicing in the District and sets the rules of professional conduct for lawyers like me, emphasizes that "litigants have a right to present their side of a dispute to the public, and the public has an interest in receiving information about matters that are in litigation. Often a lawyer involved in the litigation is in the best position to assist in furthering these legitimate objectives." The American Bar Association, the grandfather of all bar associations in the United States, adds in its trial publicity rule that "extrajudicial statements . . . may be permissible when they are made in response to statements made publicly by another party, another party's lawyer, or third persons, where a reasonable lawyer would believe a public response is required in order to avoid prejudice to the lawyer's client. When prejudicial statements have been publicly made by others, responsive statements may have the salutary effect of lessening any resulting adverse impact on the adjudicative proceeding."

In other words, if the government falsely claims that your client trades sex for favors, a lawyer may take action to undo that damage in the public sphere.

"We have a big gag order problem in certain parts of the country," says Margaret Tarkington, a law professor at Indiana University Robert H. McKinney School of Law and a leading scholar on attorney speech. "There are too many judges who issue overly broad gag orders on attorneys. These are mostly unconstitutional because they prohibit too much speech. They not only violate attorneys' free-speech rights but also negatively impact the public's right to access . . . . [C]ourts have turned to gag and sealing orders to keep things under wraps. This is concerning, because attorneys can serve as an important check on the judiciary and the court system."

I agree. Courts should strive to keep their doors open—most of all where public scrutiny is at its highest—and avoid silencing litigants unless absolutely necessary.

In addition to the false claims the prosecution made about Maria, consider the actions of Natalie Mayflower Sours Edwards, another member of the government at the time. A senior official with the US Department of the Treasury in the Financial Crimes Enforcement Network (FinCEN), Edwards had eyes on suspicious activity reports (SARs for short) which are crude red flags raised by banking institutions about transactions that *might* indicate a violation of law.

As an example, if you deposit a bunch of cash into your bank account, FinCEN might receive a SAR for that deposit. It doesn't mean you did anything wrong. In fact, it likely means you *didn't* do anything wrong. According to The Bank Policy Institute, a nonpartisan public policy, research, and advocacy group representing the nation's leading banks, just a sample of the largest banks reviewed in 2017 filed over 640,000 SARs. Of those, the banks received feedback from law enforcement on 4 percent. Approximately 90 to 95 percent of the people the banks alerted the government about had broken no rule at all. A tiny subset of the 4 percent of SARs that received follow-ups resulted in arrest and conviction.

Why are we wading into the weeds of banking administration? Because Natalie Edwards, a senior official at FinCEN, illegally disclosed Maria's SARs to the public, suggesting they were incriminating. Maria had committed no financial crimes and had passed no money to anyone in the service of any crime at all, yet these SARs were released in a way that ultimately smeared her. The truth is that a review of Maria's banking activities would show no illegal, much less remarkable activity. She was a Russian national with a bank account back home. It's hardly surprising that some of her international transactions triggered reports. In fact, when Maria sent money home, it was so her family members could help pay off her Russian bank-issued credit cards.

Natalie Edwards would eventually be prosecuted for her felony, which is all well and good, but Judge Chutkan barred us from speaking to the media to explain what had happened. Government actors literally broke the law, harming a defendant, and her attorneys were prohibited from speaking publicly to defend her. The painful irony here is that the First Amendment was designed to protect people from the government, not the other way around.

But here's the sticky wicket: parties are often reluctant to challenge the propriety of gag orders even if an appeal is on strong legal footing. The reason? Appeals can be cost-prohibitive, and they carry the risk, however unfounded, that the trial judge might take offense, even subconsciously. And if you win, you just showed that the very judge presiding over your case acted unconstitutionally. Never a flattering look.

Natalie Edwards, whom journalist Sarah Ellison of *The Washington Post* called "one of the most important whistleblowers of our era," pleaded guilty to one count of conspiracy to make unauthorized disclosures of SARs and was sentenced to six months of incarceration. Contrary to Ellison's belief, Natalie Edwards was not a "whistleblower." Nothing about her SARs disclosure was akin to blowing the whistle. It was an abuse of her position. Whistleblowers are protected from prosecution because they follow the law when reporting misconduct. Edwards did no such thing. As Judge Gregory H. Woods said at her sentencing, "It should have been exceptionally clear" to Edwards "that violating her oath and exposing sensitive law enforcement information" that could be used "to tarnish the reputation and interest of innocent people was both illegal and wrong."

Here's what Judge Chutkan had to say:

"All right. With regard to imposition of a [gag] order. . . . I have to say, Mr. Saunders and Mr. Kenerson, I think it helpful to begin as you would wish to proceed, and you began this case with rather salacious allegations against Ms. Butina, who's a young woman with no criminal record. And Mr. Driscoll is right. Those allegations are notorious and have received a lot of attention and have damaged her reputation, and I'm sure her family and she are all very upset by them. And I will give you credit for walking them back, as I found out yesterday in perusing my Sunday paper, that you have taken those allegations back. I have to say that in reviewing the substance of the emails in the pleadings before me, it took approximately five minutes for me to review those emails and tell that they were jokes. It wasn't even—it was apparent on their face. And so I'm concerned that somebody in your office or over at the Department of Justice could look at those emails and conclude that they were a serious offer to trade sexual favors for other services. I'm dismayed by that. Once allegations are made, as Mr. Driscoll properly points out, it's very difficult to take back. And I credit you for publicly taking back those allegations, but I caution you not to make those—especially start out a case with those kinds of salacious claims. It really makes it very, very difficult to have a fair trial when those sorts of statements are made, and it's one of the problems in this case in trying to get a jury pool that's not tainted. So I appreciate your publicly retracting those comments, and I caution both sides from spending any more time on them."

Judge Chutkan understood the issue. Prosecutors had falsely maligned a defendant at the outset of a case in a way that was "very difficult to take back." Unfortunately, she then cautioned us (Maria's attorneys) against spending any more time on those false allegations, even though we were duty-bound to vigorously oppose any false statement that harmed our client's reputation—a duty that did not end because the government retracted its statement.

Judge Chutkan continued:

"On the other hand, Mr. Driscoll, you spent a significant amount of time making public statements about this case, including giving your opinion as to Ms. Butina's innocence or guilt, giving your own alternative explanations for the evidence in this case. And I don't anticipate that you're going to be a witness in this case, so I don't think those kinds of statements are proper. Local rule 57.7(b)(3) specifically prohibits dissemination of, and I quote, 'Any opinion as to the accused's guilt or innocence or as to the merits of the case or the evidence in the case.' Local rule 57.7(b) also prohibits a lawyer from disseminating information or opinion in connection with criminal litigation 'if there is a reasonable likelihood that such dissemination will interfere with a fair trial or otherwise prejudice the due administration of justice.' I find in this case that you have overstepped local rule 57. I understand your position that the government has made a lot of claims that you believe to be unfounded against your client, including the aforementioned claim regarding sexual favors, which it has now publicly retracted. However,

I do find that your comments have crossed the line. This is a case that's going to be tried here in the District of Columbia. When is a matter we'll turn to in a moment, but our jury pool is relatively small. Having a gag order 30 days before a trial won't help us get an impartial jury if you've gone all over the media making statements, giving explanations for the evidence in this case. So I'll tell you, the government contends that you violated 57.7(b) by naming a potential witness, discussing financial transactions involving the defendant, discussing the subject of governmental surveillance, that you've made claims regarding the government's alleged failure to produce evidence, claims regarding evidence of Ms. Butina's contact with political campaigns, and characterization of her relationship with a Russian official, among multiple other examples. And I have to agree. I understand you feel you have to zealously defend your client, and I certainly understand that. I've been in your position before."

Again, Judge Chutkan, a former defense attorney herself, understood our professional ethics, but she was critical of our media engagement because "there comes a point at which your work defending your client needs to happen in this courtroom and not on the public airwaves." She's not wrong in her criticism. It's simply that we use the mantra "innocent until proven guilty," but the words mean nothing when a defendant and her attorneys are forbidden from presenting their side of the story—especially in response to a false accusation by the government, one so exaggerated and widespread that it taints public opinion against her.

It's no doubt difficult to strike the right balance between ensuring a fair trial and protecting free speech. Both are core constitutional rights, and I sympathize with judges who preside over big cases—their job is challenging. But here's the thing: publicity regularly accompanies high-profile cases, and the public has an understandable interest in them. It comes with the territory. Litigants have a genuine interest in presenting their side of a dispute to the public, just as the public has a legitimate interest in staying informed about what's going on. That's a feature of our democracy, not a bug. So in my view, cutting off public access to the voices of those involved is almost never the right move.

Maybe this is why Bob says practicing law is often more of an art than a science.

We were in a tough spot defending a young woman and incredibly unpopular client who the government wrongly accused of using sex for influence. This singular claim created a media frenzy, where it seemed as though all news organizations had accepted and repeated the government's depiction of Maria as some type of spy-novel honeypot character who seduced her way to access and power. If that weren't enough, the aspersions continued with a senior official at FinCEN leaking confidential suspicious activity reports to the news, implying they showed banking activity of Maria's attempt to sway the 2016 presidential election on behalf of the Kremlin when they did no such thing.

I thought Judge Chutkan might be leaning toward a gag order, but I didn't expect one to issue so soon, especially right after we exposed the falsity of the government's most extreme claims. We were fewer than sixty days into the case, with no trial date in sight. Courts have plenty of ways to deal with threats to a fair trial that stop short of issuing a blanket gag order. They can use jury questionnaires, pull from larger jury pools, and have extensive qualification and selection processes. They can also adjust the trial schedule, give clear and robust jury instructions, or in the rare instance, sequester a jury. By issuing a gag order so quickly, it effectively allowed the government to freeze the false narrative it helped create. And worse, it didn't accomplish the goal of reducing risks to Maria's right to a fair trial since false and negative news coverage continued to swirl around her—this time, unchecked by counsel.

Alas, Judge Chutkan chose to block speech altogether.

"So, accordingly . . . the court will issue a special [gag] order under local rule 57.7(c), restricting the ability of the parties to release information or make statements regarding the merits of and/or evidence at issue in this case as more specifically described in local rule 57.7(b)(3)."

Once, when visiting Maria at CTF, I saw a small group of family members waiting to see an inmate. Most social visits at the DC jail are done by video, but these folks were there for an in-person visit. Unfortunately, the guards at the facility were rude that day, barking at them about how to line up and where to go or stand. Most of my interactions with the employees at this facility (and government facilities generally) are pleasant if not unmemorable. But that day was different. These particular guards demanded certain behavior and were shouting at the family to put their possessions in lockers—lockers that cost money. It was clear, to me anyway, that this family didn't have the resources for that and was scrambling to find another way to manage. There was a threat though that if they didn't "act right" or weren't compliant, they wouldn't be allowed to see their loved one. This family had taken however many buses to get to that jail, and all they wanted was to see their mother, daughter, or sister on a designated visiting day. Instead, what they found were correctional officers—city workers who serve the public—treating them cruelly when things for that family may have been at their worst.

It was a reminder that those in power must be kept in check by systems to prevent abuse, especially of the most dispossessed.

On a regular basis, the Russian government performs targeted killings, political assassinations, phony judicial proceedings, and arbitrary detentions. The government tortures and murders its own citizens like it did the Russian entrepreneur Valery Pshenichny in February 2018. While waiting in pretrial detention, Pshenichny was stabbed, beaten, electrocuted, raped, and asphyxiated. After initially claiming the man had committed suicide, the Russian government finally admitted he had been murdered. Then, as it does with so many things, the Kremlin offered hollow vows to find and punish the culprits.

Russia's record of human rights was on Maria's mind as two officers loomed outside her cell. On previous evenings, they may have flipped on the cell block lights to see if she was crying. If so, instead of offering mental health care, an officer, one that had subjected her to unnecessary strip searches, would sit down but ignore her. These officers were different though. These officers were here to take her. They didn't respond to her questions. They simply told her to pack her possessions: the books given by friends, the toiletries from the canteen, and the legal papers being used to prepare for her trial. She was instructed to carry these items into a staff room and leave them on a table. There, her jailers picked through her belongings under the hum of fluorescent lighting. One officer mentioned that it's too bad about the new prison jumpsuit she was wearing. "What a waste."

It was then Maria fell silent and feared the worst.

Under the cover of darkness, Maria was loaded into a van and spirited away. Before long, the transport turned down a long road bounded by trees. An officer reached for the radio and asked Maria what kind of music she liked. Perhaps this would be the last song she'd ever hear. Had she been in Siberia, where she grew up, August 17, 2018, might have been etched on her headstone. But she was in the United States. Because of the propaganda of her home country, she didn't realize that she was being transferred to the Alexandria city jail just across the Potomac River. Nobody told her what was happening.

When I tell people this story, it serves as a litmus test. Some believe her panic was a just punishment: similar to a mock execution, the tactic used by ISIS and a torture forbidden by the Geneva Convention. Some laugh at the madcap misunderstanding of it all, the broken government bureaucracy, not fully appreciating that though the United States doesn't carry out capital punishment in such a way, Maria comes from a country where she had been told we did. Some are seized with empathy and can understand her terror as she was driven shackled down a dark, wooded road by guards who refused to answer questions. Some are disappointed she wasn't executed. Some don't care.

After Maria had been settled in the Alexandria jail, where she would eventually be released into the general population, I visited frequently.

We see jails and prisons as holding facilities for the castaways of society, but as a defense attorney, I know that many inmates are just people fallen on hard times. Some of us know the horrors of these institutions because we watch prison dramas and legal shows on TV. Others know because we read about them in the news. We know about the violence, the death, the rape that occurs in our facilities with such a frequency that it should make us wonder why every other Western nation has taken the right path on this issue and the wealthiest among them, the United States, has decided to take a different direction. But I do wonder how many people truly understand the extent of the suffering that occurs in our jails and prison systems.

In July 2018, shortly after her initial court appearance, Maria was placed in solitary confinement upon arrival at CTF. She could not have her glasses, receive letters written in her native Russian language, or see the sun. When marshals transferred her to the Alexandria jail in August, she remained in solitary confinement. Between the two facilities, Maria was in solitary for twenty-two hours a day for sixty-seven days straight. She was relieved from her cell twice a day for two hours during which she could shower, exercise, or call her parents. To put that duration in context, "prolonged solitary confinement" is defined under the Mandela Rules, adopted by the United Nations Commission on Crime and Criminal Justice in Vienna in 2015, as a "time period in excess of 15 consecutive days."

According to *The Journal of the American Academy of Psychiatry and Law*, "Solitary confinement is recognized as difficult to withstand; indeed, psychological stressors such as isolation can be as clinically distressing as physical torture." The psychological effects of solitary include "anxiety, depression, anger, cognitive disturbances, perceptual distortions, obsessive thoughts, paranoia, and psychosis." The physical effects include migraines, profuse sweating, neck and back pain, and heart palpitations. Extreme weight loss or gain is not uncommon, and these symptoms can worsen with each trip to solitary confinement.

A US military study of the naval aviators who were imprisoned in Vietnam, John McCain being one of them, found that social isolation was as torturous as any physical abuse they had suffered. If you're familiar with the story of those aviators, you'll know that being isolated from others was as bad as having their bones shattered. Think about this fact when you consider the 48,000 inmates, or 4 percent of the incarcerated population in the United States, that are right now undergoing this torture.

What happens to those isolated is physical. We have studies that show the slowing of brain waves from those who have suffered a week or more in isolation. Fifty-seven prisoners of war in the detention camp in the former Yugoslavia showed brain abnormalities after their internment. The worst symptoms were found in those with head trauma that had rendered them unconscious or in those who had been placed in solitary. To put it bluntly, without sustained social interaction, the brain becomes as damaged as if from a violent injury. After being exposed to such torture, and there is no other name for it, a March 2014 article in the *American Journal of Public Health* found that, "Inmates in jails and prisons attempt to harm themselves in many ways, resulting in outcomes ranging from trivial to fatal." The surgeon and writer Atul Gawande put it best when he wrote, "If prolonged isolation is—as research and experience have confirmed for decades—so objectively horrifying, so intrinsically cruel, how did we end up with a prison system that may subject more of our own citizens to it than any other country in history has?"

I've heard answers to the above question, none of them satisfying. People will say that something must be done with the truly dangerous. According to a massive study performed by the Vera Institute of Justice examining eight state prison systems and two local jail systems from 2015 to 2018, "nonviolent, low-level disciplinary infractions—such as swearing, smoking, disrespecting authority, or possessing minor contraband—were among the most frequent reasons people were sent to solitary confinement." These individuals weren't the truly dangerous. But even when violence is involved, many studies have shown that the use of solitary confinement tends to increase violence within a facility, not reduce it. As noted by Daniel Mears, a criminology researcher at Florida State University, 24.2 percent of inmates held in solitary confinement committed a violent crime three years after they were released compared to 20.5 percent of inmates who were not isolated. Torture creates violence; it doesn't prevent it.

Maria was placed in "administrative segregation," solitary by another name. This happened not because she was violent or disruptive but because—well, actually, I have no idea why. The jail didn't tell us. And they're not required to. They can impose these extreme conditions any time they want, without internal review or explanation.

Solitary has measurable long-term physiological effects when it lasts longer than a few weeks. Maria was kept in solitary for a total of four months.

I have a suspicious number of square dancers in my family. For the uninitiated, a square dance consists of four paired-off couples that start each dance facing the middle of their octet. To the rhythm of the song, a caller then talks everyone through various repertoires that require dancers to come together, circle about, and jaunt back to their home spots. At its most complex, it's a wild whirligig of motion dictated by strict rules. My mother and her sisters are old hands and can promenade left when the time is right. Even my boyfriend had learned how to do-si-do at his Southern elementary school. But in my family, my beloved and departed grandmother Swersie was a pioneer and became the first Black female square dance caller to reach the national stage. She'd be the celebrity caller on cruise ships and at state conventions. She even went on national TV, showing Phil Donahue how to sashay.

When my grandmother was calling, prejudice was on a bit of a bull market, not just in the square-dancing scene but across the nation, so not everybody would let you dance with them. But she was so competent and had such a strong personality that over time people just forgot to be racist or sexist or however intolerant. She even called dances in Chicago's gay and lesbian scene, a fun intersection on a bizarre Venn diagram. Bigotry requires effort, and it's much easier to allemande left.

Sometimes in my life, I feel a bit like Swersie. Law can be like a called dance, sometimes with partners who don't wish to look you in the eye. With enough time though, with enough direction from a good caller, I can wear down any bias—hopefully before the song runs out.

One afternoon, I huddled with Bob in his office for one of our impromptu strategy sessions. We discussed Maria's anxiety that had been noticeable on each of our visits. Even after she was transferred to the Alexandria jail and released from solitary, we found a hopelessness in her, likely shaped by the anti-American propaganda about our justice system that had permeated her upbringing. Bob and I pitched ideas either to settle her nerves or find a way forward that could resolve her situation swiftly.

"Hey," I said, playing an idea through the dozen or so possibilities that could unfold. "What if . . . hear me out."

"Okay," Bob said, leaning back in his chair with his typical patience.

"So, Maria is our best witness, right?"

"Okay."

"I mean she's never lied to us, never lied to the government. And she knows all the answers to all the questions the other side has."

"Right."

"What if we—"

"—arrange a sit-down."

"Yeah. Queen for a day."

Bob considered the idea. A queen for a day or proffer session is a potentially risky game you can play with the government. The basic setup is this: your client agrees to tell prosecutors everything they know about any crimes—perhaps even their own—in exchange for a limited immunity agreement. The government promises not to use your client's words against them in any legal proceeding. But there's a catch: those words can still be used to further the investigation. So if your client admits to skimming from the till, prosecutors can't use that confession in court, but they can go get the surveillance footage and bank records to prove it. Plus, if your client lies to investigators during the session, they're in a world of hurt by opening themselves up to additional charges for making false statements. So why would a client ever agree to such a thing?

"To deescalate," Bob said.

"If they're looking for a spy, we can show they don't have one."

"Right."

"What do you think?"

Bob nodded. "Could work."

We sat. We thought. We ran through the square dance in our conversation to see how this dance could end.

"We should pitch the idea to Maria," Bob said. "If she gives the okay, we can figure out how to reach out to the government."

"I could talk to Tommy to see if they're interested."

Thomas Saunders was one of the prosecutors who entered the case alongside Erik Kenerson. I knew Tom, but I was originally introduced to him as Tommy because he was a close friend of Jack.

Chapter Fifteen

In a memorable scene from 1987's *The Untouchables*, our heroes, played by Kevin Costner and Sean Connery, arrest Al Capone's bookkeeper after a shoot-out on the Canadian side of the border. The protagonists then pressure the accountant to flip on his boss, but the bookkeeper dismisses the idea even after verbal threats and a slug to the face. Undeterred, Sean Connery, playing a Chicago beat cop, walks outside and finds the corpse of a man just gunned down in the shoot-out. Connery takes the man's body, props him against the window, and interrogates him to make the bookkeeper think the man is still alive. Connery offers the man the same deal he offered the bookkeeper, and since the corpse keeps his lips sealed, Connery shoots the man through the skull. Suddenly terrified, the bookkeeper reconsiders the offer from Chicago's finest.

My family is from Chicago, and I can't help but mention that the city has gotten a bad rap for violent crime. Does Chicago have too much crime? Absolutely. But is it the worst in the country? No. In 2024, the right-leaning outlet Wirepoints.org compiled police data from the seventy-five largest cities in the United States, and Chicago didn't even make the top ten in per capita murder rates. It ranked thirteenth, behind St. Louis, Cleveland, and Washington, DC. In fact, if you broaden the lens to include all violent crime, as the FBI did in 2019, Chicago ranked forty-fifth—behind Wichita, San Francisco, Mobile, and Houston.

So why is Chicago cloaked in infamy? Besides its history with organized crime and the public's shaky grasp of per capita statistics, the answer lies in partisan media narratives. Chicago is a major city run by Democrats. The implicit message: if Democrats can't keep you safe, vote Republican. But if that's the standard, consider the FBI's data on state-level homicide rates. In 2020, the five states with the highest per capita murder rates were Mississippi, Louisiana, Alabama, Missouri, and Arkansas. Notice anything? All are conservative-leaning, all have Republican legislatures, and all had Republican governors—except Louisiana. If crime is a reflection of political leadership, then the numbers don't support the narrative. (For the record, the five states with the lowest murder rates were New Hampshire, Vermont, Maine, Idaho, and Massachusetts.) Do I believe crime is simply a matter of which party is in power? I do not. A more plausible explanation is that the most violent states also tend to be among the poorest. But nuance doesn't drive clicks, and partisan media loves political theater.

Let's get back to *The Untouchables* because I did mention it for a reason. The protagonists of the story were trying to do something revolutionary: take down the mob. And in the beginning of their seemingly quixotic journey, they realize that to accomplish such a feat, they must get their hands dirty. "What are you prepared to do?" asks Sean Connery.

The term "nonviolent revolution" feels like an oxymoron because it practically is. How can power shift so dramatically on a large scale from one party to another without violence? Well, strong democratic institutions have a good track record for that, but when things go off the rails and the rules of democracy are thrown out, that's when things become violent.

What about Gandhi? you might say. Sure, but if Gandhi is your argument, you may wish to investigate the Indian National Army, which was anything but peaceful. Sometimes the violent alternative makes the peaceful one more palatable. Lawyers do this good cop/bad cop all the time, and the illusion of choice allows people to feel good about taking a path they wouldn't otherwise take. In *The Untouchables*, the bookkeeper learned this lesson on the Canadian border.

Most revolutions require guns, and every government knows it. But please don't read a guns rights argument into this—that would require a book unto itself. I'm simply saying that rebels need a means to foment and wage rebellion. Then, if they succeed, something curious happens: they usually reach a point, once in power, when they decide that the means of rebellion should no longer remain in the hands of the people. Gun rights for me, but not for thee. Nowhere is this better illustrated than in twentieth-century Russian history.

The Russian Civil War was sparked in 1917 by multiple factions vying for power in post-tsarist Russia. You had the Red Army, the White Army, a few Greens, and even the Black Army thrown in for good measure. In general, the Reds wanted to spread Marxism, the Whites hated the Reds, the Greens armed local peasants who fought both sides, and the Blacks were the anarchists. However, they all had one thing in common: weapons. When the Red Army won the tussle, which killed roughly ten million people, the newly installed Soviet government allowed the people to possess small firearms and bladed weapons.

The Declaration of the Rights of Working and Exploited People in January 1918 sought to "arm the working people," the rationale being that an unarmed populace is powerless against the whims of the mighty. But by December of that year, the Soviet government realized that they weren't the populace anymore; *they* were the mighty. In a new decree, they ordered citizens to surrender all firearms, swords, bayonets, and bombs. Yes, members of the Communist Party threw the proletariat a bone by allowing a single pistol or rifle for personal use, a concession that was perhaps later regretted after Sergey Kirov, a buddy of Joseph Stalin, was assassinated by Leonid Nikolayev in 1934 using his own revolver. Or maybe Stalin didn't actually regret it because he tightened his grip on the Soviet Union with the crackdown that followed. But whatever the case, all weapons were classified, categorized, and conditioned, and in March 1933, the manufacture, possession, purchase, and sale of firearms, except for smoothbore hunting weapons, was punishable by five years in prison.

In 1935, the rules applied to knives—because why not. During World War II, civilians then had to hand over their personal hunting weapons for defense against the Germans. After Stalin's death in 1953, the USSR had an oscillating wave of gun legislation. The conditions for gun ownership were softened and melee weapons were allowed again. Registration wasn't mandatory until it was again. The criminal code for penalties was eased but later enhanced.

To get a gun in Russia these days, you must pass a battery of requirements: you'll need the A-OK from both a psychiatrist and ophthalmologist, a certificate of completion in a course on gun safety, a urine test to catch any drug abusers, a special safe to house your gun, and an inspection by the police to make sure everything's in order. After a federal test and the necessary background checks, you're well on your way to purchasing a firearm for self-defense, hunting, or sporting activities.

Valery Butin, Maria's father, jumped through the necessary hoops to acquire his TOZ-34, a double-barreled long gun for home defense, hunting, and target practice. Because he only had girls, Valery likely assumed the gun hobby would remain his own within the family. Or maybe not, given Maria's early proclivities. When Maria was young, Valery noticed she possessed a keen interest in his gun safe. She'd walk around the house and be drawn like a magnet to the thick box where Valery held his weapon. At first, this fascination concerned Valery. He worried that one day his headstrong tomboy of a daughter might find herself alone and crack into the safe. She was quite clever and persistent, so Valery felt he had two choices. He could remove the gun from the house, or he could teach Maria to shoot it. He presented the options to Maria, and the decision was quick. She chose the latter.

At age ten, Valery gave Maria her first lesson in firearms. With only a plastic bottle and a couple of rounds, they trekked to a forest near their dacha, a little summer house in the country, and Valery set up the plastic bottle as a target. His goal was to teach Maria how powerful a firearm could be. He had Maria shoot the bottle with his shotgun, and like that, the thing was destroyed. He said a gun is completely dangerous in the wrong hands, but it can save your life if you know how to handle one. Until it was confiscated many years later by airport security, Maria would carry the spent round of ammunition as a reminder of her first lesson in the awful power of firearms.

As a teenager, some girls in Russia would have dolls, Maria had guns. It is unusual for any Russian to have a gun. Only 9 percent of Russian citizens have them compared to some 40 percent of Americans. And in Russia, it was especially strange for women to possess a firearm. While Maria wasn't allowed by her mother Irina to go hunting—though she would eventually hunt boar, deer, and pheasant in South Dakota many years later—she was allowed to do sporting activities. This meant firing at little orange plates or taking trips to the shooting club where Valery's friend, a shooting instructor for the police academy in Barnaul, would give them leftover ammo to practice with. They'd shoot a Makarov, a standard police pistol at a time, which was much better for Maria because the shotgun had quite the kick.

Lured by the soft glow of libertarianism, Maria floated like a moth to the philosophy of gun ownership. Libertarians see firearms as the last defense against a tyrannical government, the boogeyman of personal freedom. After graduating from college in 2010, Maria registered a group of other like-minded gun supporters composed entirely of friends and family. Together, they'd shoot, talk shop, and eventually deliver a petition to Putin's local office. It was all a bit of fun though, the natural postgrad spillover from your late-night college talk about grand plans to change the world. But an unexpected offer took Maria out of the theoretical realm and into the practical.

One day, when Maria was browsing online for a gun rights speech, she found an organization like her own but in Moscow and with actual bona fides. Excited by signs of life across the diaspora, she wrote the group's organizers to get the skinny on their activities and learn how big-city gun rights activists rolled. She didn't expect a prompt reply and was a bit startled when one came right away with an invitation to an event in Moscow. Her heart was all aflutter. There was a problem though. Moscow was a four-and-a-half-hour flight from Barnaul, not to mention that a plane ticket would cost about as much as a two-bedroom condo—not really, but awfully expensive for a college grad even one with her own furniture business. Certainly excited to make contact, Maria just couldn't take the plunge and follow the bright lights of the big city, so she politely declined. One day she'd end up in Moscow, but when the time was right.

Then the organizers emailed back and offered a free plane ticket, and the time suddenly became right. Dreams do come true, but only with a donation from a bunch of libertarians.

Moscow is a modern city with an ancient past. First documented in the twelfth century—though settled long before—Moscow would eventually become the capital of the Tsardom of Russia. Today, its population is about 50 percent larger than that of New York City. The Russian capital is home to the Bolshoi Ballet, St. Basil's Cathedral, Red Square, and the

Moscow Metro, which boasts not only chandeliers but also a pack of stray dogs that know how to navigate the metro map. In the center of Moscow, you have the Kremlin, meaning "fortress inside a city," the world's largest medieval fortress, likely first established sometime in the eleventh century. From the thirteenth century onward, it's been the central nervous system of Russia and the site of some of the most influential historical events. Today, the fortified complex holds presidential office buildings, cathedrals, and even a palace. It's a little bit like a much, much, much grander White House except the Russian president doesn't live there—Putin doesn't anyway.

For Maria, Moscow was *the place* to visit—a Russian marvel to be proud of. When she touched down, suitcase in tow, Maria met the men running the pro-guns website, and over the course of her trip, they introduced her to sponsors and even offered her money to establish her own gun-rights group in Moscow if she were willing to expand the cause nationwide. In this magical land of onion domes and savvy stray dogs, Maria's fantasies were finally—after endless *months* of chilling with friends—coming true. To Maria, every Siberian has a dream to conquer the capital, to make it in the big city. It's the New York City of Russia. It's the "if you can make it there, you can make it anywhere" kind of metropolis. And there she was with her golden ticket.

When Maria returned home, she found herself in the post–big city blahs. The water didn't taste quite right. She had outgrown her childhood home. She discussed the idea of moving to Moscow with her boyfriend Anton. They'd been dating throughout college, and he encouraged her to go and ignore the piddling excuses she presented in her list of pros and cons. Her father could help manage the furniture stores, and besides, she could always expand into Moscow. Convinced by Anton, and with the support of her family, Maria agreed to the move. If it didn't work out, Barnaul would always be there.

In preparation, Maria's planning was simple and idealistic. She'd use the money she'd socked away over the years to open an additional store in the capital. She knew furniture, and this was a surefire way to find footing. Do what you know, as they say. In the meantime, she'd make sophisticated urbanite friends, both while doing business and spreading her guns rights advocacy. These people will surely have read Alisa Rosenbaum, the Russian libertarian firebrand, and she could very well imagine all the new authors and periodicals she'd discover in her journey. She would then move into a downtown loft with Anton, who would float with other intellectual lotus-eaters. He'd be wry and charming. She'd be beautiful and clever. She *did* get the Moscow dialect and patter from her grandmother, who was born and raised in and around the capital. Remember, Maria didn't play in the streets as a young child. She spent it with her grandmother with a teacher's elocution so pure and proper. Her plan was foolproof. She had a system, an algorithm, an understanding—insider know-how and the kind of chutzpah only the young and foolhardy possess. In her case, it leaned more toward the foolhardy.

When it came to business, Maria first researched the furniture market and saw some openings in the retail space. But after a bit more research, she then discovered a little company called IKEA operating in the city. Perhaps you've heard of it? At the time, Maria had not. Imagine you handstitched your own T-shirts to hawk in the big city and then you learn about a company called Walmart that sells its shirts at half the price. I suppose no analogy was needed for IKEA, but I want to underscore the devastation that Maria felt when she discovered the Swedes had already invaded the city. The meatballs didn't help. On the Barnaul front of the war, Maria assumed that her business would hum along nicely without her. She'd staffed it appropriately and created the systems for near selfsufficiency. One thing she didn't consider: people steal. Before long, her furniture stores were on the brink of collapse because so many staff members were plundering the goods. When the cat's away.

Thankfully, Valery stepped in to help his daughter. He managed to prop up the business until Maria realized it was time to sell the venture. On the commerce side of things, Maria waved the white flag, a full surrender on the Eastern front to the marauders within her home territory, and on the Western front, she laid down her arms before a shot was even fired against the Swedish Vikings.

Sadly, the social scene saw defeats just as devastating. She found herself, as the days went by, becoming lonelier and lonelier. Yes, she lived with Anton, who was always more than willing to play *Civilization V*, a PC game about world domination, but as far as her fantasy about befriending the interesting urbanites with the best opinions on the hot new places, that didn't happen. Instead, she met no one. She was just a young woman in a city of twelve million who missed her friends back home.

As someone who's lived in big cities like New York and Boston, I think there's something soul-crushing about living among millions of people who don't even know your name.

Maria stayed in Moscow though. You know when things aren't working out, but the idea of coming back home to the sting of perceived failure is so much worse than the misery of staying put. When you wonder why your closest friend is living in a cramped studio without a bathroom in Queens, that's the reason. Sometimes, it hurts even more to walk away and reconstruct how you see yourself. At least, Maria had a little PR company and made websites. It wasn't much, but it was something.

One day, nearly crushed by the burden of loneliness, she posted a message on LiveJournal, the once American but then Russian social networking service where you can post blogs or personal diaries. Maria wrote that she wanted to form a group, like the one she had back home with fellow gun rights enthusiasts, and planned to have the group's inaugural meeting at a nearby McDonald's. To her surprise and delight, about twenty people showed up. For two hours, they sat with their Big Macs and Chicken McNuggets discussing mutual interests, figuring out their platform, and deciding what to do next. It quickly became clear that they needed to hold a public demonstration to send a message to the government, so they signed a document and set a date. When the day arrived, roughly two hundred people showed up. Journalists were there—*American* ones according to Maria—and she couldn't have been happier. Suddenly, Maria had friends. She had a purpose.

The newly formed gun-rights group met weekly. They took care of business right away with a slick logo and a proper name: the aptly branded Right to Bear Arms.

A very quick aside and the only one I'll apologize for in advance. Whenever I see the phrase *the right to bear arms*, my first thought is about a seemingly absurd but in actuality extremely humorless organization that campaigns on the single issue of grafting bear arms to their human bodies. They have a logo and everything, and if you crack a smile at their demonstrations, they'll fly into an ursine rage. Sometimes I think any single-issue organization is basically this way: a bunch of determined humans who really want bear arms.

Maria's Right to Bear Arms group went from a ragtag bunch of like-minded activists to a serious operation with semiserious finances from a rich Russian guy. Whenever I hear of a rich Russian guy handing out cash without restrictions, I imagine the story ending with a bloody execution in some bathhouse. Not here though. Funding came from a wealthy private businessman named Konstantin Nikolayev—someone who had a logical interest in Maria's gun-rights advocacy because his wife Svetlana Nikolayeva was the CEO of a domestic gun manufacturer called ORSIS. The Nikolayevs then hired a PR firm to give Maria a makeover. She was encouraged to color her hair. Soon after, this young, wonkish woman from Siberia became a firebrand for Russian guns.

Her group was allowed to move into an abandoned production plant, an agricultural chemical factory that used to manufacture pesticide. Not an ideal spot to run your new nonprofit, but the Right to Bear Arms did get a promise that the factory would be scrubbed clean. Of course, no such promise was ever fulfilled. But Maria's group was composed of a bunch of scrappers so they cleaned the place themselves. Over the next four or five years, the Right to Bear Arms (are you thinking about bears?) built out their office and warehouse. They had flags, boxes, pencils, and all the honey they could eat. Maria absolutely loved it.

In the beginning, the organization was difficult to run. Sure, Maria had a complimentary cancer-inducing factory, but resources were somewhat limited. Besides the teeming volunteers, Maria had two people on her payroll: a girl who helped out and Dimitry Kislov, a friend and great guy according to Maria. Technically, Dimitry was the executive director of the organization, but really, he ran the press center. Actually, it was entirely him. The government would later claim Maria was trying to sleep with him—because the feds didn't understand a joke and basic texting. They eventually withdrew the salacious accusation, but not before the media picked it up. The media, by the way, rarely makes retractions for falsehoods they didn't create but only repeated from court filings. Maybe that's why a lie can travel around the world and back again while the truth is lacing up its boots, according to Mark Twain. Small correction, since I like to make them: Twain didn't say that.

Anyway, the Right to Bear Arms group grew fast, and as the founder and chairwoman of the organization, Maria had to deal with growing pains along the way. For example, she once had to quell a competitor inside the group, one Sergei Dubov, who tried to oust her from her top spot. Maria describes Sergei as a real-life giant who worked as a security guard for very rich Russians. (Again, bathhouse executions?) According to Maria, Sergei only really wanted to be on TV, to enhance his public persona, which was something Maria had little interest in at the time, so Sergei organized a few disgruntled workers to defeat her in the upcoming election. In the end, Maria won the vote, and the uprising was quelled with good old-fashioned democracy. The way Maria tells the story, the competition was not about size but about mind. I guess she's saying she outwitted Sergei.

Aside from the occasional insurrection and constant fundraising, the Right to Bear Arms engaged in two different activities. The first involved practical instruction. In essence, they were a shooting club with instructors at different locations, all focused on educating the public about gun safety and how to handle a firearm. Its second mission involved advocacy work. The group fought for gun rights by writing various reports, holding events, and lobbying parliament to pass legislation on the use of firearms for self-defense, chiefly in the home. When you get down to it, they wanted gun access to be a fundamental part of Russian life like it is in the United States. To advance that cause, they published a report on national gun law reforms, which made a big splash in the media probably because it was presented to the Russian Senate (called the Federation Council) by someone powerful and well connected. Who, you might ask? Senator Aleksandr Torshin, the Russian official who, spoiler alert, would end up being the reason why Maria went to prison in the United States.

Chapter Sixteen

I'd had dinner with AUSA Tom Saunders (Tommy to me) well before hearing the name Maria Butina. I'd seen him at parties and run into him here and there. A friend of a friend, Tommy was smart and charismatic. He had a good sense of humor and knew how to tell a good story.

After Maria had given us the green light to engage with the government, I reached out to Tommy or maybe I should call him Saunders considering his posture at the time. Courteous as always, Saunders suggested we meet outside the Greene Turtle, a sports bar in Chinatown. I was a bit surprised by the suggestion—I figured we'd just chat on the phone—but he wanted to meet in person. Perhaps he'd be between meetings, and the Greene Turtle was a convenient enough landmark for us to coordinate a meet. Or maybe for Saunders, who had recently made the transition to the National Security Section, talking on the phone made him nervous. The Russians might be listening.

There he was standing on the corner of 6th and F Street NW. The area was quiet for an otherwise busy district outside a massive sports arena. We shook hands and then walked back to the Triple Nickle, a local nickname for the old US Attorney's office building in DC—so named for its street address 555 Fourth Street NW.

"Are the phones really that unsecure?" I asked.

Saunders had no idea, but after I asked him if Bob and I were being tapped, Saunders said he couldn't be sure but thought it'd be better to assume we were. The advice didn't surprise me. My boyfriend had been photographed outside our apartment by a man with a telephoto lens lurking across the street. Perhaps the shutterbug wanted a few pics of our dog or the lovely row homes, but as my boyfriend continued across the street, the photographer locked on to him.

Saunders asked the reason for the meeting.

"I wanted to connect because the Maria we know is very different from the Maria we've read about in your filings. I'd like you guys to meet her."

Saunders listened.

"At one point," I said, "I think the government expressed an interest in interviewing her. Are you still interested?"

Saunders said he'd take it back to his team, and they'd be in touch.

"I'm glad you're on the case," I said. "Even though we're adversaries, it's nice to know there's a colleague and friend on the other side. Should things ever go sideways, don't hesitate to use me as a bridge."

With that, we gave friendly goodbyes, and he stepped into the Triple Nickle.

Later, we'd get a proffer letter, spelling out the terms for our queen for a day, which would really take months.

Along with Bob and me, Maria talked to the FBI special agents and prosecutors in regular sit-downs in a building on the campus of the Alexandria jail. There, in a small conference room, the government asked every question imaginable. They went through Maria's entire life, through every important interaction, through every document and text message. By November 2018, we were close to an end and almost ready for a possible plea deal. But a curious thing happened: Maria was put back in solitary confinement. Then we received a phone call from the Russian Consulate. The Russians wanted to meet, but about what? They wouldn't say over the phone. I suppose the phone-tapping anxiety swings both ways.

Bob and I met Nikolai and Max, the two Russian consular officers, at our office. The men were like US foreign service officers who help Americans when they get in pickles or are dealing with crises overseas. We'd met both of them a few times before, having crossed paths in court or to help facilitate their welfare checks on Maria for consular assistance, but this meeting felt different. Both were middle-aged, maybe in their forties though it was difficult to say. Nikolai wore glasses and seemed to have the more Asian features of perhaps someone from Eastern Russia. Max appeared Caucasian with a widow's peak of backswept hair.

"We love your cafeteria downstairs," Nikolai said in his distinctly Russian-English accent, confirmed by a steady nod and smile from Max.

Bob and I thanked them as we traded glances with each other. We didn't have a cafeteria downstairs. We didn't have a cafeteria anywhere nearby, but it wasn't long before we realized they meant café and were referring to the Pret A Manger, a British coffee shop that sells sandwiches, pastries, and soups on the corner. I mean, they weren't wrong. The almond croissants are pretty good.

Once we had dispensed with the pleasantries, the diplomats launched into the reason for our meeting. They wanted to know why Maria had been placed back in solitary confinement. They were concerned about her being tortured. They then mentioned something unexpected: the 2018 G20 Buenos Aires summit. The Group of Twenty (or G20) is an international faire la fete involving the largest economies of the world. As the big man on campus, the United States struts into these once-a-year to-dos like we own the place. But Russia is number nine on the list of the GDP big britches—or at least they were at the time—and since the United States and other world leaders voted to expel them from the G8 (now G7), an even more exclusive group of economic powerhouses, the Kremlin always seemed eager to attend these meetings for international recognition and credibility. (Tiny footnote: Russia was kicked out of the G8 after they annexed Crimea from Ukraine in 2014.)

What does the G20 have to do with us? As the officers explained, President Putin might have an opportunity to interface with President Trump at their scheduled bilateral meeting in Buenos Aires to grease the wheels for a possible prisoner exchange. Ah, a potential diplomatic result to get Maria straight on a flight bound for Moscow.

We thanked the diplomats for their time and told them we'd think about what they said. Lawyers can be sphinxlike when surprises are sprung.

Certainly, we already knew from public reporting that Putin and Trump had plans to meet at the G20, and the thought of a diplomatic resolution to Maria's case did cross our minds. But even then, we could see the potential pitfalls. The State Department would have to know and participate in any such negotiation. And if the prosecution ever got wind of Putin's involvement in a potential prisoner exchange involving Maria, they would almost surely leap to the conclusion that she was better connected than she was, and more of an asset than she appeared.

Take Brittney Griner, for example, the basketball player we exchanged for releasing a bona fide Russian arms dealer. Swaps are made for all sorts of reasons. Maria was just the poster child in Russia for US overzealousness. If a deal were to be struck, it would be made at the highest levels without the involvement of the prosecutors looking to further their careers with a notch in their belts. But the risk of prosecutors using the prospect of a prisoner swap against her was undeniable. Ultimately, we could only explain the landscape to our client. Lawyers are bound to present all possible legal options along with our earnest recommendations, and as with everything else, it would be Maria's decision how to proceed.

After the Russians left our office, Bob and I half-joked about hiring a team to sweep the conference room for bugs or search for dropped pens with hidden microphones. Half-joked. This was starting to become remarkably similar to a John Grisham novel veering into Tom Clancy territory.

Back in Bob's office, we walked through the many implications of a prisoner swap. We wondered whether it was feasible and if we could be involved with this. We thought about the Logan Act—a federal law that criminalizes negotiation by unauthorized American citizens with foreign governments having a dispute with the United States. We thought about whether we had an obligation to inform our government. We considered our legal ethics, broad duty of confidentiality, and foundational responsibility to do-no-harm to the client.

But if there's one thing almost every lawyer I know has in common, it's this: we're a risk-averse bunch. We want all the i's to possess their tittles, and even just the appearance of impropriety rankles us. So Bob and I decided to talk to Maria about it, and if she was interested in pursuing this, we'd get her permission to alert our own government about a possible request from Russia. We realized that telling the prosecutors might derail our progress, especially if a prisoner exchange proved unworkable. Instead, after getting the green light from our client, we reached out to the one person we thought could deliver a message to the right people without hurting Maria:

the former CIA station chief in Moscow, the guy we'd met serendipitously in the Fox News green room, who knew she wasn't a spy.

Bob's meeting with the former station chief was prompt and a bit clandestine. They met at a local hotel in the city, and after turning off their phones, Bob shared what he had learned with the ex–CIA chief. The man thanked him and said he knew just the right people to pass the information to.

About a day or so later, Bob got an email from him that read, "You have the thanks of a grateful nation."

"That's it! That's all it says?" I asked.

"That's it," Bob said.

So we waited.

On November 29, 2018, the day before the G20 summit in Buenos Aires, President Donald Trump announced he was canceling his planned meeting with Russian President Vladimir Putin. The reason: Russia had seized three Ukrainian naval ships and twenty-four Ukrainian sailors operating in international waters near the Kerch Strait, off Crimea. Trump tweeted, "Based on the fact that the ships and sailors have not been returned to Ukraine from Russia, I have decided it would be best for all parties concerned to cancel my previously scheduled meeting in Argentina with President Vladimir Putin."

Except the meeting did take place.

Trump spoke with Putin in Buenos Aires without US aides present. The White House described it as an "informal conversation." But *The Financial Times* reported that, according to people familiar with their discussion, the exchange "appeared longer and more substantive than the White House has acknowledged."

What was discussed? According to Putin, they talked about Ukraine.

Was anything else broached? I don't know. But I can tell you this much: Maria remained in pretrial detention in Alexandria. Ukraine's two dozen sailors remained in custody in Moscow. And one month later—on December 28, 2018—former US Marine Paul Whelan was arrested in Russia on suspicion of espionage. That arrest came just eight days after Putin's year-end press conference, where he specifically addressed Maria's case and remarked, "The law of retaliation states, 'An eye for an eye or a tooth for a tooth.' . . . But we will not arrest innocent people simply to exchange them for someone else later on."

Draw your own conclusions.

Our meetings with the government continued—with the familiar faces of Kenerson, Helson, Ball, and Saunders. Maria told them the same stories she had told us many times, the same stories she told the Senate before that, and this time, she had all the evidence to point to, the text messages to explain. The government was satisfied, not because she helped them uncover secrets or crimes or Russian operations—she did none of that because she knew none of that. No, they were satisfied because she was telling the truth.

"Truth is my best defender," Maria said.

In a moment of frustration about how things had unfolded for her, Special Agent Helson mentioned how this whole situation could have been avoided if Maria had responded when they had reached out. Maria was confused. She *had* talked to the FBI. She turned over her electronics. She talked to the Senate.

Yes, Helson went on to explain that they had requested a meeting prior to her testifying before the Senate and surrendering electronics, but these requests went unanswered. Stunned, Maria asked who they left the message with. Helson claimed it was the lawyer at another law firm Maria had been working with at the time. I've been unable to verify if the FBI did in fact make a request to meet with Maria through counsel. But according to Helson, the alleged communication bungle was partly the reason for the FBI's increased scrutiny and later arrest. Helson's unverified version is plausible because our FBI agents will sometimes meet with foreign students studying in this country to sniff out foreign intelligence threats or give warnings to protect unwitting students from crossing any lines.

Maria never got that meeting though. She could have been in South Dakota, starting her new postgrad life. Instead, she was sitting in a jail jumpsuit, telling federal agents the same story she would have told them months earlier—only now, the stakes had changed. The government couldn't let her go. Why? Because of the story they created and let run wild in the media.

According to the zeitgeist on cable news, which we had tried to tamp down, the government had nabbed a Russian spy. To legitimate journalists, they had grabbed a full-fledged Russian agent working on behalf of a high-ranking figure in the Russian government. The US intelligence community, backed by evidence gathered by Special Counsel Robert Mueller, had concluded that the Kremlin had set out to interfere with the 2016 election. With all that machinery, the government couldn't just walk away from the whole thing. Not now.

That left us with two options: go to trial or take a plea deal. A trial would be long and expensive—but more than that, it would take months, even over a year, just to get to a trial date. The government would have asked the court to pause her right to a speedy trial, and the court likely would have agreed. In the meantime, she'd be stuck sitting in a cell. Sure, Maria wasn't footing the bill as it was—lawyers do pro bono work all the time. Bob and I were fully prepared to go to trial and had no issue doing so if that's what Maria wanted. But the real problem with moving forward wasn't time or money. It was the climate in Washington.

Democrats wanted blood. I knew this because my entire bubble outside of work was saturated with that liberal bloodlust. Donald Trump was the true target, but in the wake of Robert Mueller's Russia investigation, anything remotely related to the Russkies was, de facto, Public Enemy Number One.

Washington was a high-risk venue, and Bob and I feared that what we were seeing on cable news was what we'd see in the jury box: McCarthyism cavorting as condescension. We'd seen it a hundred times in our own social lives—people with zero knowledge of the facts, other than the innuendo that had been fed to them, speaking with absolute certainty about guilt and truth. We were talented lawyers. But it becomes a very different task, and a much more daunting one, when the jury pool walks in primed against you and your client.

Maria felt the same way. She hated having her good intentions second-guessed. She didn't trust putting her fate in the hands of twelve strangers. She missed her family. She wanted to go home. She wanted the nightmare to end.

That left the plea agreement—which, honestly, wasn't as objectionable as it sounds. From our research, we believed her conduct should yield a minimal sentence. And even if Maria pled to a felony, it wouldn't really change her job prospects in this country. She was headed back to Russia on a one-way ticket. Even if we had taken the case to trial and won, there was zero chance the US government would have let her stay or allowed her to return here.

We all want to believe that innocent defendants don't plead guilty to crimes they didn't commit. But they do. It's difficult to imagine an innocent person feeling so compelled to accept their own wrongful conviction—though it happens every year, often in exchange for a lesser offense or reduced sentence to avoid some horrible outcome like a mandatory minimum.

We didn't have to worry about that here, though, because Maria's conduct, unbeknownst to her at the time, fit within the broad language of the antiquated statute she was charged under. She did share her political impressions with Aleksandr Torshin, but there was nothing secret about them. In truth, they were amateurish, cobbled-together summaries of Wikipedia entries and American news articles translated into Russian. For example, when Scott Walker announced his presidential candidacy, Torshin asked Maria to "write [him] something brief" on it, which she did. She read American news, translated it, and passed it along. She was never paid for this. She was never trained for this. She wasn't passing secrets or stealing classified information. And she could have said no without any fallout. But because she shared her impressions at Torshin's request without first informing the Attorney General, she technically violated the law. Her only misstep was failing to notify the US government that she was sharing open-source information with someone affiliated with the Russian government. That, she could plead to, and so she did.

Because Maria chose to plead guilty and cooperate with authorities, the government agreed to seek a downward departure at sentencing, asking the judge to impose a reduced sentence. You only get a downward departure when you tell the truth. In its court filings, the government acknowledged that Maria had cooperated by assisting in other criminal investigations. And she did—just not in the way you might think. She knew of no dead drops, secrets, covert operations, or spycraft. She simply answered the government's questions. Her cooperation led to no additional charges, except for one brought against her ex-boyfriend Paul, who was later charged with offenses Maria knew nothing about. And what's clear is this: the government believed everything she told them.

My future in-laws had a beautiful house nestled in a beachside community on the panhandle of Florida. If you've seen *The Truman Show* starring Jim Carrey, then you know the place. Usually a retreat for holidays or a few weeks in the summer, Santa Rosa Beach, for a full seven months during the height of the coronavirus pandemic, became our through-the-looking-glass paradise where COVID wasn't acknowledged and people without masks in pastel-colored clothing wandered about as if a pandemic wasn't killing hundreds each day. The emergency rooms were a different story.

All of that would be a couple years later though.

In 2018, during the Thanksgiving holiday, Brendan and I decamped to that beachside neighborhood, and there in a too-perfect park, holding a bag of our dog's poop, Brendan proposed marriage, and I said yes. We popped champagne with both sets of our parents and enjoyed a sunset in paradise.

It was also there I received a call from a jailhouse counselor.

"I'm calling from the Alexandria Detention Center in regard to Maria Butina," she said. "I just spoke with her today. And she asked me to call you."

I had represented dozens of defendants and had never received such a call before.

"Is everything okay?" I asked.

Apparently, Maria was crying and quite upset because she was administratively segregated. Again.

Why, was my first thought. Maria had been in solitary at CTF in DC and then again in Alexandria following her transfer to that facility. But they had ultimately screened and placed her in general population where she was, by all accounts, doing very well. She was happier there, tutoring other inmates to acquire their GEDs. She had even been entrusted with bathroom cleaning duties as a jail trusty. I knew Maria was well liked by both guards and prisoners, so her change in status was both perplexing and concerning.

Right away, I called Bob who suggested we reach out to Chief Deputy Joseph Pankey, who was in charge of the facility. Our messages were not immediately returned, so we sent an email. Meanwhile, we believed we had uncovered the reason for her sudden housing change—something never formally entered into the Alexandria jail's computer system but instead scribbled on a piece of tape posted at the guard stand. Apparently, Maria had passed Bob's phone number to another inmate who was being discharged. That action violated no jail rule or regulation. I read the entire handbook to be sure.

Solitary confinement is typically reserved for a specific purpose. Sometimes, it's used for management reasons, like when an inmate is having trouble adjusting to general population, is disruptive, or is believed to pose a safety risk. It can also be used for protective custody, to shield vulnerable individuals like informants or former police officers. Alternatively, restrictive housing may be imposed as a disciplinary measure for violating jail rules.

How did Maria giving another inmate her lawyer's phone number fit into any of those buckets? I finally got Deputy Chief Pankey and Captain Craig Davie of the Alexandria Sheriff's Office on the phone to explain. The conversation was less than edifying. They confirmed that Maria was well-adjusted, had been doing just fine in general population, and had broken no institutional rules or regulations—major or minor. And yet, they insisted she had been "placed in ad seg for her own safety."

I've heard that before. It reminded me of that courtroom scene in *A Few Good Men*, when Tom Cruise's character presses Jack Nicholson's: if it had been made crystal clear that the private was not to be touched, and orders are always followed, then why would he be in any danger? Here too, something wasn't right. What exactly? Your guess is as good as mine.

I do have two of them, though. Neither is particularly charitable. The first—and, in my view, the far less likely—possibility was that Maria was on the cusp of a plea deal with the government. Prosecutors favor plea agreements and often push for them, but not always in above board ways. Using solitary confinement during stalled plea negotiations to pressure a defendant into accepting a plea deal crosses both legal and ethical lines. Is it possible? I've heard stories of that kind of coercion happening before, but I didn't buy it. I think there was another explanation. The second—and what I believe is the more plausible one—is this: When Bob's phone number was found in the possession of the departing inmate, I believe jail officials flagged it, confiscated it, and alerted the FBI special agents, who in turn notified the prosecution team. To the paranoid and suspicious—or perhaps just overzealous—a phone number passed from one inmate under a gag order to an ungagged, departing inmate may have looked like an attempt to circumvent that order, with the help of counsel. As best I can piece together, the government's theory, as strained as it was, seemed to be that counsel might use the ungagged inmate to coordinate a media interview or public statement about Maria. That wasn't happening, of course. Bob had no role in that. But when you're looking through a dirty window, everything looks dirty.

There was no plan or attempt to violate the gag order, but I can imagine the prosecution was looking for one. To put a semi-charitable spin on it, I can also imagine a prosecutor not wanting to derail a potential plea deal with a gag order violation that might upend the whole process. Still, there was no gag order violation, no rule infraction, and no intent to commit one. That made Maria's housing change improper because her jailers had essentially used administrative segregation as a pretense for punishment. Jail officials did not follow established procedures. They didn't even document her housing change in the computer system.

Back in Washington, Bob and I reached out to colleagues within the Civil Rights Division of the Department of Justice who shared our concerns about the overuse of restrictive housing and pointed us to DOJ's latest guidance and recommendations for reducing the use of this practice.

We then reached out to Chief Deputy US Marshal Lamont Ruffin to seek options for reevaluation or release back to general population. Yet, although Chief Deputy Ruffin acknowledged that the US Marshals Service was responsible for the safe, secure, and humane housing of Maria as a federal pretrial detainee, we were told that they would not get involved absent a court order. Their advice: take it up with the judge. We went ahead and did exactly that.

We asked the court to return Maria to general population—or at least review the decision that confined her to a cell no larger than a parking space for twenty-two hours a day. Even if Judge Chutkan ruled against us, we expected she'd at least find out why Maria had been placed in solitary. Judges are uniquely positioned to cut through crap to get the truth. So we filed our motion, which was initially unopposed by the government yet then later opposed for reasons not understood by us.

What's troubling is that our request for judicial oversight—our effort to understand why Maria, convicted of nothing, was once again being held in conditions widely recognized as cruel and psychologically destructive, including by our own Justice Department and every leading prison reform scholar and medical expert—was denied.

Denied.

Judge Chutkan, the one person with the power to fix it, and the very person the marshals told us to go to, chose not to act. She didn't request briefing, a proffer, or evidence. She didn't ask for an explanation from the marshals, the jail, or the government. She just declined to hear it. Why? Because the court believed it should defer to the everyday decisions of the jail.

Here's the twist: federal judges *can* and *do* intervene when pretrial detainees face alleged mistreatment. Maria was in the Alexandria Detention Center only because the court committed her to the marshals, who sent her there. That connection carries responsibility—principally under the Due Process Clause, which prohibits punishment or conditions that amount to punishment before conviction. We argued that Maria's placement in ad seg wasn't for safety or management—it was punishment.

The court didn't act.

That kind of judicial passivity contrasts sharply with how similar issues have been handled, including in the January 6 Capitol breach cases that would come years later. In one instance, Judge Royce Lamberth held jail officials in contempt for denying medical care to a pretrial detainee and referred the matter to the Justice Department for civil rights investigation. The matter brought much-needed attention to the conditions of pretrial confinement, including the overuse of solitary and restrictive housing.

Lawmakers ranging from Senator Elizabeth Warren to Representative Marjorie Taylor Greene voiced concerns about the psychological toll caused by such conditions.

In January 2019, the Alexandria jail moved Maria back in gen pop, but not without strings. To leave ad seg, they made her sign a "contract" with all sorts of conditions like agreeing not to disrespect staff, petition other inmates to contact the media, or talk about stuff unrelated to her case. The consequence for violating these terms? Back to solitary—another round of unconstitutional punishment, all before conviction. In case you're wondering, they transferred Maria back to gen pop after she changed her plea to guilty on December 13, 2018. I'm not suggesting it was coordinated, and I don't believe it was, but a more cynical observer might wonder.

In the new year, my fiancé and I were invited by Bob and his wife Rosie to their home in Northern Virginia. Bob and I had been working so closely together for many months, and we've each talked about our significant others so many times, but this was the first time we'd all broken bread. I have a sneaking suspicion that Rosie was the instigator of our visit, and I'm glad she was.

We sat in their dining room, ate the best rice and beans we've ever had—from Rosie's Cuban heritage—and talked about everything in our lives but Maria. Mostly, we discussed the past. Bob, Rosie, and Brendan had all gone to Georgetown University. I was the odd man out having attended the University of Virginia. But it was nice to hear them track the creep of time through old professors they had or traditions they held. We talked about creative pursuits—Rosie is a poet and Brendan is a writer. We talked about the Church and communities, parents and siblings, children and dogs. We talked about travel. We talked about life.

This particular chapter in our life stories was soon to be closed, and the strange pressure cooker of national frenzy had forged in us new outlooks. All that was left was to craft our sentencing recommendation and deliver an allocution, the speech the defense gives at the time of sentencing. It was the most daunting task of my career, but I knew everyone in that dining room, no matter the outcome of sentencing, would be there to help.

Chapter Seventeen

How did Maria's orbit overlap with the Russian Senator Aleksandr Torshin? Torshin appeared on Maria's horizon in the way most people did during that time: he attended a meeting of the Right to Bear Arms. The guy was an active Twitter user and a gun owner interested in expanding those rights. Even though Torshin was the former acting chairman of the Russian Senate, Maria had no clue who the guy was standing among the thrum of supporters. To her, he appeared as a gregarious, salt-and-pepper-haired, mid-level bureaucrat or a bespectacled bank manager who might deny her a loan. And she wasn't far off. The difference was that he had basically been the boss of the legislature—and later, the Central Bank of Russia. Someone eventually pointed him out, and when Maria learned that his interests aligned with hers, they became fast friends.

In Russia, considerable friends often come with considerable baggage, and Torshin was no different. The man had been accused of being linked to organized crime, thanks to his relationship with convicted money launderer Alexander Romanov of the Taganskaya outfit. Torshin and Romanov became friends in 1995 while working together at the Bank of Russia. Torshin was the State Secretary there, and Romanov worked beneath him. Though they met in a business capacity, Torshin says Romanov is a personal friend instead of a business associate. That might be because Romanov's business wasn't strictly legal. The Taganskaya gang, Romanov's crew, harkens back to Moscow's criminal underworld of the 1980s. They started off as a low-level crime syndicate that stole cars and pushed drugs, but as they moved into racketeering—an illegal activity involving blackmail, coercion, or extortion to collect "profit" from a victim—they found themselves sliding into a specialized criminal industry called "raids." In the 2000s, the gang used their muscle to take over companies. It's kind of like corporate raiders in the United States but ignoring all the pesky details about corporate governance or federal law. In 2005, Romanov served time in a Russian prison for his financial dealings with the Taganskaya gang. He got a three-year sentence for fraud but was soon granted parole. Shortly thereafter, he moved to Spain. To enjoy the fine Rioja or seafood paella? Perhaps, but really, he was establishing a number of companies that took fictitious loans in order to launder more money for the Taganskaya clan.

According to Spanish investigators, Torshin played a key role in Romanov's money laundering operation. As a high-ranking politician and banking bigwig in Russia, he was thought to have helped direct gang members through financial and real estate transactions. Spanish police even saw him as outranking Romanov within the Taganskaya crime syndicate, citing months of wiretapped conversations and seized documents in which Romanov referred to Torshin as his "godfather" or "boss" and appeared to be taking orders from him. When authorities seized Romanov's properties, they suspected the majority of them really belonged to Torshin.

On August 21, 2013, Torshin was reportedly set to attend Romanov's birthday party in Mallorca. Just as Spanish cops were ready to move—cuffs in hand—hoping to arrest Torshin the moment he stepped foot on Spanish soil, the Russian senator changed his mind and never got on the plane. Spanish authorities believe he received a warning from the Russian General Prosecutor's Office. Not the best time to vacation, apparently, with the Spanish Civil Guard sniffing around. As for Romanov, Spanish law enforcement nabbed him in December 2013. He received a prison sentence of nearly four years, along with a fine of over 4 million euros for money laundering and possessing fake documents.

Torshin was Maria's connection to Russian politics. After they solidified both a professional and a personal relationship, Torshin lent his name and prestige to her gun-rights group. In July 2012, he submitted a report to the Duma that recommended the parliament adopt a version of the "Castle Doctrine," which would allow the use of firearms for home self-defense. The bill got a lot of press attention, mainly because it was presented by an important man, but it never passed. Such a measure would require the approval of Putin, and as something of a historian himself, he likely understands the role firearms have played in revolutions. They're somewhat of a sine qua non as we've covered.

Beyond educating the public and pushing for new laws, Maria wanted her group to gain real power and influence so they could make the changes they were fighting for. That meant climbing the nonprofit ladder in Russia.

There's a hierarchy there that I don't fully understand, but it starts with local groups. These are your mom-and-pop soup kitchens and church gaggles. One level up, where the Right to Bear Arms stood, were regional organizations. They had some pull, but nothing like the "All Russian" national groups that spanned and operated across the entire country. That was the big league where Maria and her crew wanted to be (and would later reach). Of course, if you were ambitious, as Maria always was, you had your sights set on the international groups at the top, the real who's who of nonprofit work. At the time, the Right to Bear Arms still had a couple rungs left to climb, and to do that, they needed more media attention. The proposed legislation was a good start, but now it was time to get the international media interested.

In the fall of 2013, the third year of the Right to Bear Arms, Maria planned their annual meeting with an eye on raising its status by inviting international guests. There were no fancy invitations with calligraphy and gold-embossed double-headed eagles or anything. Maria merely emailed a list of people who might show up. While she couldn't offer them air travel, she could extend free lodging at what she believed was one of the fanciest hotels in Moscow: the Marriott Courtyard.

I think this is a cute little detail about Maria's eagerness to impress, and if you know her as I do, it comes off as an earnest attempt to do just that.

The folks on the international invite list came from a variety of countries: Greece, Estonia, Latvia, and Israel. But the pièce de résistance was the invitation to some members of the NRA, the holy grail of guns rights activism. Maria was quite ambitious to invite the crème de la crème of the gun rights advocacy group, and to potentially shake loose a representative from the American bastion of gun enthusiasts, Maria approached her best connection: Torshin. Maria knew that Torshin was an NRA member who had traveled to multiple NRA annual meetings, back when the guy could travel outside of Russia without fear of extradition, so she asked if he might put her in touch with someone at the NRA. Yes, it seemed. Torshin gave Maria a business card for a guy who might attend their meeting, one David Keene, the very president of the NRA. Not too shabby. She got an email back from Paul Erickson asking for more time to consider the invitation. Evidently, Keene had recently had knee surgery, and Erickson was a friend helping him out as he recovered. But it wasn't long before an RSVP came back in the affirmative.

Maria was the only one in her organization who could speak English, so over the next few weeks, she Skyped with Keene and Erickson to figure out the visa quandary they had found themselves in. Turns out they thought one could just apply and receive a visa in a day or two. It takes weeks, apparently, but the hiccup gave them an opportunity to get to know each other. The trio all acted professionally, yet still managed to have a good time laughing and joking as they filled out paperwork. I suppose this was the meet-cute for Maria and Erickson. On second thought, there were many stages in their relationship. Perhaps this was the visa application for the meet-cute to come. Eventually, all was worked out and the NRA duo landed in Moscow to attend the event. Both Keene and Erickson stayed for two nights in the finest accommodations provided by the Right to Bear Arms, and Keene was introduced as the guest of honor at its 2013 annual conference.

"There are no peoples that are more alike than Americans and Russians," Keene said in his speech.

"We value the same kinds of things," Keene said. "We need to work together."

During the event, Maria stressed over every detail. She was the time-keeper, the gatekeeper, and the bookkeeper, and with her superpower of speaking the English language, she was often the only translator, the universal Babel fish within that collective of member nations. Her nonstop efforts to wrangle gun rights enthusiasts and manage international reporters left her restless at night and irritable by day. Bless your heart if you were to ask her an inane question, and God help you if you were so bold as to place your hand on her, even a benign tap on the shoulder could inspire a volcanic eruption. Yes, she may have been a Gorgon, whose gaze you'd rather avoid, but in her mind she was the fire and fury for those few days—and once it was over, she'd drink vodka with her supporters to unwind and show her appreciation. Vodka, the best Russian spackle to repair the deepest of fissures.

After the official itinerary was completed—the speeches given, the panels depaneled—Maria still had to deal with the endless logistics of coordinating travel, transfers, or return trips to the airport for guests who had arrived from all over. It was during this frenzy that someone touched her back and mumbled something in a foreign accent. That was two strikes with one pitch, and in this game, in which only one could get you thrown out, the batter was in trouble. God help the poor mumbling tapper. Incensed, Maria spun on her heel ready to swear to high heaven all of the best Russian curse words when she found the poor idiot smiling back at her. It was Paul Erickson. With his dopey grin, he mumbled again—something in what approximated the local language, but to Maria was just a mush bowl of Cyrillic syllables. His Russian was so dreadful that she told him to speak in English.

"I was trying to fix your gun belt," he said in words approximating that.

Ah. Paul was trying to adjust her shooting belt stretched across her lower back. Remember, this was a gun rights convention. When you attend the cowboy corral, you wear your Stetson. After Paul repeated the sentence in English, Maria relaxed, just a bit, and thanked him. There was something winning about Paul. At first, they simply laughed on Skype and filled out visa forms, the way most couples do when finding love. But when he arrived to accompany his friend, Paul was a most disarming guest, and during a stressful event, a spritz of cold water on a hot day. Perhaps this was their actual meet-cute, but either way, their journey together was just beginning.

The Right to Bear Arms organizers took different foreign guests to various restaurants around the city. Maria was paired with David Keene and Paul Erickson, the NRA VIPs, and she invited them to a nice restaurant next to the Foreign Ministry. Keene couldn't go due to lingering pain from his knee surgery, so Erickson went for the both of them. At dinner, Maria saw an extra dimension to this man who had only, until then, appeared affable and personable. She found Paul had a sharp intellect—was an Ivy

Leaguer as well—which, for Maria, was quite the turn-on. "He had a beautiful mind," she said, high praise from a Russian stingy with any praise at all. That evening, there was no physical romance between them, no kiss or wandering hands, just professional conversation. And yet, something romantic had begun. The bullet had been loaded in the chamber if the pin had not been cocked.

The next morning, Erickson and Keene flew out, but before they left, Maria had asked Erickson to give her a call once they were on the plane. Sure enough, Erickson gave Maria a call just like she'd asked, and for some reason, that small bit of housekeeping had an unexpected impact on her. I suppose it showed that Erickson was reliable or perhaps thinking of her. Whatever the case, the gesture stuck. It was the cherry on top of a successful weekend, not just for her gun rights group, but also her relationship with this American.

After that, Erickson went to Israel, or he said he did. Who knows. He would send Maria a picture of himself, but in the picture, he was in Afghanistan with a lot more hair. Perhaps Erickson's reports should be taken with a grain of salt, though when you're falling for someone, fraud can appear as flirting.

Maria was a tough and independent Russian woman, a national leader with a gun holster strapped to her back, yet here was this guy from the United States who, to Maria, was not only a gentleman but someone who took a caring interest in her. Adjusting her gun belt was apparently a rare act of kindness in Russia. Or perhaps it was just that Anton, her boyfriend, did no such thing. While Maria labored away with her PR company and her gun rights organization, Anton sat at home and played *Civilization V*. As much as he enjoyed the computer game about world domination, Maria wished to dominate the real world, and between the two of them, she was the only one living in practical reality. Besides, surviving in Moscow was not easy, and the bills for groceries and rent added up.

Enter Mr. Paul Erickson.

"Love is evil. It will make you fall in love with a goat," a Russian saying goes. They have a way with the unpleasant.

Who was this Paul Erickson? Raised in South Dakota, Erickson first dipped his toes into politics while in college. In 1980, as a student at the University of South Dakota, he coordinated a youth campaign for Republican Representative Jim Abdnor. That early taste of political life sent him to Washington, where he spent a year serving as treasurer of the College Republicans—a group where he worked alongside a real blue book of scandal-plagued conservatives, like Jack Abramoff, who later wrote, "To every college Republican who contacted the national office, Paul Erickson was by far the most impressive person they had ever encountered in politics." In case you're not familiar with the source of this ringing endorsement, Abramoff is the guy who went on to lobby for Native American tribes and in the process racked up multiple felonies—conspiracy, fraud, and tax evasion.

This was the company Erickson kept, and he would eventually find his own legal troubles decades later. In 2019, Erickson pleaded guilty to wire fraud and money laundering tied to fraudulent investment schemes that spanned more than twenty years, from 1996 to 2018. He defrauded over $5 million from dozens of people, including his own family members, friends, and even his godmother. But that's all in the future, and we're looking in the past.

After Erickson's year in Washington, he transferred from the University of South Dakota to Yale, where he earned a degree in economics and political science. In 1988, he graduated from the University of Virginia School of Law.

In that same year, at the Republican National Convention, George H. W. Bush spoke a line to uproarious applause from his supporters in the crowd: "Read my lips: no new taxes." Back in the day, Republicans didn't really lean into culture war issues as much as they do now, so keeping a lid on tax hikes for wealthy people was their neon sign. But by 1990, Bush struck a deal with the Democratic-controlled Congress that ended up increasing taxes, which, you know, was the opposite of what he promised his supporters. And boy was he met with opposition—Erickson among them, since he joined Bush's primary challenger Pat Buchanan, as his national political director and campaign manager for the 1992 presidential race. It was somewhat of a hopeless bid as no incumbent president has ever lost a primary, but maybe Erickson saw himself as a spoiler. Biographer Timothy Stanley would later write that Erickson was "the best there was at the price Pat could afford," which I think is a rather monstrous compliment. Anyway, Buchanan and his best-he-could-get campaign manager would lose the race. From there, Erickson worked as an advisor on two failed campaigns for Mitt Romney. To round out his CV, Erickson also joined the board of the American Conservative Union (which organizes CPAC) and befriended Andrew Breitbart, the founder of the right-wing news website that bears his name.

Does Erickson have any personal references for this résumé? Sure does. South Dakota Republican political consultant Casey Phillips described Erickson as a well-connected matchmaker in conservative politics. "He likes to put people in touch with people. He's a person that's at the center of relationships all over the place." Stephen Moore of the Club for Growth praised Erickson's "clever and creative ideas." But former South Dakota State Representative Lee Schoenbeck offered a sharper view, calling Erickson "the single biggest phony I've ever met in South Dakota politics."

Maria started dating Erickson first by Skype and text. They kept up their chats for a few months, and she described it not as love but something more intellectual. But that all changed when they decided to meet in Israel to celebrate New Year's Eve in 2014. The whole event appeared rather innocent. Erickson took a dancing class in Tel Aviv because Maria loves dancing. They trekked up a mountain in crisp jacket weather. They opened a bottle of champagne on a little lighthouse balcony. Then they walked back to their hotel along the beach, leaving funny little footprints in the sand. For Maria, it was the best and only actual romance she'd had in her life. She felt—for the first time—in love.

Their relationship developed from there. She planned to visit the NRA in the States, and this time Erickson helped *her* complete the documents to obtain a visa. She traveled to a cabin in South Dakota. She saw the huge mountains and fields. She saw bison. The place smelled like Siberia, except when the wind blew from the sausage factory. If Israel was their Act I, South Dakota was their Act II. From then on, Maria would travel back and forth to the United States. She'd go to conferences, and Erickson would be her guide. He came to Altai Krai to meet Maria's parents, and they had a wonderful trip to the Altai Mountains. He came to visit her on the Fourth of July, and somehow, though it was illegal, she found a way to have fireworks during their special day. All the residents thought it was a bombing, but to Maria that terror was just the price to pay for true love. Maria would do so many little things for him, and he would send her little gifts. Life was perfect. I mean, there was of course Anton, her boyfriend, but life was perfect for Maria.

When you fall out of love with someone, it happens slowly. You may realize it suddenly one day when you come home and see this stranger whom you know well sitting in the shell of someone you once loved. You don't scream at them or despise them when you fall out of love. Those emotions are just the other side of the same coin of affection. No, if you've fallen out of love with someone, they become a ghost in your life over the weeks and months. Sometimes you forget they live with you. Sometimes you see a cereal bowl in the sink or hear the television turn on in the next room and you remember, "Oh, that's right. Someone else lives here." It's not hate you feel. It's nothing, which is why it's so difficult to move on. They're just there haunting the space.

Maria had lost interest in Anton a long time ago. He was a bad boyfriend, she admitted—but probably the best she'd ever had. They first grew close in college after Anton's father died. When Maria tried to help him through the process, her own grandfather passed away. Bound by mutual loss, they came together. But then in Moscow, her gun rights work allowed her to grow. She was out front, speaking for an organization picking up steam, while Anton stayed the same—or even regressed—back at the apartment. They became roommates instead of boyfriend and girlfriend. She was meeting Russian senators and NRA presidents, and he was playing video games. Maria broke up with Anton because he didn't want to mature. He never worked. He was clever, but he didn't clean. On occasion, he was supportive, but it wasn't enough. With Erickson, Maria found someone who was not only smart and pragmatic. He was romantic. At least, she thought so.

Chapter Eighteen

In the 1970s, while James Bamford was getting his law degree, he testified before a Senate select committee and blew the whistle on the NSA for illegally spying on US citizens. What followed were sweeping reforms to prevent future government abuse. Bamford would go on to be a journalist, writing for *The New York Times*, *The Atlantic*, and *Harper's*. He'd win the National Magazine Award for his work in *Rolling Stone*. He'd be nominated for an Emmy as a producer for PBS. According to *The New York Times*, Bamford is "the nation's premier journalist on the subject of the National Security Agency." *The New Yorker* called him "the NSA's chief chronicler."

On February 11, 2019, after Judge Chutkan had lifted Maria's gag order and after months of research, Bamford published an article on Maria's case in *The New Republic* titled "The Spy Who Wasn't."

"The government's case against Butina is extremely flimsy," Bamford wrote, "and appears to have been driven largely by a desire for publicity. In fact, federal prosecutors were forced to retract the most attention-grabbing allegation in the case—that Butina used sex to gain access and influence. That Butina's prosecution was launched by the National Security Section of the District of Columbia federal prosecutor's office, led by Gregg Maisel, is telling in itself: According to a source close to the Mueller investigation, the special counsel's office had declined to pursue the case, even though it would have clearly fit under its mandate. Despite the lack of evidence against Butina, however, prosecutors—abetted by an uncritical media willing to buy into the idea of a Russian agent infiltrating conservative political circles—were intent on getting a win. In the context of the Mueller investigation, and in the environment that arose after Trump's election, an idealistic young Russian meeting with influential American political figures sounded enough like a spy to move forward."

Later in the article, Bamford wrote, "A senior CIA official who held one of the highest jobs in the agency's Clandestine Service, and who worked closely with the FBI on many spy cases, offered a cynical view of the bureau's counterintelligence work. 'They want to generate headlines. They don't care if the information is credible or not,' he said, asking to remain anonymous because of his past clandestine work. 'I feel sorry for Butina; she got caught up in this whole vortex. They're just interested in putting another notch in their belt, and they don't care who gets hurt in the process.'"

When one of the nation's leading journalists covering national security and intelligence—someone who has a degree in law and knows about the abuses committed by the United States government—savages the prosecution so thoroughly, it's devastating.

As the sentencing hearing for Maria approached, we suspected the government was getting nervous that the story they had built, sometimes through false statements, would fall apart in the face of public scrutiny. They hadn't nabbed a serious player in Russia's scheme to interfere with the 2016 presidential election. They knew it. We knew it. And they knew we knew it. But they wanted to make sure the public remained fooled. In service of this farce, on April 19, 2019, a week before the sentencing hearing, the prosecution filed its sentencing materials with the court attaching a declaration from Robert Anderson Jr.

Anderson was once the Assistant Director of the FBI's Counterintelligence Division and Executive Assistant Director of the FBI's Criminal, Cyber, and Response and Services Branch. This is the same Anderson who, in response to the North Korean cyberattack on Sony Pictures Entertainment, questioned: "Is this an act of war?"

An *act of war*. Exposing confidential emails that showed Hollywood producer Scott Rudin calling Angelina Jolie a "minimally talented spoiled brat" was an act of war. Look, I get it, protecting intellectual property, especially for a company as iconic as Sony, is no small matter. Cybersecurity is serious business. But suggesting that was a national security crisis on par with war? That's the Robert Anderson we're talking about.

Just as we were trying to put Maria's actions in their true context and quiet the anti-Russian war drum prosecutors had beaten, Anderson was the guy the prosecution wanted to debut for sentencing. Why? Apparently,

Anderson was brought in as an expert witness to help the government raise the curtain on its latest theory: that Maria was part of a deliberate Russian intelligence effort to "spot and assess" Americans. This was, it seemed, their new position—and it was the first we'd heard about it. It wasn't in any court filings. It hadn't come up during the many months we had been in contact with them. Yet suddenly, this was their story. Even though the government remained quite certain Maria wasn't a spy, had never been employed by the Russian government, had no intelligence training, and had no connection to any foreign intelligence operation in the United States, they now wanted to paint her as a low-level operative anyway—just close enough to suggest a vague connection to intelligence work to try to justify their prosecution, but not enough that they'd have to prove anything concrete at sentencing.

We filed a motion to strike the Anderson declaration on April 21, 2019. Not long after, Bob fired off a curt email to the government while I got on the phone with Kenerson the night before our hearing.

"Why are you doing this?" I asked. "You know she's not a spy."

Kenerson agreed but said there was a need to impress upon the court that Maria wasn't just someone who failed to inform the Attorney General about what she was doing. (Actually, she was.) They wanted the court to know the intelligence goals of the Russian Federation—goals that Maria knew nothing about. The way to do that? Use a guy who'd never met or evaluated Maria—not once. The same guy whose reaction to the Sony hack wasn't exactly a masterclass in measured thinking. The kind of judgment that has no place in a courtroom.

It was clear how much the Bamford article had stung the government's ego.

I encouraged Kenerson not to involve Anderson. It was then I got the impression that using Anderson was not something Kenerson wished to do or would have done, but that leadership had required it. I understood the position he was in. Kenerson had to follow direction and the policy decisions of his department.

"You know," I said to Kenerson, "Maria asked me moments ago whether it was all rigged. She wondered whether you guys had already spoken to the judge privately to tell her what to do. I said, 'No, something like that would never happen here.' But it bothered me that the question even had to be asked. And yet, I can't fault her for asking it given every-thing that's gone wrong in this case.

"Don't transform what should be a straightforward sentencing hearing into a sideshow over Anderson. Maria's done everything you've asked of her. She's answered all of your questions. She's explained everything. You believe her. Let her go home."

It wouldn't have gone well for the government had they called Anderson to the stand anyway. We were ready to cross-examine him, and I explained all this to Kenerson. We planned to expose Anderson's circular logic, flawed assumptions, and unsupportable conclusions about Maria. Then we would have called Special Agent Kevin Helson to the stand, the lead case agent who actually investigated and interviewed Maria. He would have confirmed that, during her fifty-plus hours of interviews with the government, no federal agent or investigator ever suggested or directly raised the prospect that Maria was a "spot-and-assess" operative helping Russia identify and recruit vulnerable Americans. And we would have had him repeat the things he told all of us in the proffer sessions—statements that would have dismantled whatever reliability Anderson's opinions and written declaration still carried.

On April 26, 2019, Judge Chutkan's courtroom was packed. Bob and I sat with Maria on our side. Kenerson, Saunders, and the government were on theirs. Journalists from every major news organization were there. The Russian consular officers were there. James Bamford was there. My fiancé was there. Our best friend Jack. Their side was rife with DOJ attorneys supporting "Team America." Their witness Robert Anderson was there. Special Agent Michelle Ball was there. Courtroom sketch artists, law clerks and judicial interns were in the jury box.

Know who was missing? One person: Helson.

It didn't matter though. The government decided not to call Anderson but instead make him available should we or the court wish to question him. No one did, so the government proceeded.

The prosecution agreed that Maria's extensive cooperation warranted a reduced sentence. They said that an appropriate sentence in this case would have been twenty-four months of incarceration, prior to taking her cooperation into account. But with her assistance they recommended that the court impose a sentence of eighteen months.

I stood before Judge Chutkan, the prosecution, and the news-consuming world to deliver my allocution.

"I have a few prepared remarks," I said.

"That's fine," Judge Chutkan replied. "I'll just ask that you speak—when we read, we tend to speed up, and for the sake of my court reporter, if you could slow down a bit. Thank you."

"Sure," I said.

"For the past nine months, I've gotten to know Maria well. It's been impossible to speak with her without sensing some regret. She never wished to break any law. She never wished to lie. She never lied, and she never acted maliciously. Even so, she knows she violated an important statute, and for this she's being sentenced.

"Before I tell the story of the actions Maria took that has led to this moment, I'd like to first begin by addressing what's on everyone's mind. The case against Maria is certainly timely. America is looking for enemies wherever we can find them. We feel wronged, and we should feel wronged, about the attacks on our democracy perpetrated by those who wish to cause us harm. Our laws exist for a reason: so we can have a government free from undue influence.

"But here's the fact I wish to stress to the Court. Maria is not a spy. She's not intelligence. She's never been employed by the Russian government. She knows of no secret codes, safe houses, illegals. She has never engaged in covert activity, and she has never lied to our government. I mention all this because, while many of us may be skeptical and untrusting, and I understand that feeling, the point is that Maria is not a proxy for the Russian government. She's not a proxy for the Russian 12 who were indicted and remain at large."

During my argument, Judge Chutkan pulled out a fan—one a debutante might use—and flitted it gently as I spoke. She smiled, nodded, and listened with such focus that it felt less like arguing before a judge and more like speaking to an adoring aunt or someone genuinely rooting for me. There was a quiet sense of recognition between us. Judge Chutkan was born in Jamaica, like my family on my mother's side, and something about her felt familiar. What stood out even more was the contrast between how she treated me compared to Bob. Perhaps it was because Bob was a partner at the firm, more experienced, and the one who had "crossed the line" in the public defense of Maria that led to the gag order. Or maybe it was something else—I don't know. Bob didn't seem to mind. Still, I don't like it when people are terse with him; he's one of the most charitable people I know. That said, I'll admit—I liked being the favored one in that moment.

"Even so," I continued, "Maria did commit a serious crime for which she has deep remorse. The reason she's here today is because she failed to notify our government before agreeing to act as an agent of a Russian official. Agent of a Russian official. I appreciate how that sounds. It's easy to let your mind wander and draw conclusions.

"But, of course, there are many agents of foreign governments acting lawfully in the United States. The difference between those agents and Maria is that they notified our government in advance, while Maria did not. So when our government calls Maria an agent, they are not calling her an intelligence agent. They are not calling her a secret agent. In truth, nothing about Maria has been secret. She's answered every single question posed to her by our federal government, and she's been answering these questions before she was even arrested. As we put in our memo, Maria voluntarily produced thousands of pages of documents and voluntarily appeared before this same body, a Senate intel committee, answering all of its questions for a voluntary deposition for an eight-hour time period. When the FBI carried out a search warrant, she gave the agents all of her electronics and passwords. She had nothing to hide. And when the FBI seized her computer and phone devices again with her arrest, they requested her passwords once more, and she had not changed them.

"So what happened? Well, a lot of things have been said, and Maria has explained everything. But her crime really comes down to this, and it's very simple. During Maria's time in the United States, and unbeknownst to her, she was committing a felony, conspiracy to violate § 951. While in this country, she maintained close contact with her family and friends from Russia. One of them was Aleksandr Torshin, an official who used to work at the Russian Central Bank. They discussed vacations and their daily lives, but Maria also took advice from him and did things for him. I don't mean to trivialize or rehash all the details which you have available to you, but the context for these things is somewhat important.

"So, for example, she bought clothes for his grandchildren. She was also invited to a presidential campaign announcement, and she described the event to him because he asked about it. Maria complied by translating a Wikipedia page she copy-pasted into a Twitter direct message. This is how they communicated back and forth, and it was all unsecured."

I watched Judge Chutkan's eyes glance over to the government's table. In my mind, it was as if she was surprised to hear that Maria and Torshin communicated through ordinary, unsecured means and thus was looking for a reaction from one of the prosecutors to fact-check what I had said. Presumably she saw no such reaction because she turned back to me seemingly satisfied.

"Before starting school, Maria made these business cards that listed her as a special assistant to Torshin. The title was made up. While traveling on a trip with him to the U.S. for an NRA event, there was a point when the host at a front desk asked: One hotel room or two? This made her uncomfortable. She wanted to be appreciated for her intellect, not her gender, so she asked Torshin for permission to make the card and phony title, to keep anyone from mistaking her relationship with him for a romantic one ever again, and he said okay.

"Once in school, Maria met her share of discrimination on the American University campus, especially after the 2016 election. This didn't deter her, though. She grew to love the United States. You know, she tells a story. One of the first stories she told me was that when she got here, she went to a grocery store, and she felt like it looked like a museum."

"Mr. Carry," Judge Chutkan interrupted, "you just said she met her share of discrimination on the American University campus. What are you referring to?"

I was referring to a character letter written by one of Maria's classmates.

In it, she described how peers treated Maria poorly at school—due in part to the climate of heightened Russophobia that hung over Washington and the university campus, and also in response to a February 2017 article in *The Daily Beast*, which cast her in a negative light. That piece portrayed Maria as a shady figure who shifted identities depending on her audience: sometimes a grad student, and, at other times, a gun rights advocate, Russian Central Bank staffer or liaison between Russia and Washington insiders in Republican political circles. Because of that article, Maria had few friends. Those around her questioned her motivations and presumed she was in the United States for illegitimate or even sinister reasons. Yet, as I explained to the judge—paraphrasing her classmate's letter—had they really known Maria, they would have seen someone who was consistent, genuine, and kind, not shady or shadowy.

Despite all that, I continued, Maria still "wanted to learn as much as she could about this country, and she admired our work ethic and ideals. And she knew this country to be good and just. In fact, she wished to live here. But she also loved her home, her family. She wanted a foot in both worlds. She thought perhaps she could work for a think tank; perhaps she could start a foundation or be the go-to consultant for anything American or Russian. These are the kinds of things that she had in mind as a potential career. Graduation was inevitable, so she continued to share her political thoughts and ideas with her American contacts and Torshin, although not under orders or for money.

"When the government tells this story, they stress words and phrases like 'agenda' and 'Russian interests' and 'unofficial transmitter of communications.' They're in the Statement of Offense. And we don't walk them back, but I believe the government has highlighted these words to make her actions appear more nefarious than they were. Her agenda was better relations between Russia and the United States. The Russian interests she was pursuing was all the same. And as an unofficial transmitter of communications, this means that she had conversations with like-minded people at Friendship Dinners and other civic society events about how to improve relations. These Friendship Dinners weren't a bad thing. It's not like they were plotting behind the scenes about how to infect the American government with a Manchurian candidate. No. They were cultural exchanges, attended mostly by artists, movie directors, philanthropists, and political wonks. They talked about world history and U.S.-Russian affairs. They talked about peace. And Maria shared her thoughts and ideas with them as they did with her. The Friendship Dinners were publicized and out in the open, and they were organized with her help by an American philanthropist who she met and has long been interested in restoring the relations with the U.S. and Russia as a legacy to his father, which was an equal interest of Maria's."

"You're referring to Mr. O'Neill," Judge Chutkan said.

Yes, I was referring to George O'Neill Jr., who doubled as the second unindicted, unnamed American who appeared in the charging documents and submitted a generous character letter on Maria's behalf in aid of sentencing.

"All right," Judge Chutkan said.

"Maria never stole any documents, bribed any officials, funneled money to the NRA, or lied to any investigators. And she just can't see how anyone would think she's a spotter. I'll also note that some have cast doubt on the seriousness of a gun rights group in a country that doesn't allow such rights. I don't normally like to inject myself into argument, but I'll remind those same people that there was a time in this country when women did not have the right to vote, and I didn't have the right to marry. Rights advocacy is a bedrock principle of being American. Her gun advocacy wasn't a pretext, it was sincere, and the written testimonials from the wrongly convicted people she helped as part of her work should show that. I also take issue with how the government has characterized some of her time in the U.S., as though she was only interested in her diplomacy activities versus school. Maria came to the United States for school, and she was a straight-A student at AU. And I mean a near 4.0. She held two internships, did work-study for professors, studied at the library every day, participated in class, took her coursework seriously, did all of her exams, and graduated with high marks.

"When Maria was arrested, it had been stated that she was using her education as a cover for nefarious or clandestine ends. This is not true. Maria's main interest in coming to the United States was to pursue graduate work, but as an admirer of both this country and her home, she hoped for a better relationship between the two nations. For this reason, and for this reason alone, Maria pursued peacebuilding by organizing dinners between Americans and Russians who wanted better relations.

"In the end, Maria didn't notify our government in advance of her activities, although she would have committed no crime if she had. Regardless, Maria has confessed to her crime. She recognizes that her good ends were sought using unlawful means. She admits that her activities triggered a duty to notify the Attorney General and that she failed to provide that notice. For this, she is remorseful. This remorse, which I know many Americans will be suspicious of, is not merely because she is currently in jail where she has spent most—some of her time in solitary confinement. No. Maria is filled with regret because she has accidentally harmed a country that she loved and admired, a country where she saw a future for herself, a country where she was moving to South Dakota to begin an American life. These hopes have obviously been undone by her own actions. But Maria understands why this is so, and her contrition is honest, like everything else about her.

"Judge, like you, I used to be a public defender."

Chutkan smiled brightly back at me. She knew what it meant to be a public defender. It's demanding and far from glamorous, but it matters.

"I loved the work," I added, "and continue to help when I can because I can appreciate, in the words of Bryan Stevenson, that each of us is more than the worst thing we've ever done. In my eight years practicing law, I have met no one, and I've never said this before, but no one more emblematic of that belief than Maria."

And that had truly been how much Maria had impressed me.

"She has learned a valuable lesson," I said. "Given the high-profile nature of this case, she has felt the depths of shame and humiliation. She has felt the weight of being called a felon—which now she is—a foreign agent, and to some in the news, a spy. These are brands that she will bear for the rest of her days, and she knows what they will mean for her future. She has languished in solitary confinement. Other than brief trips for transport, Maria has gone outside only once. She has served a sobering night in Central Cell Block, weeks in the DC jail, and months in the Alexandria Detention Center. She has been justly punished.

"Finally, I appreciate the sometimes higher range sentences for § 951 that the government points out for offenders, but this case is distinguishable. Maria stole no sensitive information. She did no covert activity. She never lied to our government. There are no multiple counts here. She cooperated immensely. All of Maria's many good qualities as well, which are reflected in the many character letters you have seen, should not be overshadowed by her aberrant act. So I ask that you impose a sentence of time served."

In other words, I was asking Judge Chutkan to impose a sentence of approximately nine months—time Maria already spent in custody awaiting sentencing, so she could be released immediately and go home. I then made myself available for any questions the judge had and ended my allocution.

"Thank you, Mr. Carry," Judge Chutkan said.

Maria then stood up to approach the podium to address the judge. I stood beside her as she asked for mercy. At times, her words hit me harder than I expected, and I felt myself fighting back a tear.

Yes, it's a professional relationship. You're the lawyer, they're the client. But when you spend that much time with someone—defending them, fighting for them, and seeing them at their lowest after almost everyone else has written them off—it changes. They become more than a client. Then you witness the constant indignities of jail and a broken system, and that, too, changes you. Bob and I visited Maria often while she was in solitary confinement, so she could get out of her cell, have some human contact, and keep up her spirits. Having no family nearby, even our significant others Rosie and Brendan came for visits. We saw her so frequently that some of the guards began greeting me by name and appeared supportive, as if hoping for a good outcome. One later told me as much during a jail visit after sentencing.

By the time Maria stood to speak, the weight of it all had peaked. Emotions were high. And in that moment, standing beside her, listening to her statement—even though I'd heard it before, helped her shape it, and rehearsed it with her—it hit differently.

When she finished, we walked back to counsel's table in silence and sat quietly. The courtroom remained still as we waited for the judge to speak.

In practice, judges consider the arguments from both sides before fashioning a sentence. Typically, they'll take a brief recess to retreat to chambers and reflect on everything that's been said. Judge Chutkan, however, though it may have been her custom, was poised to proceed immediately.

"Sentencing is the most difficult part of this job," she said. "After considering the departures and hearing statements made by counsel and Ms. Butina, statements which I believe were sincerely made, on both sides, I must now consider the relevant factors set out by Congress in 18 U.S.C. § 3553(a) and ensure that I impose a sentence sufficient but not greater than necessary to comply with the purposes of sentencing. These purposes include the need for the sentence imposed to reflect the seriousness of the offense, to promote respect for the law, and to provide just punishment for the offense. The sentence should also deter criminal conduct, protect the public from future crimes by the defendant, and promote rehabilitation.

"I must consider in each case the nature and circumstances of the offense, the history and characteristics of the defendant, the types of sentences available, and the need to avoid unwarranted sentence disparities among defendants with similar records who have been found guilty of similar conduct. I've considered all of these factors in deciding what the appropriate sentence is in this case, and I will discuss some of them now. With regard to the nature of the offense, as Mr. Anderson, who is the former Assistant Director of the FBI's Counterintelligence Division, noted in his declaration, the United States is Russia's primary target for malign and intrusive intelligence operations.

"In targeting the United States, and I quote, 'Russia works to obtain not only classified material or trade secrets, but also to collect any information that could, by itself or in conjunction with other efforts, assist the Russian government in increasing its geopolitical power or undermining and harming that of the United States.' Contrary to defense counsel assertions in its sentencing memorandum, this was no mere failure to provide the U.S. government with required information.

"While it is certainly true that Ms. Butina was not engaged in any espionage activity, and while I certainly agree that she was a legitimate and hard-working student at the same time as she was engaging efforts, she was not simply seeking to learn about the U.S. political system. She was seeking to collect information about individuals and organizations that could be helpful to the Russian government, and she was doing this under the direction of a Russian official for the benefit of the Russian government at a time when the Russian government was acting to interfere and affect the United States' political and electoral process."

According to a recent biographical piece on Judge Chutkan in *The New York Times*, that framing "struck some legal observers as gratuitous," given that even federal prosecutors had not accused Maria of directly conspiring with Russia to meddle in the 2016 election. The remark also blurred the lines by seeming to punish her for conduct she hadn't committed—let alone been accused of. In fact, Maria didn't appear anywhere in the then publicized version of the Robert Mueller report: *On the Investigation into Russian Interference in the 2016 Presidential Election.*

Judge Chutkan continued, "[Maria's] activities organizing Gun Rights Organization visits to Russia, U.S.-Russia Friendship Dinners, were all used to establish back-channel lines of communication to advance Russian interests. The conduct was sophisticated and penetrated deep into political organizations. Ms. Butina was likely able to establish the contacts she did precisely because she did not reveal herself to be an agent of a foreign government. This case is not simply about failing to notify the Attorney General. Yes, it may be true that had Ms. Butina alerted the Attorney General, her conduct might have been legal. But it is because she did not register that her conduct was so dangerous and her crime a threat to our country's democratic institutions.

"One of the things that Ms. Butina should have learned during her studies in this country is that she was able to participate in our political system and make connections because this is a country where our constitution protects individuals' freedoms to associate, gather, and exchange ideas, free from governmental interference. But this is also a country where the rule of law means something, and our laws require her to declare her true business in this country, which was to gather information and develop relationships that could be used to Russia's advantage. This was no simple misunderstanding by an overeager foreign student. There can be no doubt, as Mr. Anderson noted in his declaration, that the offense that

Ms. Butina has pled to is serious and jeopardized this country's national security.

"Turning to Ms. Butina's characteristics as an offender. It is apparent to this court, from hearing from Ms. Butina, from hearing from Mr. Carry, Mr. Driscoll, over the last nine months, and from reading all of the letters submitted on your behalf, Ms. Butina, that you are an intelligent, personable, kind, and hard-working person who is a devoted daughter, sister, granddaughter, and who impressed people wherever she went. It is also clear to this court that you were a legitimate and engaged student at American University and that you—you know, in a language that is not your own, you managed to graduate with a 3.91 grade point average, and that is to your credit. I also accept and understand that you have acknowledged your wrongdoing and have fully accepted responsibility for it. You have provided the government with substantial assistance and cooperation, resulting in their filing of a downward departure letter. You are well educated, you have no prior convictions, you don't have a prior history of criminal activity, and I will tell you that I have no doubt that you will not have any further criminal activity in your future.

"I do also understand that on completion of your sentence, should I sign the order of removal, you may be immediately subject to removal. You have a strong support network, which is evidenced by the many letters that the Court has received from your family, your friends, your former professors, your support network, priests, your former colleagues—one former colleague at American University, and others. No doubt you have suffered greatly because of the national attention that this case has received, including some salacious details that were proven to be incorrect. And in the era of Google, those will be difficult to overcome. So I take those factors into consideration, and I take your absolute—what I take to be your absolute sincerity and remorse into consideration.

"Ms. Butina faces a maximum sentence of five years of imprisonment. She has been held for a little over nine months. Her counsel asks for her to be sentenced to time served, and she and the government have agreed to an order of removal, which will hopefully prevent her from spending additional prison time beyond her sentence awaiting deportation proceedings. The government, after moving for a downward departure, asks for a sentence of 18 months of incarceration, which will mean that, with the time she has already been held, she would serve an additional nine months less any potential institutional good-time credit.

"In addition to the nature and circumstances of the offense and history and characteristics of Ms. Butina, I also have to consider the purposes of sentencing, among other factors, and one of the specific factors in 3553(a) is the need to avoid unwarranted sentence disparity. However, because there is not a sufficiently analogous sentencing guideline in this case, the Court was unable to find reliable national or DC Circuit statistics for mean and median sentences, and neither the government nor the defense has provided any. What is clear, however, is that sentences for violation of 18 U.S.C. § 951 and conspiracies to commit that offense vary greatly. The Court's sentence is in line with a number of cases that the Court has reviewed.

"If you could stand."

Maria stood. We stood with her.

"It is the judgment of this court that you, Maria Butina, are hereby committed to the custody of the Bureau of Prisons for a term of 18 months on Count 1. You are further ordered to pay a special assessment of $100. The Court finds that you do not have the ability to pay a fine and therefore waives imposition of a fine in this case."

Her words came out clearly and methodically, but I barely registered them.

Eighteen months. That's what I heard. That's what I kept hearing, replaying my own allocution in my head. I thought about what Maria had said—her pleas for mercy—and how this prosecution had reshaped her life: "I came to the U.S. not under any orders but with hope, and now nothing remains but penitence." I thought of Maria's family, and the too-few supporters in the courtroom gallery. I thought of whether I'd missed something. Of whether I said too much, or too little. Of whether there was still something left to say, even now.

Avoiding sentencing disparities had seemed important to the judge. I'd prepared a chart with various sentencing data—oh, my chart, I remembered. But I hadn't shown it to her. Maybe I could show it to her now. Maybe I could get her to reconsider.

The judge kept speaking.

"Pursuant to 18 U.S.C. § 3742, Ms. Butina, you have a right to appeal the sentence imposed by the Court if the period of imprisonment is longer than the statutory maximum or the sentence departs upward from the applicable sentencing guideline range. If you choose to appeal, you must file any appeal within 14 days after the Court enters judgment. As defined in 28 U.S.C. § 2255, you also have the right to challenge the conviction entered or sentence imposed if new and currently unavailable information becomes available to you, or on a claim that you received ineffective assistance of counsel in entering a plea of guilty to the offense of conviction or in connection with sentencing. If you are unable to afford the cost of an appeal, you may request permission from the court to file an appeal without cost to you."

But I wasn't listening. Not really. Everything felt suspended. I saw Bob and Maria just standing there, motionless. None of us moved—caught in a shared stillness—while I tried to process whether there was anything more I could do, or could have done, even though I already knew the answer. My thoughts then returned to Maria, and with them, a sense of resignation.

Judge Chutkan spoke again.

"Are there any objections to the sentence imposed that are not already noted on the record? Mr. Kenerson?"

"No, Your Honor," Kenerson said.

The judge turned to us. Bob's voice answered.

"Other than noted, no," he said.

"All right. As set forth in the plea agreement, the government pledged to move to dismiss the remaining count of the indictment against Ms. Butina. Does the government wish to do so now?"

"Yes, Your Honor," Kenerson said. "We move to dismiss the remaining count."

"The motion is granted."

And the case was complete. Maria was sentenced to an additional nine months—which she spent in a federal penitentiary in Tallahassee, Florida—minus any good time credit before being sent back to Russia.

Chapter Nineteen

After five years of running the Right to Bear Arms, Maria had secured only modest gains on the legislative front. They got laws passed allowing gun owners to transport more rounds of ammunition, and they got a new rule to keep their guns in certain conditions. However, for the big things they wanted, like having the right to own pistols for self-defense, those never got through. Maria had plumbed her contacts, exploited the media, and roused the rabble, but in the end, there was no pathway forward because Russia isn't a democracy. For critical issues like civilian gun ownership, you'd need the approval of the man at the top, and the chances of Putin allowing the public to take matters into their own hands didn't seem likely. Seeing no pathway forward, Maria felt the group needed a fresh pair of eyes, new leadership to steer the ship. At the same time, she needed the chance to find perspective. She'd been mired in gun rights issues for half a decade, and this was her chance to rediscover the other things out there in the world. So, placing a new guy in charge, Maria stepped back to become a normal member of the group that she founded in that McDonald's five years ago. She gave the new leader specific instructions about her role moving forward. She was happy to answer his questions, but she couldn't advise him on the best path forward. He was in charge.

Suddenly, free from the gun-rights shackles, Maria needed a new passion and direction in life, so she threw her hat into the job market. It was promptly thrown back. At first, she applied to be a TV host at multiple stations, a job I didn't even know one could apply for. And maybe you can't because nobody even wanted her résumé. TV stardom was out—for now. Next on her list was academia. She spent the previous five years educating the public about gun rights and proper firearm usage, so surely, she could get a job as a teacher. She took a good look at the Russian education system and didn't like what she saw. She glanced abroad—perhaps Germany would be a good place to park oneself—but the problem was that her German was so scheisse that Deutschland was a nein. As she searched for positions in education, she realized she was looking on the wrong side of the student/teacher coin. A graduate degree could give her more heft wherever she wanted to go, so she looked at law school in Russia. Yet as her romance with Erickson developed—thinking she'd soon be married—she considered graduate schools in the United States. As she tossed the idea around, she began to fall in love with it. Not only would she be closer to her one-and-only, the United States also had the best schools in the world—along with the United Kingdom—she reluctantly admits.

Ultimately, Maria applied to a few schools in the United States, deciding not to tell her parents unless she was accepted. Maria claimed Harvard admitted her to their master's program in something or other, but it was way too expensive. She also applied to the master's program at American University's School of International Service. She got in, and since the price was right, it seemed like a perfect fit. In addition, Erickson often visited Washington, DC, where American University is located, and the curriculum's focus on global politics and security made it even more ideal. Maria ended up choosing to study international affairs at American because she figured that if she and Erickson could find neutral ground despite being from such different circumstances, then maybe their respective nations could find the same.

The first course she took dug into the US-Russian relationship. Inspired, she began thinking about a future in diplomacy, maybe even founding a pro-Russian think tank to foster dialogue that could help unite the two countries. Her thinking, however, was naive. The United States and Russia are adversaries not because we don't have avenues of dialogue. We're adversaries because one country is a democracy and the other is merely cloaked in the trappings of democracy. These two political philosophies stand in opposition. You may notice that the United States isn't particularly close with many nondemocratic countries. If you really want the United States and Russia to be friends, you'll need a real democracy in Russia, or authoritarianism in the United States. Either of those alterations will make the bespoke glove of friendship fit like, well, a glove.

Leaving Moscow wasn't easy for Maria. Her mother was anxious—partly because of the distance, partly because of the stereotypes—but both parents had met Paul and thought he would take care of her. Maria had her own worries. She would miss her friends, her family even more, her little sister especially, but high on the list of things she was loath to leave was her apartment. Over the years, she had turned it into a little art gallery filled with drawings and paintings. Before heading out, she gave those creations to her friends or colleagues from the Right to Bear Arms. Once all the goodbyes were said, the artwork given away, the last hugs shared, her things packed, and the final glance around the apartment taken, she made her way to the airport on her own—which seems fitting for someone so independent.

Maria believed her life was about to change. And it would. Moving to the United States, she wanted an adventure. She wanted to change the world.

Chapter Twenty

Paul Erickson, Maria's former boyfriend, was indicted in South Dakota on February 5, 2019, for wire fraud and money laundering. In July 2020, a federal judge sentenced him to seven years in federal prison. On January 13, 2021, a week before Donald Trump left office, the president granted Erickson a full and unconditional pardon. The president also wiped out $3 million in restitution Erickson would have had to pay.

On January 10, 2023, James Bamford released his nonfiction bestseller *Spyfail: Foreign Spies, Moles, Saboteurs, and the Collapse of America's Counterintelligence.* The book explores how politics, special interests, and corruption play roles in our intelligence services. In the final chapter of the book, appropriately titled "The Scapegoat," Bamford tells Maria's story.

"As the bureau would eventually discover," he wrote, "there was absolutely no evidence of any kind showing massive amounts of Russian money flowing to the NRA or Trump, let alone via Maria Butina. And Butina's only contribution to the NRA was her annual dues. Nor was any money flowing from the Kremlin to Butina, who had to continuously borrow money to pay for her tuition. With her family in Siberia unable to help, she was not even able to make the payments for her final semester."

Bamford took aim at "crack counterspies, Kevin Helson, forty-five, a slow-talking former blood and fingerprint analyst from Tennessee, and Michelle Ball, thirty-three, a perky brunette with a sideswept bang, large dimples, and a toothy smile. Fresh out of the FBI Academy, she had spent the previous five years as a local anchor and reporter for a Biloxi, Mississippi, TV station. . . . There is no indication she knew anything about Russia or espionage, except what she may have watched on *The Americans.*"

Bamford explained how Mueller and his team, the special counsel investigators tasked with examining Russian involvement in the 2016 US election, had zero interest in Maria because "there had never been anything suspicious about her." And yet somehow, one of the supposed smoking guns in the case was an old email from March 2015 between Maria and her then boyfriend Paul Erickson. She'd been tossing around grad school ideas and floated a starry-eyed plan for a "Diplomacy Project" to improve US-Russia relations. She sketched out a rough budget, guessing it might cost around $125,000 to cover travel, conferences, and maybe even a trip to the Republican National Convention. But it was all talk. As Bamford pointed out: "what was never mentioned by Helson was that nothing ever happened. It was simply idle chatter, wishful thinking, idealistic dreaming, nothing more." Sure, Maria had a sincere interest in diplomacy and peace, but that wasn't the whole story. Like most long-distance couples, she and Erickson were also just trying to come up with ways to see each other and be in the same place.

Bamford ended the chapter with a stark reminder about the consequences of unjust legal treatment. He wrote, "Butina had come to the United States five years earlier as an idealistic graduate student, hoping to someday find a way to create better relations between the United States and Russia. It was her childhood dream. She left bitter and forever scarred by a country that politically and publicly abused her."

Suppression of *Brady* material is a violation of due process. During Maria's incarceration, Patrick Byrne, the then CEO of Overstock, publicly disclosed he had been serving as a government informant, feeding information about Maria to what he called the "men in black" since 2015. According to Patrick, after being tasked with pursuing a relationship with her, he informed the government that Maria was an age-appropriate idealist who was not working for the Russians.

This information was not turned over to Bob and me, and if it exists, it would be a clear example of a failure to disclose *Brady* material. The Office of Professional Responsibility (OPR) is responsible for investigating the conduct of Justice Department employees who are accused of professional misconduct. OPR declined to open a matter or pursue action.

Since presiding over Maria's case, Judge Chutkan has handled other highly publicized matters. In 2024, she presided over Special Counsel Jack Smith's prosecution of former President Donald Trump on charges of trying to subvert the 2020 election. Following a string of statements posted on Trump's social media account that criticized potential witnesses, court personnel, and Jack Smith and his team, Judge Chutkan issued a gag order. An appeals court upheld most of the restrictions in the gag order but pared back some of the excesses that swept in more protected speech than necessary.

After Trump won the 2024 election, Jack Smith asked Judge Chutkan to dismiss all charges against the once and future president citing a Department of Justice policy that prohibits prosecuting a president while in office. She granted the request and dismissed the charges.

After Maria's sentencing, I parked outside my apartment and gave Tommy a call. He picked up, and we talked about grabbing drinks once everything settled down. We also spoke briefly about the case. He was kind and gracious, neither gloating nor rubbing it in. He recognized how hard we had worked on this case and that Maria meant a lot to us. Out of curiosity, I asked if he had anticipated this outcome. Having handled many sentencing hearings, you develop a sense of likely outcomes, and I was caught off guard by this result. He was, too. He mentioned he didn't expect the judge to adopt the government's sentencing recommendation, but he also didn't think we'd get what we requested either.

Tommy is still at the US Attorney's Office for the District of Columbia, and we remain friends and good colleagues today.

Upon completing her sentence, Maria flew back to Russia as what felt to her like the most famous woman in Moscow, and to me the unexpected champion of the Russian people. For a while, I kept in touch with her and her family, trading the occasional message, birthday greeting, or holiday well-wish. And in the beginning, Maria laid low and spent time with family, but she had always been ambitious. Since she was suddenly a celebrity, she used her newfound fame to land a gig for the online version of RT, state television.

In 2021, Maria would throw her hat in the ring for the State Duma, which is like the US House of Representatives. Running in the Kirov Oblast against headwinds antagonistic to Putin's United Russia party, she was seen as a government mouthpiece and lost her race. However, the governor appointed her to the Duma, where she currently serves.

In the spring of 2021, Russia began amassing military forces along the Ukrainian border. The invasion followed on the morning of February 24, 2022. Branded by Putin as a "special military operation," missiles and airstrikes peppered Ukraine, including the capital Kyiv, paving the way for a massive ground assault. Though the operation into Ukraine had started eight years earlier with the seizure of Crimea and parts of the Donbas, in February 2022 the war began in earnest.

Russia thought their victory over the former Soviet republic would be swift and that citizens would lay down their arms, though war persists. As part of the United States' efforts to impose costs on the Russian Federation for its war against Ukraine, the US Department of Treasury's Office of Foreign Assets Control (OFAC) sanctioned hundreds of enablers believed to support the Kremlin's invasion. These sanctions covered all 450 members of the Russian State Duma, all 170 members of the Federation Council, and 47 Russian governors. Among the State Duma members sanctioned: Maria Butina. Since her addition to the OFAC list, we've fallen out of touch. Not completely—every so often she'll send a quick, friendly text to share a life update or say hello, and I'll respond. But the rhythm of regular, meaningful contact is gone. The last real conversation we had was before the invasion.

"We keep winning," Bob said to me in 2021, a few years after Maria's sentence. He was talking about our more recent cases, which kept breaking our way. "I feel like we paid our dues with Maria—when everything that could go wrong did go wrong—and now we're riding a wave of karmic correction."

Slivers of Bob's rich beliefs reveal themselves when he discusses fate. I feel the same way though. We see our lives as stories, and we imagine the threads of kismet weaving through our choices and actions. For Maria's case, we suffered professionally through a road of trials, a hero's journey of sorts involving constant setbacks with the government hydra. The chips of fate were so stacked against our client, the Russophobia so palpable, that it was a dispiriting battle. Still, in our resurrection to the ordinary world, Bob and I had returned with a metaphorical elixir or, from Bob's perspective, divine providence.

In the years following Maria's sentence, Bob and I handled other high-profile cases, and our reputations were forged through excellence in our craft, our legal prose, and our temperament. We represented a White House Chief of Staff and CEO of a publicly traded company. We stood among a small set of attorneys representing multiple clients before the House Select Committee to Investigate the January 6th Attack on the United States Capitol. We helped many witnesses chart the rocky shoals of grand jury subpoenas from Special Counsel Jack Smith's investigations into President Donald Trump. And we helped resolve headline-grabbing criminal and civil cases.

I like to think our recent accomplishments are because we stuck to first principles of logic, concision, and merit, but maybe Bob's right. Maybe it's because of karma. Perhaps we have simply entered the third act of our story, our dénouement. In a way, everyone in our case found favor, depending on how you interpret it.

Also, I married the love of my life. He'll be happy to know I mentioned him.

"You were duped!"

Liberals, often with a touch of frenzy, will corner me at a social event, where I must dodge attempts to draw me into argument. They want to educate me on the topic of Maria Butina. If I'm truly cornered, I might remind my would-be elucidator their starting premises are wrong and their facts are misinformed. Eventually, they'll admit I know more about the law and the evidence, but where they double down is on the matter of the personal psyche. You see, these wizards of the human condition, and only those who agree with them, possess the innate ability to judge evil, and they alone are quite certain that *this woman*, whom they've never met, is wicked. They want everyone to know their moral compass is true and that justice should never be granted to villains.

I find myself lucky these people with perfect moral compasses are always far away from the gears of justice.

As children, we look for heroes and villains in the stories we're told. We search for clear lessons, for guideposts on how to navigate our lives—be mindful, be patient, be kind. Over time, as we mature, the guideposts become less decipherable, appearing to point in many directions at once. This is not a flaw of human development; it *is* human development. With experience, we find nuance where once we found black and white, and we find that those who act with wisdom do so without dogmatism—kind of like the Dunning–Kruger effect of morality. I have found that in my years as an attorney, a husband, and a man, villains don't spring fully realized from the ether, and heroes aren't always heroic. If you step past the facades of fairy tales, you find the richest stories are the ones that explain our regrettable acts—not just our heroic feats.

It's a curious thing, but goodness in the world becomes much sharper when viewed with nuanced thought. I look less to the foibles and sins in the individual than I do to the sins in the system that have allowed bad acts to emerge. This is not an abrogation of personal responsibility, far from it, but I endeavor to make the ideal place that allows people to be their best selves.

No man or woman is perfect, and more importantly, few have been truly tested. But of course, we are always met by the boisterous loud-mouths of proverbial surety on both sides of the aisle. The more they huff and puff, the more they push and prod, and the less they ask questions, the more I know where they stand on the spectrum. When we dump people into buckets of moral certitude, when we are positive to dislike someone based on a hunch, we find ourselves in the land of prejudice. Here's a bad question: Is that person morally fit? Here's a better question: How can we prevent moral injustices? It is our systems that save us rather than our gut intuition about *who* can save us. This is the foundation of any good justice system, including our own, and these are the waters I sail.

Here's a truth I hope you'll carry with you when you read or watch the news about court cases or criminal convictions: All people require good representation, and you should be happy when those who have committed the most heinous of acts have the strongest representation. Because without that, we have no justice.

Acknowledgments

I'm grateful to Maria for trusting me with this story, for allowing me to share it, and for letting me stand by her side. Thanks also to my family and friends for their support along the way—your encouragement, patience, and perspective meant more than you know. To my colleagues and mentors, thank you. I'm especially grateful for the quiet moments that made writing possible—and for the chaos that gave me something to write about. And to Bob, thank you for asking, "Do you wanna go?" I'm glad I said yes.

Criminal Complaint and Affidavit in Support of Application for a Criminal Complaint

Case 1:18-cr-00218-TSC   Document 1   Filed 07/14/18   Page 1 of 1

AO 91 (Rev. 08/09) Criminal Complaint

UNITED STATES DISTRICT COURT
for the
District of Columbia

United States of America	)
v.	)
Mariia Butina	) Case No.
also known as Maria Butina	)
DOB:	)
	)
Defendant(s)	

CRIMINAL COMPLAINT

I, the complainant in this case, state that the following is true to the best of my knowledge and belief.
On or about the date(s) of ___Between 2015 and Feb. 2017___ in the county of _____ in the
_____ District of ____Columbia____ , the defendant(s) violated:

Code Section	*Offense Description*
18 U.S.C. § 371	Conspiracy
	See Appendix A, which is incorporated herein.

This criminal complaint is based on these facts:
SEE ATTACHED AFFIDAVIT

☑ Continued on the attached sheet.

_____
Complainant's signature

Kevin Helson, Special Agent
Printed name and title

Sworn to before me and signed in my presence.

Date: ___07/14/2018___

_____
Judge's signature

City and state: ___Washington, D.C.___

Deborah A. Robinson, U.S. Magistrate Judge
Printed name and title

IN THE UNITED STATES DISTRICT COURT
FOR THE DISTRICT OF COLUMBIA

IN THE MATTER OF AN APPLICATION FOR CRIMINAL COMPLAINT FOR MARIIA BUTINA, ALSO KNOWN AS MARIA BUTINA	Case No. _____

AFFIDAVIT IN SUPPORT OF
AN APPLICATION FOR A CRIMINAL COMPLAINT

I, Kevin Helson, being first duly sworn, hereby depose and state that I am a Special Agent

with the Federal Bureau of Investigation (FBI) and charge as follows:

THE FBI INVESTIGATION

1.   The bases of my knowledge for the facts alleged herein are as follows. I have been a

Special Agent with the FBI for 15 years. Currently, I am assigned to the Counterintelligence

Division within the Washington Field Office of the FBI. The focus of my counter intelligence

efforts has been the investigation of the foreign intelligence activities of the Russian Federation. I

have learned the facts contained in this affidavit from, among other sources, my personal

participation in this investigation, my discussions with other law enforcement agents, searches that

have been conducted, surveillance that has been conducted, and reviews of documents, electronic

items, and other evidentiary materials.

2.   In the course of this investigation, the FBI has employed a variety of lawful

investigative methods, including the acquisition of Rule 41 search warrants of two premises, which

included authorization to search electronic devices. One of those searches included a laptop

computer belonging to MARIIA BUTINA, a/k/a "Maria Butina" ("BUTINA"), (hereinafter

"BUTINA's Laptop") and an iPhone belonging to BUTINA (hereinafter "BUTINA's iPhone").

Because this affidavit is being submitted for the limited purpose of establishing probable cause, it

does not include every fact that I have learned during the course of this investigation. Further, any statements related herein are related in substance and in part only. Finally, certain items related herein were translated by FBI linguists from Russian to English.

BACKGROUND

Title 18, U.S. Code, sections 371 (Conspiracy) and 951 (Agents of Foreign Governments)

3. Title 18 of the United States Code, section 371 (Conspiracy to Commit Offense or to Defraud United States), makes it a criminal offense for any person(s) to conspire together with one or more others either to commit an offense against the United States or to defraud the United States, or any agency thereof, in any manner or for any purpose.

4. Title 18 of the United States Code, section 951 (Agents of Foreign Governments), makes it a criminal offense for any person, other than a diplomatic or consular official or attaché, to act in the United States as an agent of a foreign government without prior notification to the Attorney General, as required by law. For purposes of this law, the term "agent of a foreign government" includes an individual who agrees to operate within the United States subject to the direction or control of a foreign government or official.

Relevant Persons and Definitions

5. Defendant BUTINA is a Russian citizen who entered the United States in August 2016 on an F-1 Student Visa. Before and after her arrival in the United States, BUTINA served as Special Assistant to the RUSSIAN OFFICIAL. Conspiring together, BUTINA and the RUSSIAN OFFICIAL took various overt acts in furtherance of the conspiracy and to effect the illegal purpose thereof.

6. The RUSSIAN OFFICIAL is a Russian citizen and a high-level official in the Russian government. The RUSSIAN OFFICIAL was previously a member of the legislature of the Russian Federation and later became a top official at the Russian Central Bank. The RUSSIAN OFFICIAL directed BUTINA's activities in furtherance of the conspiracy.

2

7.   U.S. Person 1 is a United States citizen and an American political operative. BUTINA established contact with U.S. Person 1 in Moscow in or around 2013. U.S. Person 1 worked with BUTINA to jointly arrange introductions to U.S. persons having influence in American politics, including an organization promoting gun rights (hereinafter "GUN RIGHTS ORGANIZATION"), for the purpose of advancing the agenda of the Russian Federation.

8.   U.S. Person 2 is a United States citizen who was included among the participants in a series of email communications in 2016 and 2017 that reveal BUTINA's efforts to arrange a series of dinners in the District of Columbia and New York City involving Russian nationals and U.S. persons having influence in American politics (hereinafter "friendship and dialogue dinners"). BUTINA told U.S. Person 2 that the RUSSIAN OFFICIAL was "very much impressed by you" and that "the Russians will support the efforts from our side."

9.   The Ministry of Foreign Affairs of the Russian Federation (MFA) is the Russian government agency with primary responsibility for the Russian Federation's foreign relations and foreign policy.

Actions of the Russian Federation

10.   The Russian Federation, or Russia, is one of the leading state intelligence threats to U.S. interests, based on its capabilities, intent, and broad operational scope. Penetrating the U.S. national decision-making apparatus and the Intelligence Community are primary objectives for numerous foreign intelligence entities, including Russia. The objective of the Russian Federation leadership is to expand its sphere of influence and strength, and it targets the United States and U.S. allies to further that goal.

11.   Russian influence operations are a threat to U.S. interests as they are low-cost, relatively low-risk, and deniable ways to shape foreign perceptions and to influence populations. Moscow seeks to create wedges that reduce trust and confidence in democratic processes, degrade

3

democratization efforts, weaken U.S. partnerships with European allies, undermine Western sanctions, encourage anti-U.S. political views, and counter efforts to bring Ukraine and other former Soviet states into European institutions.

12.   In 2018, pursuant to Executive Order 13661, the U.S. Department of the Treasury's Office of Foreign Assets Control (OFAC), in consultation with the U.S. Department of State, listed seven Russian oligarchs and 12 companies they own or control, 17 senior Russian government officials, including the RUSSIAN OFFICIAL, and a state-owned Russian weapons trading company and its subsidiary, a Russian bank, as specially designated nationals. OFAC sanctioned the RUSSIAN OFFICIAL for being an Official of the Government of the Russian Federation. In sanctioning these entities, U.S. Treasury Secretary Steven T. Mnuchin announced:

> The Russian government engages in a range of malign activity around the globe, including continuing to occupy Crimea and instigate violence in eastern Ukraine, supplying the Assad regime with material and weaponry as they bomb their own civilians, attempting to subvert Western democracies, and malicious cyber activities. Russian oligarchs and elites who profit from this corrupt system will no longer be insulated from the consequences of their government's destabilizing activities.

THE DEFENDANT'S ACTIVITIES ON BEHALF OF RUSSIA

13.   As detailed below, the FBI's investigation has revealed that BUTINA, the defendant, was working in the United States at the direction of the RUSSIAN OFFICIAL.

14.   The FBI's investigation has further revealed that BUTINA and the RUSSIAN OFFICIAL took steps to develop relationships with American politicians in order to establish private, or as she called them, "back channel" lines of communication. These lines could be used by the Russian Federation to penetrate the U.S. national decision-making apparatus to advance the agenda of the Russian Federation.

15.   The FBI's investigation has also revealed that BUTINA and the RUSSIAN

OFFICIAL planned to advance Moscow's long-term strategic objectives in the United States, in part, by establishing relationships with American political organizations, including the GUN RIGHTS ORGANIZATION. Based on my training, experience and familiarity with this investigation, I believe that BUTINA and the RUSSIAN OFFICIAL took these steps in order to infiltrate those groups and advance the interests of the Russian Federation.

16.   The Russian influence operation included, among other things, (i) taskings from the RUSSIAN OFFICIAL to BUTINA; (ii) meetings between BUTINA and U.S. politicians and political candidates; (iii) BUTINA's attendance at events sponsored by special interest groups, also attended by U.S. politicians and political candidates; and (iv) BUTINA's reporting back to Moscow through the RUSSIAN OFFICIAL the results of the various encounters with the U.S. politicians and political candidates.

Laying the Groundwork in Russia

17.   During the course of her work as a covert Russian agent, BUTINA regularly met and communicated with the RUSSIAN OFFICIAL and U.S. Person 1 to plan and develop the contours of the influence operation.

18.   On or about March 24, 2015, BUTINA emailed U.S. Person 1 with the subject line of "The Second Pozner."[1] The body of this email also contained a project proposal. BUTINA noted to U.S. Person 1 in the email that she was sending the "Google Translator text. Maybe I could translate it myself but it would take at least a day because the text is very specific." She went on to note that she "will be happy to answer to any your questions [sic] and follow your recommendations before a [sic] finally send it." The first line of the proposal reads, "Project Description 'Diplomacy.'" It goes on to state that a major U.S. political party [hereinafter

---

[1]   I believe that this statement likely refers to Vladimir Pozner, a propagandist who served in the disinformation department of the Soviet KGB and who often appeared on Western television to explain the views of the Soviet Union during the Cold War.

"POLITICAL PARTY 1"], would likely obtain control over the U.S. government after the 2016

elections; that POLITICAL PARTY 1 is "traditionally associated with negative and aggressive

foreign policy, particularly with regards to Russia. However, now with the right to negotiate seems

best to build konstruktivnyh [sic] relations;" and that "[c]entral place and influence in the

[POLITICAL PARTY 1] plays the [GUN RIGHTS ORGANIZATION]. The [GUN RIGHTS

ORGANIZATION] [is] the largest sponsor of the elections to the US congress, as well as a sponsor

of The CPAC conference and other events."

     19.   The March 24, 2015 email further highlighted BUTINA's relationship with the GUN

RIGHTS ORGANIZATION's leadership, including her attendance at events in the United States

and BUTINA's and the RUSSIAN OFFICIAL's connections to officials of the GUN RIGHTS

ORGANIZATION. BUTINA described recent visits to the United States, including references to

instances when she was introduced to POLITICAL PARTY 1 leaders as a "representative of

informal diplomacy" of the Russian Federation. BUTINA's project proposal concluded by noting,

"[t]he resulting status needs to be strengthened is in the current time interval, before the

presidential election in 2016," and requesting a budget of $125,000 for BUTINA to participate in

"all upcoming major conferences" of POLITICAL PARTY 1.

     20.   In late March 2015, U.S. Person 1 replied to BUTINA via email with the subject

"Potential American Contacts":

> Dear Maria,
>
>   * * *
>
> Your challenge in your "special project" will be to balance two opposing
> imperatives: Your desire to communicate that you speak for Russian
> interests that will be ascendant (still around) in a post-Putin world while
> simultaneously doing nothing to criticize the President or speed the arrival
> of his successor.
>
> This restriction is easily understood in private meetings with political and
> business leaders. It will SEVERELY limit your interactions with media.

> Most of the potential "guest appearances" listed under media will only be possible if you're willing to be more candid (honest) than is politically prudent for you. But ALL of the media personalities listed would be interested in meeting you "off the record" – though your patrons / sponsors may not fully understand the power of such meetings if you do not appear on television, radio, or print as you do in Russia.

> * * *

> [T]here is NO limit as to how many American companies that you can meet—at the highest levels—if you are able to represent that you are a potential line of communication into future Russian Federation governments.

In this email, U.S. Person 1 listed potential media, business, and political contacts, and closed with,

"Everyone on this list understands (to some degree) U.S. / Russian relations under President Obama and President Putin. Everyone on this list would like to better understand U.S. / Russian relations under new presidents for each country. YOU can provide commentary on both— if you're willing to take that risk."

   21.   Also in late March 2015, U.S. Person 1 emailed BUTINA, with the subject line "Your Plan Forward." In this email, U.S. Person 1 told BUTINA that

> If you were to sit down with your special friends and make a list of ALL the most important contacts you could find in America for a time when the political situation between the U.S. and Russia will change, you could NOT do better than the list that I just emailed you. NO one – certainly not the "official" Russian Federation public relations representative in New York – could build a better list. And for a variety of current political reasons, the current Russian ambassadors to the United States and United Nations do not even try.

> YOU HAVE ALREADY MET ALL OF THE AMERICANS necessary to introduce you to EVERYONE on that list. . . .

> If you had NOT spent the last year attending conferences in America, it would take you ANOTHER year to be able to meet the names on that list. What you have done is prepare all of the groundwork (necessary introductions) in order to be introduced to everyone on that list. All that is needed is for your friends to provide you with the financial resources to spend the time in America to TAKE ALL OF THESE MEETINGS. I and your friends in America can't make it any easier for you than that.

Your potential sponsors either understand this or they don't. The names of all of the people that impress your friends by listing them. All that your friends need to know is that meetings with the names on MY list would not be possible without the unknown names in your "business card" notebook. Keep them focused on who you are NOW able to meet, NOT the people you have ALREADY met.

22.   Your affiant has reviewed a number of .pdf documents stored in BUTINA's Laptop containing Twitter direct messages between BUTINA and the RUSSIAN OFFICIAL that reflect direction and coordination of BUTINA's efforts by the RUSSIAN OFFICIAL. The direct messages between BUTINA and the RUSSIAN OFFICIAL in the latter half of 2015 include:

- A conversation between the RUSSIAN OFFICIAL and BUTINA regarding an article published by BUTINA in *The National Interest* on or about June 12, 2015, which argued that certain U.S. politicians and Russians share many common interests. BUTINA asked the RUSSIAN OFFICIAL to look at the article, and the RUSSIAN OFFICIAL said it was very good;

- A request by the RUSSIAN OFFICIAL for BUTINA to "write [him] something brief" about a political event in the United States which she was scheduled to attend. BUTINA provided that write-up the next day, which included descriptions of her speaking to a political candidate on the night of the announcement, as well as BUTINA's previous private meeting with the candidate at the 2015 annual GUN RIGHTS ORGANIZATION members' meeting;

- Discussions about the RUSSIAN OFFICIAL's anticipated attendance at a National Prayer Breakfast (including whether he had received approval to attend from the MFA), and providing the RUSSIAN OFFICIAL with

8

biographies of U.S. politicians and executives of the GUN RIGHTS
ORGANIZATION;

- Discussions about the RUSSIAN OFFICIAL's plans to meet with a U.S.
Congressman during a Congressional Delegation trip to Moscow in August
2015. In that conversation, BUTINA noted that she has the RUSSIAN
OFFICIAL's diplomatic passport and can purchase a plane ticket for him
from St. Petersburg to Moscow; and

- A statement from BUTINA to the RUSSIAN OFFICIAL that the latter "has
the responsibility of a serious mission – restoration of relations between
countries." BUTINA continued by saying that this is a long game and that
"maybe, by inviting the [GUN RIGHTS ORGANIZATION] here, you have
prevented a conflict between two great nations. [] although, I think, this is
the very beginning of the journey."

23.   Based on my training, experience, and familiarity with this investigation, I believe
that the above-described email and Twitter conversations represent BUTINA's plan to conduct
activities as an illegal agent of the Russian Federation in the United States through a Russian
influence operation.

Acts in the United States

24.   BUTINA's efforts in the United States to promote the political interests of the
Russian Federation were diverse and multifaceted, including BUTINA's efforts to organize a
series of "friendship and dialogue" dinners, some of which are believed to have taken place in the
District of Columbia, as well as BUTINA's attendance at two National Prayer Breakfasts in the
District of Columbia.

25.   On or about January 19, 2016, BUTINA and the Russian Representative exchanged

Case 1:18-cr-00218-TSC   Document 1-1   Filed 07/14/18   Page 10 of 17

Twitter direct messages regarding logistics for the 2016 National Prayer Breakfast. The RUSSIAN

OFFICIAL noted that the MFA had given approval for his attendance.

26.   On February 4, 2016, both BUTINA and the RUSSIAN OFFICIAL attended the

2016 National Prayer Breakfast in the District of Columbia.

27.   A series of email communications (also known as "email strings") spanning

March 10 and 11, 2016 and involving BUTINA, U.S. Person 1, and U.S. Person 2 reveal

BUTINA's efforts to arrange the "friendship and dialogue" dinners in the District of Columbia

and New York City near the end of May 2016.   U.S. Person 1 provided a list to BUTINA of

American individuals and noted that this list would serve as "a good start for Maria's first briefing

for [the RUSSIAN OFFICIAL's] Friday morning in Moscow." BUTINA expressed her gratitude

to U.S. Person 1 and noted that she had received the list before her meeting with the RUSSIAN

OFFICIAL, and "that [w]e confirm the Dates! [the RUSSIAN OFFICIAL] is working on the best

third person from the Russian side now." Additionally, BUTINA told U.S. Person 2 that the

RUSSIAN OFFICIAL had expressed to her that he was "very much impressed by you and

expresses his great appreciation for what you are doing to restore relations between the two

countries. He also wants you to know that Russians will support the efforts from our side. That

is all I can tell you for now. More information next week!"

28.   On March 14, 2016, BUTINA emailed U.S. Person 2 and said that the RUSSIAN

OFFICIAL confirmed to her "his desire in our Russian-American project," and that a

representative of the Russian Presidential administration had expressed approval "for building this

communication channel." BUTINA additionally assured U.S. Person 2 that he should not worry

as "all that we needed is <<yes>> from Putin's side. The rest is easier."

29.   On March 30, 2016, BUTINA sent an email thanking an associate of the organizer

of the 2017 Prayer Breakfast for meeting with her and the RUSSIAN OFFICIAL in Moscow. In

this email, BUTINA noted that the RUSSIAN OFFICIAL "suggested to President Putin that he

consider coming to the Prayer Breakfast next year, Feb 2017, and Pres. Putin did not say 'no'!"

BUTINA observed that she believed that there were a number of conditions that should be met in

order for President Putin to attend, including a personal invitation from the President of the United

States and the attendance of at least fifteen other world leaders or heads of state. In a later March

email, the organizer of the 2017 National Prayer Breakfast promised BUTINA he would provide

ten seats at the 2017 event.

30.   On September 16, 2016, BUTINA sent an email to U.S. Person 1 and U.S. Person 2

regarding organizing another Russian-American "friendship and dialogue" dinner in the District

of Columbia. BUTINA suggested scheduling the next dinner at the beginning of October 2016,

because "we only have 2 month left before the US elections and it's the time for building an

advisors team on Russia for a new president. I am seriously worry that the candidates some

upcoming day will suddenly realize that 'now' is the time to do something with Russia and will

look for advisory among currently popular radically oppositional to Russia crowd of experts. Bad

things happen than. I believe we can prevent it." [sic]

31.   On October 4, 2016, U.S. Person 1 sent an email to an acquaintance. The email

covered a number of topics. Within the email, U.S. Person 1 stated, "Unrelated to specific

presidential campaigns, I've been involved in securing a VERY private line of communication

between the Kremlin and key POLITICAL PARTY 1 leaders through, of all conduits, the [GUN

RIGHTS ORGANIZATION]." Based on my training, experience, and familiarity with this

investigation, I believe that this email describes U.S. Person 1's involvement in BUTINA's efforts

to establish a "back channel" communication for representatives of the Government of Russia.

32.   On October 5, 2016, BUTINA and the RUSSIAN OFFICIAL exchanged the

Case 1:18-cr-00218-TSC   Document 1-1   Filed 07/14/18   Page 12 of 17

following direct messages on Twitter:

> BUTINA: Time will tell. We made our bet. I am following our game. I will be connecting the people from the prayer breakfast to this group. Most importantly, you get better. Everything else we will win.

> RUSSIAN OFFICIAL: No doubt! Of course we will win, but I (you are right) need to beat the illness first and get out of the hospital (I made an attempt today – it didn't work). And it is not about winning today's fight (although we are striving for it) but to win the entire battle. This is the battle for the future, it cannot be lost! Or everyone will lose.

> BUTINA: True! But don't try to get out right now: the doctors ordered you to stay for a reason. Better finish the treatment. Please do not risk it. You have a key role and you know it. I will not manage without you.

> RUSSIAN OFFICIAL: No! This is a mistake. Your political star has risen in the sky. Now it is important to rise to the zenith and not burn out (fall) prematurely.

> BUTINA: Oh well. I am just starting in this field. I still have to learn and learn from you! These are not just words! Harsh and impetuous moves will ruin everything early.

> RUSSIAN OFFICIAL: This is hard to teach. Patience and cold blood + faith in yourself. And everything will definitely turn out.

> * * *

> BUTINA: By your recommendation, I am setting up the groundwork here but I am really in need of mentoring. Or the energy might to towards the wrong direction. Yesterday's dinner showed that American society is broken in relation to Russia. This is now the dividing line of opinions, the crucial one in the election race. [POLITICAL PARTY 1] are for us, [another major U.S. political party] – against – 50/50. Our move here is very important." [sic]

33.   During the October 5, 2016 Twitter direct communications, BUTINA and the

RUSSIAN OFFICIAL also discussed other potential steps to take in the operation. The RUSSIAN

OFFICIAL asked about how the "Russia-USA friendship society" looked at that time. BUTINA

responded, "It's not alive. We are currently 'underground' both here and there. Now, private

clubs and quite [sic] influence on people making decisions is the trend. No publicity." She continued, "Advisor – is the profession of the current day. Even a secret advisor. Right now the Administration here is flexible – and there is the idea, so that the right thoughts would dominate."

34.   Following this October 5, 2016 Twitter conversation, BUTINA and the RUSSIAN OFFICIAL discussed whether BUTINA should volunteer to serve as a U.S. election observer from Russia and agreed that the risk was too high.   The RUSSIAN OFFICIAL expressed the opinion that "the risk of provocation is too high and the 'media hype' which comes after it," and BUTINA agreed by responding, "Only incognito! Right now everything has to be quiet and careful."

35.   In October 2016, BUTINA and the RUSSIAN OFFICIAL intermittently communicated to discuss the topics of the 2017 National Prayer Breakfast invitation and the upcoming elections via Twitter direct message.   On October 17, 2016, BUTINA asked the RUSSIAN OFFICIAL for a list of ten individuals from Russia who would be attending the National Prayer Breakfast. BUTINA further suggested to the RUSSIAN OFFICIAL that it would be a good idea to invite the Russian Ambassador and noted that it "needs to be somebody influential from Russia, it would be better [if it were someone] from the Kremlin or RPC [Russian Orthodox Church] of course."

36.   In a series of November 8 and 9, 2016 Twitter direct messages, the RUSSIAN OFFICIAL and BUTINA discussed the results of the U.S. Presidential election as they were announced. As part of that same Twitter conversation, BUTINA told the RUSSIAN OFFICIAL, ". . . I'm going to sleep. It's 3 am here. I am ready for further orders." The RUSSIAN OFFICIAL responded, "Think about in which areas of life we could go towards bringing us closer. ISIS – understandably, what else we need to look at the American agenda." After speculating about who might be nominated as Secretary of State, BUTINA suggested a phone call to discuss, and the RUSSIAN OFFICIAL noted that he liked the idea, but was worried that "all our phones are being listened to!" BUTINA suggested that they talk via WhatsApp.

37.   On November 11, 2016, BUTINA sent the RUSSIAN OFFICIAL a direct message via Twitter, in which she predicted who might be named Secretary of State and asked the RUSSIAN OFFICIAL to find out how "our people" felt about that potential nomination.

38.   Also on November 11, 2016, BUTINA sent the RUSSIAN OFFICIAL a direct message via Twitter which included a screen shot of two "reports" in Russian. One report proposed ways to establish dialogue with U.S. politicians through a conference. The proposal stated that "[t]he conference must be presented as a private initiative, not a government undertaking." The proposal also suggested that BUTINA and a number of political officials and U.S. Congressmen should participate. In this report, BUTINA noted to the RUSSIAN OFFICIAL, under the heading "advantages," that "[t]he event will get wide coverage in the press; it will be the first positive event regarding Russia in Washington (currently, all of them are anti-Russian and anti-Putin). The event does not pose any risks because no government officials from either country will attend; yet it creates a foundation for further talks on the level of government officials."

39.   In a November 12, 2016 Twitter direct message, the RUSSIAN OFFICIAL acknowledged reading the proposal referenced above and informed BUTINA that "they" won't go for it. He told BUTINA that he could not reach an MFA contact and noted "[p]eople are waiting for the formed decisions. I will try to clarify this subject on Monday one more time." Based on my training, experience, and familiarity with this investigation, I believe these messages are the RUSSIAN OFFICIAL relaying the Russian Federation's instructions to its agent, BUTINA.

40.   On November 30, 2016, BUTINA emailed U.S. Person 1 regarding the Russian delegation to the 2017 National Prayer Breakfast. BUTINA stated that the "[p]eople in the list are handpicked by [the RUSSIAN OFFICIAL] and me and are VERY influential in Russia. They are coming to establish a back channel of communication... Let's think if our [U.S. Person 2's first name] would like to meet with them..." (ellipses in original)

14

41. On December 1, 2016, U.S. Person 1 emailed BUTINA with instructions for "what is required to book the Russian delegation hotel rooms in the Washington Hilton – the actual venue of the National Prayer Breakfast." The email listed rooms and prices, and U.S. Person 1 noted, "To be safe, I'd ask [the RUSSIAN OFFICIAL] to place US $3500 on one of your Russian charge cards in order to pay these deposits."

42. In a December 26, 2016 email, the RUSSIAN OFFICIAL told BUTINA that the MFA had no objection to his trip to attend the National Prayer Breakfast, but "it does not mean that everything is settled. . . . Officially, only ambassadors will be invited. There will be no state leaders and delegations." BUTINA replied, "The response from the MFA is perfect.[] I am serious."

43. On January 5, 2017, BUTINA was forwarded a copy of an email between U.S. Person 1 and U.S. Person 2 regarding the 2017 National Prayer Breakfast in which U.S. Person 1 attached a list of Russian visitors, including 12 Russian guests, noting, "In addition to delegation leader [the RUSSIAN OFFICIAL], the list is populated by important political advisors to Russian President Putin, university presidents, mayors, and substantial private businessmen."

44. On January 26, 2017, BUTINA and the RUSSIAN OFFICIAL communicated via Twitter direct message about the RUSSIAN OFFICIAL delivering a speech the night before the National Prayer Breakfast. BUTINA told the Russian Representative that "[t]he only thing I ask is to somehow mention me. This is very important for me for negotiations with the breakfast committee. They need to see me not as the delegation 'organization committee' but as your partner and colleague." The Russian Representative agreed as to the "need to stress [BUTINA's] status as a key figure."

45. On February 2, 2017, BUTINA and the RUSSIAN OFFICIAL attended the 2017 National Prayer Breakfast in the District of Columbia.

Case 1:18-cr-00218-TSC   Document 1-1   Filed 07/14/18   Page 16 of 17

46.   On February 6, 2017, BUTINA emailed a National Prayer Breakfast organizer to thank him for "the gift of you [sic] precious time during the National Prayer Breakfast week – and for the very private meeting that followed. A new relationship between two countries always begins better when it begins in faith. Once you have a chance to rest after last week's events, I have *important information for you to further* this new relationship. I would appreciate one brief additional meeting with you to explain these new developments. I remain in Washington, D.C. pursuing my Master's Degree at American University. My schedule is your schedule!" (emphasis added)

48.   On February 8, 2017, BUTINA emailed U.S. Person 2 to thank him and noted, "Our delegation cannot stop chatting about your wonderful dinner. My dearest President has received 'the message' about your group initiatives and your constructive and kind attention to the Russians."

49.   At no time did BUTINA notify the Attorney General, whose office in the Department of Justice is located in the District of Columbia, that she would and did act in the United States as an agent of a foreign government.

CONCLUSION

50.   For the reasons stated above, there is probable cause to believe that BUTINA conspired with one or more persons to violate 18 U.S.C. § 951, in violation of 18 U.S.C. § 371.

51.   I declare under the penalty of perjury that the information provided above is true and correct to the best of my knowledge.

Respectfully submitted,

_____

KEVIN HELSON
Special Agent

16

Federal Bureau of Investigation

Subscribed and sworn to before me
on

_____

THE HONORABLE DEBORAH A. ROBINSON
UNITED STATES MAGISTRATE JUDGE

Indictment

Appendix B 209

IN THE UNITED STATES DISTRICT COURT
FOR THE DISTRICT OF COLUMBIA

Holding a Criminal Term
Grand Jury Sworn in on May 3, 2018

UNITED STATES OF AMERICA	:	CRIMINAL NO.
	:	
v.	:	
	:	
MARIIA BUTINA,	:	VIOLATIONS:
Also known as:	:	
Maria Butina,	:	18 U.S.C. § 371
	:	(Conspiracy)
Defendant.	:	
	:	18 U.S.C. § 951
	:	(Agents of Foreign Governments)

INDICTMENT

The Grand Jury charges that:

COUNT ONE

General Allegations

At all times material to this Indictment:

1.   **MARIIA BUTINA, also known as "MARIA BUTINA" ("BUTINA")**, was a Russian citizen who entered the United States in August 2016 on an F-1 Student Visa.   On the visa application to the U.S. Department of State, **BUTINA** declared under penalty of perjury that while she had been previously employed as Special Assistant to the RUSSIAN OFFICIAL, this employment had ended on May 20, 2016.   Despite her attestation, **BUTINA** continued to act under the direction and control of the RUSSIAN OFFICIAL for the purpose of advancing the interests of the Russian Federation after she entered the United States.

2.   The RUSSIAN OFFICIAL, whose identity is known to the grand jury, was a Russian citizen and a high-level official in the Russian government.   The RUSSIAN OFFICIAL

was previously a member of the legislature of the Russian Federation and later became a top official at the Russian Central Bank. In April 2018, pursuant to Executive Order 13661, the U.S. Department of the Treasury's Office of Foreign Assets Control (OFAC), in consultation with the U.S. Department of State, sanctioned the RUSSIAN OFFICIAL.

3.   U.S. Person 1, whose identity is known to the grand jury, was a United States citizen and an American political operative. U.S. Person 1 worked with **BUTINA** to arrange introductions to U.S. persons having influence in American politics, including an organization promoting gun rights (hereinafter "GUN RIGHTS ORGANIZATION"), for the purpose of advancing the interests of the Russian Federation.

4.   At no time was **BUTINA** a duly accredited diplomatic or consular officer; an officially and publicly acknowledged and sponsored official or representative of the Russian Federation; or an officially and publicly acknowledged and sponsored staff member or employee thereof.

5.   At no time did **BUTINA** notify the Attorney General, whose office in the Department of Justice is located in the District of Columbia, that she would and did act in the United States as an agent of a foreign government and official.

The Conspiracy

6.   Beginning no later than in or around 2015, and possibly earlier, and continuing up until the present, in the District of Columbia and elsewhere, **BUTINA** and others known and unknown to the grand jury, including the RUSSIAN OFFICIAL, knowingly did combine, conspire, confederate, and agree together and with each other to commit an offense against the United States,

2

to wit, Title 18, United States Code, Section 951, in violation of Title 18, United States Code, Section 371.

Objects of the Conspiracy

7.   The objects of the conspiracy were:

a.   To act in the United States as an agent of a foreign government, specifically the Russian Federation, without prior notification to the Attorney General;

b.   To act in the United States as an agent of a foreign government official, specifically the RUSSIAN OFFICIAL, without prior notification to the Attorney General;

c.   To exploit personal connections with U.S. persons having influence in American politics in an effort to advance the interests of the Russian Federation, without prior notification to the Attorney General; and

d.   To infiltrate organizations active in American politics in an effort to advance the interests of the Russian Federation, without prior notification to the Attorney General.

Manner and Means of the Conspiracy

8.   **BUTINA** and her conspirators would and did use the following manner and means, among others, to accomplish the objects of the conspiracy:

a.   While acting under the direction and control of an official of the Russian Federation, **BUTINA** would meet in person and communicate via electronic means with that official for the purpose of developing and executing a plan to identify and exploit personal connections with U.S. persons having influence in

3

American politics, who were in positions to advance the interests of the Russian Federation.

b. For the purpose of advancing the interests of the Russian Federation, **BUTINA** established a relationship with U.S. Person 1 in Moscow who, thereafter, would work with **BUTINA** in the United States to arrange introductions to U.S. persons having influence in American politics.

c. While residing in the United States, **BUTINA** would work on behalf of the RUSSIAN OFFICIAL by attempting to establish unofficial lines of communications with U.S. politicians and political organizations for the purpose of advancing the interests of the Russian Federation.

d. **BUTINA** would communicate via email, Twitter direct message, and other means with the RUSSIAN OFFICIAL, and others, to send reports, seek direction, and receive orders in furtherance of the conspiracy.

Overt Acts

9.   In furtherance of this conspiracy, and to accomplish its purposes and objects, at least one of the conspirators committed or caused to be committed, in the District of Columbia, and elsewhere, at least one of the following overt acts, among others:

a. On or about March 14, 2016, **BUTINA** emailed a U.S. person in an effort to develop, maintain, and exploit a relationship in furtherance of the conspiracy.

b. In or around August 2016, **BUTINA** entered the United States on an F-1 Student Visa for the claimed purpose of attending university full time in the District of Columbia, while continuing to act as an agent on behalf of the Russian Federation and the RUSSIAN OFFICIAL.

4

Case 1:18-cr-00218-TSC   Document 7   Filed 07/17/18   Page 5 of 6

c. On or about September 26, 2016, **BUTINA** emailed a U.S. person to organize an event for the purpose of influencing the views of U.S. officials, as those views relate to the Russian Federation.

d. On or about November 11, 2016, **BUTINA** sent the RUSSIAN OFFICIAL a Russian-language report that proposed ways to establish dialogue with U.S. politicians through a conference.

e. On or about February 2, 2017, **BUTINA** and the RUSSIAN OFFICIAL attended the National Prayer Breakfast in the District of Columbia, along with a delegation from the Russian Federation.

(**Conspiracy to Act as an Agent of a Foreign Government** in violation of Title 18, United States Code, Sections 371 and 951.)

COUNT TWO

10.   The allegations set forth in paragraphs 1 through 5 of Count One of this indictment are realleged and incorporated by reference herein.

11.   Between in or around January 2015 and up to and including the present, in the District of Columbia and elsewhere, defendant **MARIIA BUTINA, also known as "MARIA BUTINA,"** did act within the United States as an agent of a foreign government, without prior notification to the Attorney General, whose office in the Department of Justice is located in the District of Columbia.

(Agents of Foreign Governments in violation of Title 18, United States Code, Section 951)

A TRUE BILL

FOREPERSON

Jessie K Liu // DAC
Attorney of the United States in
and for the District of Columbia

Statement by Maria Butina at Sentencing—Court Transcript, April 26, 2019

1

UNITED STATES DISTRICT COURT
FOR THE DISTRICT OF COLUMBIA

UNITED STATES OF AMERICA,   .
                    .
        Plaintiff,   .   CR No. 18-0218 (TSC)
                    .
   v.   .
                    .
MARIIA BUTINA, a/k/a   .   Washington, D.C.
MARIA BUTINA,   .   Friday, April 26, 2019
                    .   10:07 a.m.
        Defendant.   .
. . . .

TRANSCRIPT OF SENTENCING
BEFORE THE HONORABLE TANYA S. CHUTKAN
UNITED STATES DISTRICT JUDGE

<u>APPEARANCES</u>:

For the Government: ERIK M. KENERSON, AUSA
                          THOMAS N. SAUNDERS, AUSA
                          U.S. Attorney's Office
                          National Security Section
                          555 Fourth Street, NW
                          Washington, DC 20530

                          WILLIAM MACKIE, ESQ.
                          U.S. Department of Justice
                          National Security Division
                          950 Pennsylvania Avenue, NW
                          RFK Building, Suite 7700
                          Washington, DC 20530

For the Defendant: ROBERT N. DRISCOLL, ESQ.
                          ALFRED D. CARRY, ESQ.
                          McGlinchey Stafford, PLLC
                          1275 Pennsylvania Avenue, NW
                          Suite 420
                          Washington, DC 20004

Court Reporter: BRYAN A. WAYNE, RPR, CRR
                          U.S. Courthouse, Room 4704-A
                          333 Constitution Avenue, NW
                          Washington, DC 20001

1

2

3

4

5

6

7   THE DEFENDANT: Thank you very much for this

8   opportunity to speak in front of you.

9   Dear Judge, I came to the U.S. like many others, to better

10   my life. For me, that meant getting an academic degree, and I

11   had no doubt that the best way to do that was here. I wanted

12   a future career in the international policy. At the same time,

13   I wished to mend relations while improving my own resume. So

14   I sought to build bridges between my motherland and the country

15   I grew to love. It was for these actions and my own ignorance

16   that I deeply sorry and hope to be shown mercy. Never did I

17   wish to hurt anyone.

18   My parents discovered my arrest on the morning news they

19   watch in their rural house in a Siberian village. I love them

20   dearly, but it harmed them morally and financially. They are

21   suffering from all of that. I destroyed my own life as well.

22   I came to the U.S. not under any orders but with hope, and now

23   nothing remains but penitence.

24   If I had known to register as a foreign agent, I would

25   have done so without delay. I never lied or held any secrets.

1   I never injured someone or committed other crimes. I just

2   didn't register because I didn't know to. Ignorance of law,

3   however, is not an excuse, in the U.S. or in Russia. And so I

4   humbly request forgiveness.

5   The United States has always been kind to me, and while it

6   has never been my intent to harm the American people, I did just

7   that by not notifying your government of my actions in advance.

8   I deeply regret this crime not merely because it has scarred me,

9   my beloved friends and my cherished family, but, ironically, it

10 has harmed my attempts to improve the relationships between the

11 two countries.

12   For all the international scandal my arrest has caused, I

13 feel ashamed and embarrassed. My parents taught me the virtue

14 of higher education, how to live life lawfully, and how to be

15 good and kind to others. I have three degrees, but now I'm a

16 convicted felon with no job, no money, and no freedom.

17   My reputation is ruined both here in the United States

18 and abroad. And while I know that I'm not this evil person

19 who has been depicted in the media, I am responsible for these

20 consequences. My personal ambitions and thinking, my choices,

21 put me in this situation, and I'm sorry for all the alarm my

22 behavior has become the reason for.

23   Just an apology will never be enough for my mistakes, dear

24 Judge, because instead of building peace, I created discord.

25 I cannot change the past, though I've surely tried. I have

1   helped the U.S. government in any way they have requested,

2   even before my arrest, by aiding the U.S. Senate Intelligence

3   Committee last spring, by aiding FBI agents, and recently by

4   aiding the U.S. Attorney's Office. I still hold the whisper

5   in my heart to one day return to this country, but I know this

6   wish is only a dream.

7   Dear Judge Chutkan, over the last nine months, I've learned

8   humility. I've met and shared stories with some remarkable

9   other women, each flawed and struggling in their own way, but

10 still good in their own way. As a Christian, God has carried

11 me through so much and gave me so much. My attorneys fighting

12 for me were not getting paid.

13   My family and the few friends who generously talked

14 to me during days or nights while on breaks on my solitary

15 confinement, I've seen those who have never had visitors or any

16 money, even for a 30-seconds phone call. I've seen others who

17 have waited along with me in the visitation room, and their

18 visitors has never come. I'm so grateful for what I have, dear

19 judge.

20   I've also kept a quote on my windowsill from my cell that

21 says, "When you go through deep waters, I'll be with you." God

22 has carried me through this uneasy but deserved experience. It

23 is my penance. Now I beg for mercy, for the chance to go home

24 and restart my life. Please accept my apologies and allow me to

25 begin again. Thank you.

Index